Swift 2 By Example

Create robust and extensible iOS apps using
the advanced features of Swift 2

Giordano Scalzo

[PACKT] open source

PUBLISHING   community experience distilled

BIRMINGHAM - MUMBAI

Swift 2 By Example

First published: March 2016

Production reference: 1080316

Published by Packt Publishing Ltd.
Livery Place
35 Livery Street
Birmingham B3 2PB, UK.

ISBN 978-1-78588-292-0

www.packtpub.com

Credits

Author
Giordano Scalzo

Reviewer
Hugo Solis

Commissioning Editor
Veena Pagare

Acquisition Editor
Reshma Raman

Content Development Editor
Divij Kotian

Technical Editor
Vishal Mewada

Copy Editor
Stuti Srivastava

Project Coordinator
Nikhil Nair

Proofreader
Safis Editing

Indexer
Tejal Daruwale Soni

Production Coordinator
Manu Joseph

Cover Work
Manu Joseph

About the Author

Giordano Scalzo is a developer with 20 years of programming experience, since the days of the ZXSpectrum.

He has worked in C++, Java, .Net, Ruby, Python, and in so many other programming languages he has forgotten the names.

After years of backend development, over the past 5 years Giordano has developed extensively for iOS, releasing more than 20 apps — apps that he wrote for clients, enterprise applications, or on his own.

Currently, he is a contractor in London, where — through his company, Effective Code Ltd, `http://effectivecode.co.uk` — he delivers code for iOS, aiming at quality and reliability.

In his spare time, when he is not crafting retro game clones for iOS, he writes his thoughts at `http://giordanoscalzo.com`.

I'd like to thank my better half, Valentina, who lovingly supports me in everything I do: without you, none of this would have been possible.

Thanks to my bright future, Mattia and Luca, for giving me lots of smiles and hugs when I needed them.

Finally, my gratitude goes to my Mum and Dad, who gave my curiosity the right push, along with the support to follow my passions, which began the day they bought me a ZXSpectrum.

About the Reviewer

Hugo Solis is an assistant professor in the Physics department at the University of Costa Rica. His current research interests are computational cosmology, complexity and the influence of hydrogen on material properties. He has wide experience with languages including C/C++ and Python for scientific programming and visualization. He is a member of the Free Software Foundation, and he has contributed code to some free software projects. He has also been a technical reviewer for *Mastering Object-oriented Python*, *Learning Object-oriented Programming*, and *Kivy: Interactive Applications in Python* and is the author of *Kivy Cookbook*, *Packt Publishing*. Currently, he is in charge of the Institute of Food Technologists, a Costa Rican scientific nonprofit organization for the multidisciplinary practice of Physics (`http://iftucr.org`).

I'd like to thank Katty Sanchez, my beloved mother, for her support and cutting-edge thoughts.

www.PacktPub.com

eBooks, discount offers, and more

Did you know that Packt offers eBook versions of every book published, with PDF and ePub files available? You can upgrade to the eBook version at www.PacktPub.com and as a print book customer, you are entitled to a discount on the eBook copy. Get in touch with us at customercare@packtpub.com for more details.

At www.PacktPub.com, you can also read a collection of free technical articles, sign up for a range of free newsletters and receive exclusive discounts and offers on Packt books and eBooks.

https://www2.packtpub.com/books/subscription/packtlib

Do you need instant solutions to your IT questions? PacktLib is Packt's online digital book library. Here, you can search, access, and read Packt's entire library of books.

Why subscribe?

- Fully searchable across every book published by Packt
- Copy and paste, print, and bookmark content
- On demand and accessible via a web browser

Table of Contents

Preface	**vii**
Chapter 1: Welcome to the World of Swift	**1**
The first look at Swift	**2**
Let's go to the playground	2
The building blocks – variables and constants	5
Collecting variables in containers	8
Controlling the flow	10
Transforming the values using functions	14
Structs – custom compound types	16
Classes – common behavior objects	20
Loose coupling with protocols	22
Composing objects using protocol extensions	22
Checking the existence of an optional value	24
Enumerations on steroids	25
Extended pattern matching	27
Catching errors	29
Swift functional programming patterns	33
Summary	37
Chapter 2: Building a Guess the Number App	**39**
The app is...	**39**
Building a skeleton app	41
Adding the graphics components	43
Connecting the dots	47
Adding the code	52
Summary	56

Chapter 3: A Memory Game in Swift — 59

The app is… — 59
Building the skeleton of the app — 60
The menu screen — 61
  Implementing the basic menu screen — 61
  Creating a nice menu screen — 64
The game screen — 66
  The structure — 66
  Adding a collection view — 68
  Sizing the components — 70
Connecting the dataSource and the delegate — 71
Implementing a deck of cards — 73
  What we are expecting — 73
  The card entity — 74
  Crafting the deck — 75
  Shuffling the deck — 76
  Finishing the deck — 77
  Put the cards on the table — 78
  Adding the assets — 78
  The CardCell structure — 79
  Handling touches — 81
Finishing the game — 82
  Implementing the game logic — 82
  We got a pair — 84
  We made the wrong move — 85
  Et voilà! The game is completed — 86
Summary — 86

Chapter 4: A TodoList App in Swift — 87

The app is… — 87
Building a skeleton app — 90
  Implementing an empty app — 90
  Adding third-party libraries with CocoaPods — 98
  Implementing the Todos view controller — 99
Building the Todos screen — 103
  Adding entities — 103
  Implementing datastore — 104
  Connecting datastore and View Controller — 105
  Configuring tableView — 106
  Finishing touches — 108
  Swipe that cell! — 109

Adding a Todo task | **112**
The add a Todo view | 113
The add a Todo View Controller | 120
Finishing TodoDatastore | 127
List View Controller | 128
Where do we go from here? | 131
Summary | **132**

Chapter 5: A Pretty Weather App | **133**
The app is… | **133**
Building the skeleton | **135**
Creating the project | 136
Adding assets | 137
Implementing the UI | **140**
The UI in blocks | 140
Completing the UI | **145**
Implementing CurrentWeatherView | 145
Building WeatherHourlyForecastView | 148
Seeing the next day's forecast in WeatherDaysForecastView | 152
Blurring the background | **156**
Downloading the background image | **159**
Searching in Flickr | 159
Geolocalising the app | **162**
Using Core Location | 162
Retrieving the actual forecast | **165**
Getting the forecast from OpenWeatherMap | 165
Rendering CurrentWeatherView | 168
Rendering WeatherHourlyForecastView | 171
Rendering WeatherDaysForecastView | 172
Connecting to the server | **173**
Where do we go from here? | **178**
Summary | **179**

Chapter 6: Flappy Swift | **181**
The app is… | **181**
Building the skeleton of the app | **182**
Creating the project | 182
Implementing the menu | 184
A stage for a bird | **189**
SpriteKit in a nutshell | 189
Explaining the code | 190

Simulating a three-dimensional world using parallax	191
How to implement scrolling	193
A flying bird	**196**
Adding the Bird node	196
Making the bird flap	199
Pipes!	**201**
Implementing the pipes node	201
Making the components interact	**206**
Setting up the collision-detection engine	206
Completing the game	**212**
Colliding with pipes	212
Adding the score	213
Adding a restart pop-up	214
Summary	**216**
Chapter 7: Polishing Flappy Swift	**217**
Adding juiciness	**217**
Let there be sounds!	217
Playing the soundtrack	219
Shaking the screen!	221
Integrating with Game Center	**223**
What Game Center provides	223
Setting up Game Center	223
Creating an app record on iTunes Connect	224
Enabling Game Center	226
Creating fake user accounts to test Game Center	229
Authenticating a player	230
Summary	**236**
Chapter 8: Cube Runner	**237**
The app is…	**237**
Introduction to SceneKit	**238**
What is SceneKit?	238
Building an empty scene	239
Adding a green torus	241
Let there be light!	242
Let's make it move!	242
Implementing Cube Runner	**243**
The game skeleton	243
Implementing the menu	245
Flying in a 3D world	**249**
Setting up a scene	249

Adding a fighter	252
Texturing the world	254
Make it move	256
Adding cubes	257
Adding more obstacles	263
Adding a few touches	**264**
The score	264
Let's add music	266
Summary	**268**
Chapter 9: Completing Cube Runner	**269**
Creating a real game	**269**
Detecting collisions	269
Game over!	272
Adding the juice	275
Game Center	279
Summary	**282**
Chapter 10: ASAP – an E-commerce App in Swift	**283**
The app is…	**283**
The first requirement: login and registration	284
The second requirement: the products grid	285
The third requirement: the open cart	286
The skeleton app and register screen	**286**
The skeleton app	286
The ASAP e-commerce store	**298**
The e-commerce product list	299
The product cell	303
Parsing and storing products	307
The ASAP cart	**311**
Adding a product to the cart	312
Removing items from cart and checkout	316
Summary	**325**
Chapter 11: ASAPServer, a Server in Swift	**327**
The interface of the ASAP Server	**327**
One skeleton server for two OSes	**328**
An OS X skeleton server	328
Preparing the OS X environment	328
The HelloWorld skeleton server	329
Preparing the Linux environment	332
The ASAPServer	**335**
The Products	335

The cart   336
The order   337
Connecting the ASAP app   **338**
The products   338
The Cart   340
The order   343
Summary   **344**
Index   **345**

Preface

The introduction of Swift during WWDC 2014 surprised the whole community of iOS developers, who were waiting to be introduced to the new API from iOS 8, not to be transformed into beginners.

Besides the surprise, most of them understood that this would have been a great opportunity to create a new world of libraries, patterns, best practices, and so on. On the other hand, communities of programmers in different languages, who were intimidated by the rough first impact of Objective-C, started to be attracted by Swift, which — with its friendly syntax — was less intimidating.

After a year, Swift 2.0 has proven to be a huge improvement over the first version, enriched by a lot of new features and strengthened by its use in thousands of new apps. It is finally ready for production!

In WWDC 2015, Apple made another surprising announcement: Swift will be open source and there will be versions for different operating systems, beginning with Linux and Windows. This opens up a whole new scenario, where it will be possible to implement both client and the server apps with the same language.

This book will introduce you the world of app development using the new features in Swift 2, and it will show you how to build Linux apps in Swift in order to create server counterparts of your mobile apps.

Through simple step-by-step chapters, the book will teach you how to build both utility and game apps; while building them, you'll learn the basics of Swift and iOS.

What this book covers

Chapter 1, Welcome to the World of Swift, introduces the Swift syntax and the most important features provided by the language.

Chapter 2, Building a Guess the Number App, introduces Xcode, its project file, and the different editors required to build an app; a simple game app will be created to demonstrate these.

Chapter 3, A Memory Game in Swift, shows the creation of a complete game app, with images and animations, without using any Game framework but with only the fundamental iOS libraries.

Chapter 4, A TodoList App in Swift, teaches you how to create a real-world utility app, handling the library dependencies with Cocoapods.

Chapter 5, A Pretty Weather App, shows you how to create a nice looking app that retrieves data from third-party servers.

Chapter 6, Flappy Swift, covers SpriteKit, the 2D iOS game engine.

Chapter 7, Polishing Flappy Swift, completes the game, adding Game Center support and various entertaining touches.

Chapter 8, Cube Runner, covers SceneKit and 3D programming, implementing a 3D endless runner with a space theme.

Chapter 9, Completing Cube Runner, finalizes the game and adds Game Center support.

Chapter 10, ASAP – an E-commerce App in Swift, implements an ecommerce app that uses local storage to store the products.

Chapter 11, ASAPServer, a Server in Swift, is a follow-up to the previous chapter, where we'll implement a backend server for Linux to handle the requests of the ASAP e-commerce app.

What you need for this book

In order to get the most out of this book, there are a few essentials you will need:

- A Mac computer running OS X 10.11.2 or higher
- A basic knowledge of programming

- Xcode 7.2 or higher
- An iPhone 5s or higher (an app uses CoreMotion that doesn't work in the simulator)

Who this book is for

This book is ideal for those who want to learn how to develop apps in Swift, starting the right way. Whether you are an expert Objective-C programmer or are new to this platform, you'll quickly grasp the code for real-world apps and discover how to use Swift effectively. Prior experience in the development of Apple devices would be helpful, but it is not mandatory.

Conventions

In this book, you will find a number of text styles that distinguish between different kinds of information. Here are some examples of these styles and an explanation of their meaning.

Code words in text, database table names, folder names, filenames, file extensions, pathnames, dummy URLs, user input, and Twitter handles are shown as follows: "We can include other contexts through the use of the include directive."

A block of code is set as follows:

```
let mainWindow = UIWindow(frame: UIScreen.mainScreen().bounds)
mainWindow.backgroundColor = UIColor.whiteColor()
mainWindow.rootViewController = navigatorViewController
mainWindow.makeKeyAndVisible()
window = mainWindow
return true
```

When we wish to draw your attention to a particular part of a code block, the relevant lines or items are set in bold:

```
let mainWindow = UIWindow(frame: UIScreen.mainScreen().bounds)
mainWindow.backgroundColor = UIColor.whiteColor()
mainWindow.rootViewController = navigatorViewController
mainWindow.makeKeyAndVisible()
window = mainWindow
return true
```

New terms and **important words** are shown in bold. Words that you see on the screen, for example, in menus or dialog boxes, appear in the text like this: "Clicking the **Next** button moves you to the next screen."

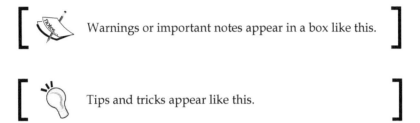

> Warnings or important notes appear in a box like this.

> Tips and tricks appear like this.

Reader feedback

Feedback from our readers is always welcome. Let us know what you think about this book, what you liked or disliked. Reader feedback is important for us as it helps us develop titles that you will really get the most out of.

To send us general feedback, simply e-mail `feedback@packtpub.com`, and mention the book's title in the subject of your message.

If there is a topic that you have expertise in and you are interested in either writing or contributing to a book, see our author guide at `www.packtpub.com/authors`.

Customer support

Now that you are the proud owner of a Packt book, we have a number of things to help you to get the most from your purchase.

Downloading the example code

You can download the example code files for this book from your account at `http://www.packtpub.com`. If you purchased this book elsewhere, you can visit `http://www.packtpub.com/support` and register to have the files e-mailed directly to you.

You can download the code files by following these steps:

1. Log in or register to our website using your e-mail address and password.
2. Hover the mouse pointer on the **SUPPORT** tab at the top.
3. Click on **Code Downloads & Errata**.

4. Enter the name of the book in the **Search** box.

5. Select the book for which you're looking to download the code files.

6. Choose from the drop-down menu where you purchased this book from.

7. Click on **Code Download**.

Once the file is downloaded, please make sure that you unzip or extract the folder using the latest version of:

- WinRAR / 7-Zip for Windows

- Zipeg / iZip / UnRarX for Mac

- 7-Zip / PeaZip for Linux

Downloading the color images of this book

We also provide you with a PDF file that has color images of the screenshots/ diagrams used in this book. The color images will help you better understand the changes in the output. You can download this file from `http://www.packtpub.com/ sites/default/files/downloads/Swift2byExample_ColorImages.pdf`.

Errata

Although we have taken every care to ensure the accuracy of our content, mistakes do happen. If you find a mistake in one of our books—maybe a mistake in the text or the code—we would be grateful if you could report this to us. By doing so, you can save other readers from frustration and help us improve subsequent versions of this book. If you find any errata, please report them by visiting `http://www.packtpub. com/submit-errata`, selecting your book, clicking on the **Errata Submission Form** link, and entering the details of your errata. Once your errata are verified, your submission will be accepted and the errata will be uploaded to our website or added to any list of existing errata under the Errata section of that title.

To view the previously submitted errata, go to `https://www.packtpub.com/books/ content/support` and enter the name of the book in the search field. The required information will appear under the **Errata** section.

Piracy

Piracy of copyrighted material on the Internet is an ongoing problem across all media. At Packt, we take the protection of our copyright and licenses very seriously. If you come across any illegal copies of our works in any form on the Internet, please provide us with the location address or website name immediately so that we can pursue a remedy.

Please contact us at `copyright@packtpub.com` with a link to the suspected pirated material.

We appreciate your help in protecting our authors and our ability to bring you valuable content.

Questions

If you have a problem with any aspect of this book, you can contact us at `questions@packtpub.com`, and we will do our best to address the problem.

1
Welcome to the World of Swift

Swift is a language so new that even the most expert programmers have barely a year and few months of experience in it. However, it borrows most of its features from several other programming languages, such as Ruby, Python, Scala, Rust, Groovy, and even JavaScript and Haskell. So, anyone who approaches Swift will already feel at home, recognizing the patterns and features of their favorite programming languages.

Moreover, unlike Objective-C, whose learning curve is really steep for beginners, Swift is really friendly for newcomers, who can write code once they learn the basics of the language.

Nevertheless, mastering Swift when using its more advanced features, such as effectively integrating patterns of functional programming with object-oriented concepts, takes time and the best practices still need to be discovered.

Also, Swift's language is just one part of the story. In fact, a programming language without a precise goal is pretty useless. Swift is not a general-purpose language, but a language with a specific goal of building apps for iOS and OS X using the Cocoa framework.

It's in this framework that the complexity resides; Cocoa is a very big framework, with thousands of APIs and different patterns and best practices. It has changed significantly over the course of its several releases, for example, moving from the delegate pattern to the use of blocks to make components interact with loose coupling.

More than knowing the language, the real challenge is in knowing the framework. I want to stress that the aim of this chapter is just to help you get the first grasp of what Swift's constructs look like, and not to be exhaustive, so expect to find a certain degree of simplification. Also, be aware that a deeper knowledge of the language can be achieved with books that specialize only in Swift learning, whereas the goal of this book is to teach you how to build apps using Swift.

The first look at Swift

The most obvious way to describe Swift is to compare it with Objective-C, which was the reference programming language for building Cocoa apps. Objective-C is an object-oriented programming language with similarities to dynamic languages, such as Ruby or Python. It is built on top of C, to which Apple has added features to make it modern, such as blocks, properties, and an **Automatic Reference Counter** (**ARC**) to manage the memory.

Swift is an object-oriented programming language with some functional programming characteristics. It aims to flatten the learning curve for the beginner, and to also provide more advanced features for the expert, adding more checks at runtime that could help make apps safer.

Objective-C is a loosely static-typed language; every variable must have a type, but it's possible to define a variable using the id type, reaching a sort of dynamic typing, where the type is evaluated at runtime. Thanks to its powerful runtime environment, it's possible to change the structure of a class; for example, adding a method or variable at runtime. This makes Objective-C a really flexible language, but it is also difficult to manage and prone to creating subtle bugs that are difficult to catch at runtime.

Swift is a strong static-typed language. This means that the type of a variable must be set and is evaluated at compile time. It also lacks any kind of metaprogramming at runtime, but this sternness, added to the functional patterns it supports, should help programmers eliminate an entire class of bugs, allowing apps to be more robust in a faster way.

However, the best way to learn a language is to play with it, and Xcode 7 has brought forth a really nice way to do it.

Let's go to the playground

Usually, the only way to experiment and learn a language until Xcode 5 was by creating a new app and writing code inside any method of that app. Then, you would compile and run it, reading the log or stopping using the debugger.

Xcode introduced the concept of a playground, which isn't an app or a program to be built, but a source file that is constantly compiled and evaluated every time it changes.

Xcode 7 can be downloaded for free from the Mac App Store at http://www.apple.com/osx/apps/app-store/. Once it is installed, go to **File | New | Playground**, as shown in the following screenshot:

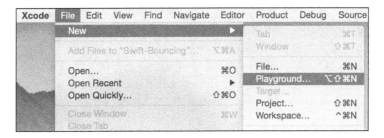

Without changing anything, you have created your first Swift program! The following screenshot shows our first program:

The playground is split into two windows: to the left is our code, and to the right is the evaluation of the code on the left-hand side.

If we change the string from **"Hello, playground"** to **"Hello, world"**, as you can see in the following screenshot, the code is compiled and run without the need to select anything from the menu. This is because the compilation is triggered by the saving operation:

If we make an error, for example, by removing the closing quote from the string, the left part presents a red dot. This dot shows the error type when we click on it. Notice that the right part still presents the result of the previous run. This screenshot displays how the playground shows an error:

```
1   // Playground - noun: a
        place where people
        can play

2

3   import Cocoa

4

5   var str = "Hello, world        Hello, world

6   |           ⊘ Unterminated string literal
```

With the `print()` function, it is possible to print messages on a debug console, which can be opened by clicking on the triangle on the bottom left, as shown in the following screenshot:

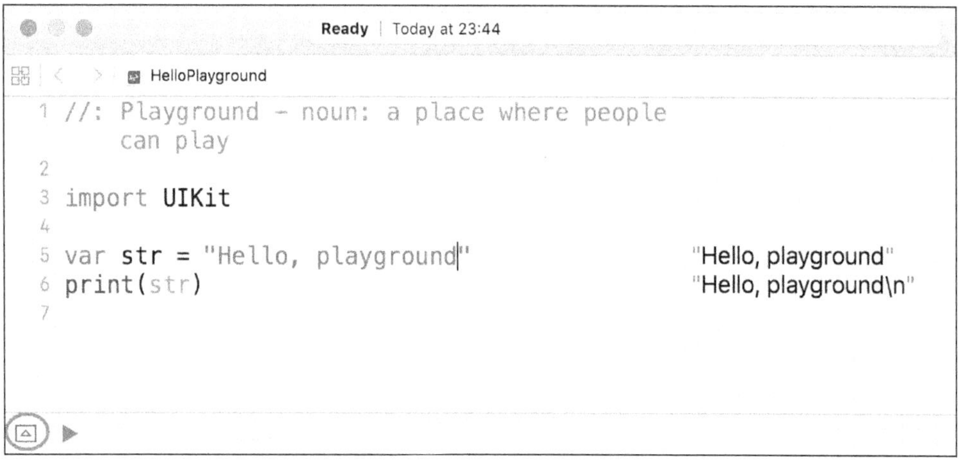

```
                            Ready  |  Today at 23:44

   <  >   ⊞ HelloPlayground

1 //: Playground - noun: a place where people
       can play
2
3 import UIKit
4
5 var str = "Hello, playground"              "Hello, playground"
6 print(str)                                  "Hello, playground\n"
7
```

The console is basically another view just below the playground view, as you can see in this screenshot:

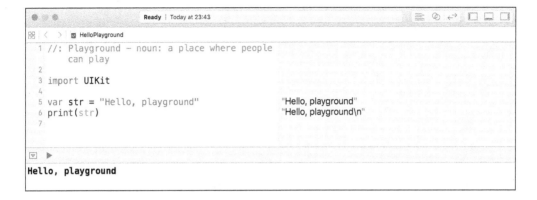

There is much more to learn about playground, but even with this much knowledge, we can dive into Swift without further ado.

The building blocks – variables and constants

As already said, Swift is a strongly typed language, which means that every variable must be declared with the type it holds:

```
let name: String = "Paul"
let age: Int = 27
```

Using the `let` keyword, we define a constant variable that cannot change its value and, as in math, the constant becomes the identity of the value itself. The following screenshot shows what the console looks like when we try to change the constant after we have defined it:

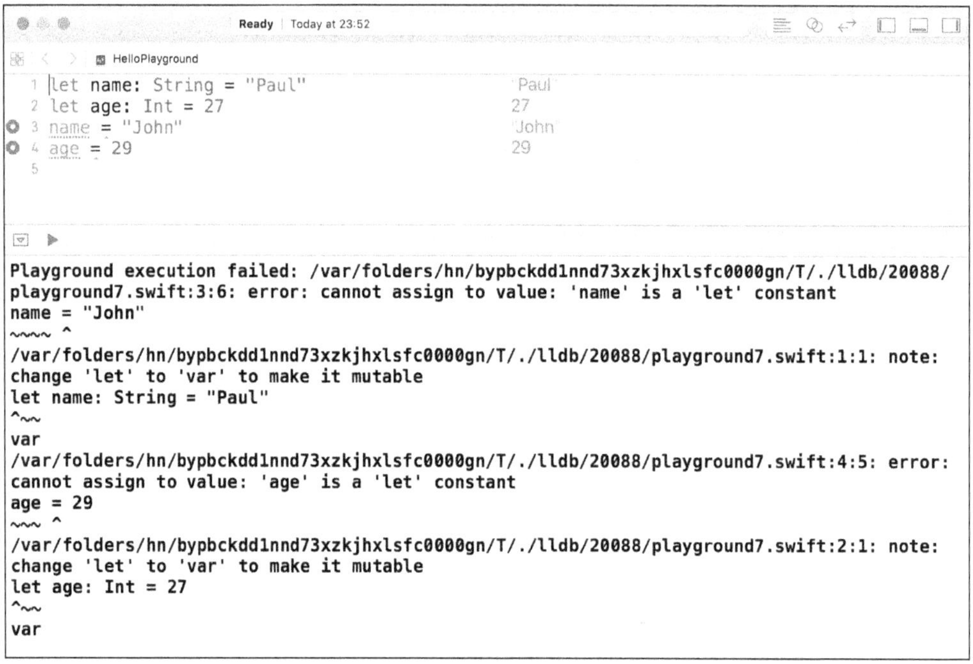

To define a variable, we can use the `var` keyword:

```
var name: String = "Paul"
var age: Int = 27
name = "John"
age = 29
```

We can change the value of a variable, paying attention to set a new value of the same kind. Otherwise, an error will be raised, as shown in this screenshot:

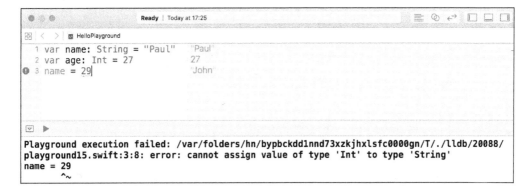

Speaking of type declaration, Swift is smarter than just requiring the type of a variable. If the value of the variable is set during its declaration, Swift can understand the type without the need for an explicit type. This feature is called **type inference**, and it allows us to create more concise code. For example, we can write code like the following:

```
let bassPlayer = "Paul"
let bassPlayerAge = 27
let guitarPlayer = "John"
let guitarPlayerAge = 29
```

Obviously, the type is mandatory if a variable is declared without being initialized:

```
var bassPlayer: String
var bassPlayerAge: Int
var guitarPlayer: String
var guitarPlayerAge: Int
```

Because it's really difficult to track all the changes made to a mutable variable, it is good practice to use constants as much as we can and use variables only to contain the status in a small and well-defined scope in which it's easy to understand whether the code is correct or not.

Collecting variables in containers

A variable is the minimum information that we can handle, but, sometimes, it is useful to group variables together. Swift provides three types of containers for this purpose: `tuple`, `array`, and `dictionary`.

A `tuple` is a limited set of heterogeneous values, like this, for example:

```
let bassPlayer = (name: "Paul", surname: "McCartney", age: 27)
```

In the declaration of a `tuple`, each piece of information is separated by a comma (`,`), each variable is a name-value pair separated by a colon (`:`), and all the elements are surrounded by a pair of parentheses.

To access the elements of a `tuple`, it is possible to use a dot notation, specifying the name of a variable:

```
bassPlayer.name     // Paul
bassPlayer.surname  // McCartney
bassPlayer.age      // 27
```

A `tuple` can also be defined as an unnamed collection, that is, without specifying the names of the elements:

```
let bassPlayer = ("Paul", "McCartney", 27)
```

In this case, to access the elements, we must use their positions inside the tuple:

```
bassPlayer.0 // Paul
bassPlayer.1 // McCartney
bassPlayer.2 // 27
```

It is also possible to unwrap the values of a `tuple` and use them in simple external values, assigning each value inside the `tuple` to specific variables:

```
let bassPlayer = ("Paul", "McCartney", 27)
let (name, surname, age) = bassPlayer
print(name)
print(surname)
print(age)
```

An `array` is an unnamed list of homogeneous values:

```
var band = ["Paul", "John"]
```

An `array` has a number of elements. These elements can be asked for using the `count` property:

```
band.count // 2
```

Each element can be accessed using square brackets (`[]`) around the index of the value:

```
band[0] // Paul
band[1] // John
```

Just as in a `tuple`, the first index starts from `0`.

Unlike Objective-C, where containers have mutable and immutable implementation, in Swift, it depends on the way in which the variable is declared with `let` or with `var`.

If an `array` is mutable, we can change the value at a particular index, but we can also add elements using the `append` method:

```
band.append("George")
band.append("Ringo")
```

Moreover, using the sum operator (+), it is possible to create a new array that contains all the elements of the two previous arrays:

```
let theBeatles = band + ["George", "Ringo"]
```

The third container Swift provides is a `dictionary`, which is a sort of named-index array. Its syntax is similar to that of a `tuple` using a name-value list separated by commas and surrounded by square brackets:

```
var band = ["bass": "Paul", "guitar": "John"]
```

Each value can be reached using the key inside the square brackets:

```
band["bass"]   // Optional("Paul")
band["guitar"] // Optional("John")
```

The value retrieved is not exactly the same value we inserted during the initialization, but it is wrapped by an optional value, which means that the result can be either a real value or `nil`. For example, if we use a key that is not present, the value returned is nil:

```
band["keyboard"] // nil
```

We'll see optional values later in this chapter. For the moment, it's enough to know that to extract the value from an optional, we must use the exclamation mark (!). Pay attention: you must do this only if you are sure that a value is inside an optional value. Otherwise, a runtime error will occur, as shown in this screenshot:

```
fatal error: unexpectedly found nil while unwrapping an Optional value
```

Controlling the flow

The most basic construct used to control the flow is the conditional check, which executes a piece of code if the condition provided is `true`:

```swift
var name = "Jim"
if name == "Paul" {
    print("Let's play the bass")
} else if name == "John" {
    print("Let's play the guitar")
} else if name == "George" {
    print("Let's play the sitar")
} else if name == "Ringo" {
    print("Let's play the drums")
} else {
    print("What do you want to play?")
}
```

The parentheses around the condition are optional but the curly braces are required, even in the case of a single statement.

The `switch` block in Swift is more powerful than in other languages. It is a nicer way of writing a chain of `if` statements:

```swift
var name = "Jim"
switch name {
case "Paul":
```

```
    print("Let's play the bass")
case "John":
    print("Let's play the guitar")
case "George":
    print("Let's play the sitar")
case "Ringo":
    print("Let's play the drums")
default:
    print("What do you want to play?")
}
```

Whereas other languages' `switch` constructs handle-only integers, in Swift, we can have different types of conditional variables.

The list of possible values must be exhaustive, and, in this case, a default case must be provided.

A case block is executed until the entered variable's value matches the case. Swift is smart enough to break a case block on completion, so you don't have to explicitly break out of the `switch` at the end of a case's code.

If you want the same behavior of case in Objective-C, which means continuing if there is no `break` command before the next `case` statement, you must add the `fallthrough` keyword, as shown here:

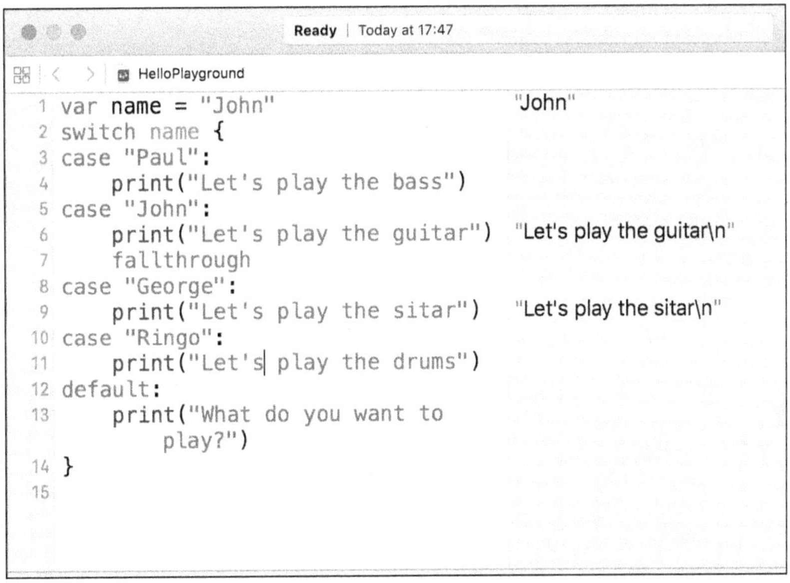

```
                                         Ready | Today at 17:47

  ⊞  <  >   🅗 HelloPlayground
 1  var name = "John"                              "John"
 2  switch name {
 3  case "Paul":
 4      print("Let's play the bass")
 5  case "John":
 6      print("Let's play the guitar")   "Let's play the guitar\n"
 7      fallthrough
 8  case "George":
 9      print("Let's play the sitar")    "Let's play the sitar\n"
10  case "Ringo":
11      print("Let's play the drums")
12  default:
13      print("What do you want to
            play?")
14  }
15
```

As said earlier, switches are more than this, but we'll see better when we implement the apps.

Swift 2 brought another keyword to manage the flow: guard.

A guard keyword is a sort of check that ensures that a certain condition is met, otherwise the function exits.

For example:

```
guard let data = db.getData() where data.count > 0 else {
    return
}
print("Data read from DB [\(data)")
```

As you can see, the role of the guard is to allow the flow only if the condition is valid; to note that the variable scoping works differently than the usual: the data variable is valid even after guard, and you can consider the variable created before the guard in the same scope as the guard itself.

Until now, we have created only linear code without jumping around or going back. It's now time to introduce the loop constructs provided by Swift. A loop is a statement that allows a block of code to be executed repeatedly, controlled by an exit condition.

The most basic kind is the while loop, where the loop is executed if a condition is true, as depicted in this screenshot:

To illustrate the `while` loop, we introduce the string format, which is a handy way to insert a part of code to evaluate inside a `string` using a backslash (\\) followed by parenthesis (()). The contained element is evaluated and the result replaces the expression. In other programming languages, this is called **interpolation**.

Another kind of `loop` is **fast enumeration**, which permits to iterate through an `array` without using an index, but by accessing the values straightaway, as shown in the following screenshot:

```
 88   <   >    🔹 HelloPlayground

  1 var theBeatles = ["Paul", "John",     ["Paul", "John", "George", "Ringo"]
       "George", "Ringo"]
  2
  3 for player in theBeatles {
  4     print("Hi \(player)")              (4 times)
  5 }
  6 |

 ▽  ▶

Hi Paul
Hi John
Hi George
Hi Ringo
```

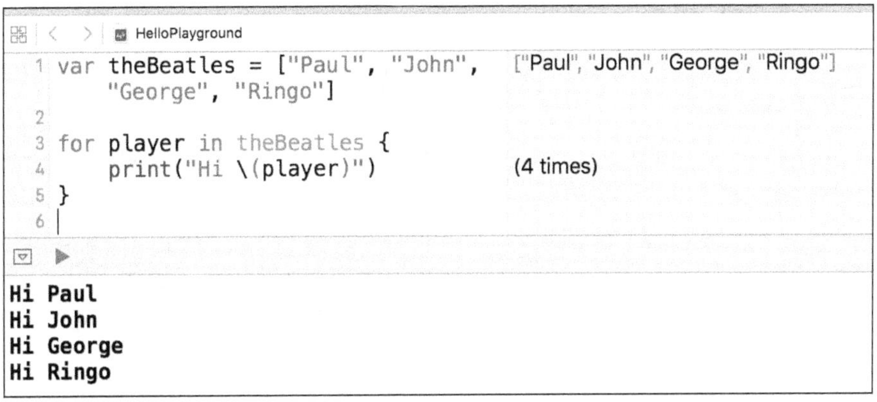

If we want to fast-enumerate through an `array`, and have also provided the index of the item, we can use the `enumerate` function. The following screenshot shows the use of `enumerate` function, which basically returns an array of tuples containing the index and the value:

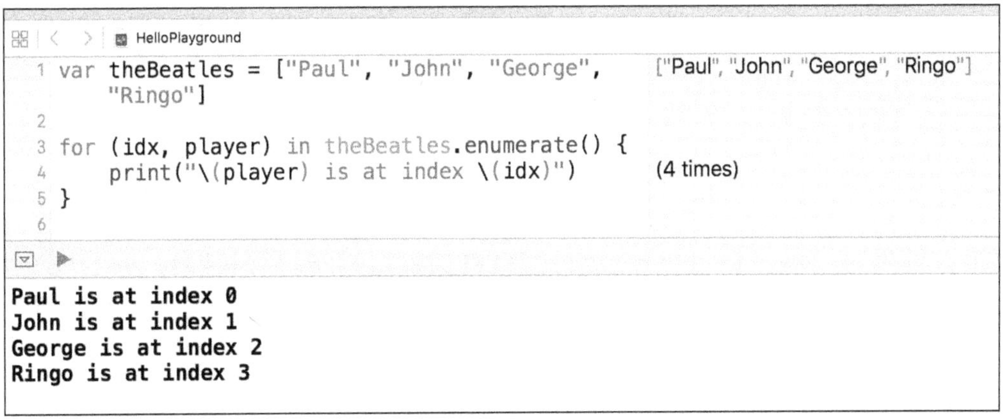

```
 88   <   >    🔹 HelloPlayground

  1 var theBeatles = ["Paul", "John", "George",   ["Paul", "John", "George", "Ringo"]
       "Ringo"]
  2
  3 for (idx, player) in theBeatles.enumerate() {
  4     print("\(player) is at index \(idx)")        (4 times)
  5 }
  6

 ▽  ▶

Paul is at index 0
John is at index 1
George is at index 2
Ringo is at index 3
```

Transforming the values using functions

Swift is a multi-paradigm language that mixes object-oriented programming with functional patterns.

The former organizes the code around objects, which are constructs with variables and functions in imperative way. This means telling the software how to execute the instructions one after the other. The latter defines the structures and elements of code as an evaluation of functions in a declarative way, which means defining what the elements are instead of how the elements behave.

These two paradigms apparently opposite give more flexibility to the developer, who can leverage one or the other depending on the context.

In Swift, functions are first-class citizens, which means that they can be assigned to variables, or they can be passed as either parameters or return values of other functions.

A function in Swift is a named block of instructions that can be initialized, executed, passed as a parameter, or returned as a return value.

A function is declared using the `func` keyword and by enclosing the code to be executed around curly braces ({ }):

```
func greet() {
    print("Hello, world!")
}
greet() // Hello, world!
```

In Swift, a function can be declared in an anonymous way; in this case, it is called a **closure**:

```
let greet = {
    print("Hello, world!")
}
greet() // Hello, world!
```

A function can have a parameter, which is defined inside parentheses:

```
func greet(name: String) {
    print("Hello, \(name)!")
}
greet("Jim") // Hello, Jim!
```

When a function is defined as a `closure`, the parameters are inside the open curly brace and the `in` keyword separates them from the block of instructions:

```
let greet = { (name: String) in
    print("Hello, \(name)!")
}
greet("Jim") // Hello, Jim!
```

A function can return a value, which is defined using the arrow (->) in the declaration:

```
func greet(name: String) -> String {
    return "Hello, \(name)!"
}
print(greet("Jim")) // Hello, Jim!
```

In a consistent manner, the closure defines the return value after the parameters:

```
let greet = { (name: String) -> String in
    return "Hello, \(name)!"
}
print(greet("Jim")) // Hello, Jim!
```

A function can have more than one parameter:

```
func greet(name: String, greeting: String) -> String {
    return "\(greeting), \(name)!"
}
print(greet("Jim", greeting: "Hi")) // Hi, Jim!
```

As we can see from this example, the parameters during the call are passed in a positional way: for the first, the label is omitted, but for the other, it is mandatory:

```
func greeting(firstname: String, surname: String) -> String {
    return "My name is \(surname), \(firstname) \(surname)"
}

greeting("James", surname:"Bond") //My name is Bond, James Bond
```

In this case, duplicating the name of the parameter in the declaration of the function and labels during calls becomes mandatory:

```
func greeting(firstname firstname: String, surname: String) -> String
{
    return "My name is \(surname), \(firstname) \(surname)"
}

greeting(surname: "Bond", firstname: "James") //My name is James, Bond
James
```

Structs – custom compound types

Earlier in this chapter, we saw how to group variables using `tuples`; starting from this concept, Swift offers a way to create complex custom types through `structs`.

A `struct` is a container of different elements with the possibility to add functions to manipulate them.

Starting from the example we used for the `tuple`, we can define a `struct` in this way:

```swift
struct Player{
    let name: String
    let surname: String
    let age: Int
    let instrument: String
}

let bassPlayer = Player(name: "Paul", surname: "McCartney",age:
27, instrument: "bass")
let guitarPlayer = Player(name: "John", surname: "Lennon", age:
29, instrument: "guitar")
```

We can access the elements of a `struct` using the dot notation that we used for the named `tuple`:

```swift
guitarPlayer.name         // John
guitarPlayer.instrument // guitar
```

This form doesn't seem much different from a `tuple`, but the `structs` are more powerful than this.

For example, we can add a function inside the `struct`:

```swift
struct Player{
    let name: String
    let surname: String
    let age: Int
    let instrument: String
    func fullname() -> String{
        return "\(name) \(surname)"
    }
}
bassPlayer.fullname()  // Paul McCartney
```

One of the basic principles of functional programming is to have functions that deal only with immutable elements: they receive immutable objects and return immutable objects.

In this way, the mutable state is not shared in different places of the program, adding complexity to the code because a variable can be mutated in different places.

The struct construct was created with this principle in mind: to enforce immutability. When a struct variable is assigned to another variable, it is assigned by copy. This means that a new struct is created with the same values as the previous struct. The same happens when a struct is passed as a function argument. The nature of the struct is also known as the **Value Type**.

On the contrary, classes (which we'll see in the next section) are *passed by reference*. This means that only the address of the object is copied and the variable points to the same object.

As just mentioned, although it is better to have immutable structs, it's possible to define variables inside a struct, making it possible to change their values:

```swift
struct Player{
    var name: String
    var surname: String
    var age: Int
    var instrument: String
    func fullname() -> String{
        return "\(name) \(surname)"
    }
}

var guitarPlayer = Player(name: "John", surname: "Lennon",
    age: 29,
    instrument: "guitar")
guitarPlayer.fullname()            // John Lennon
guitarPlayer.name    = "Joe"
guitarPlayer.surname = "Satriani"
guitarPlayer.fullname()            // Joe Satriani
```

As already said, a struct is a container of elements; these elements are called **properties**. Other related properties can be created starting from already defined properties.

A struct in Swift offers the mechanism of **computed properties** to create related properties. These are basically functions disguised as properties:

```swift
struct Player{
    var name: String
    var surname: String
    var age: Int
    var instrument: String
```

```
        var fullname: String {
            return "\(name) \(surname)"
        }
    }

    var guitarPlayer = Player(name: "John", surname: "Lennon",
        age: 29,
        instrument: "guitar")

    print(guitarPlayer.fullname) //John Lennon
```

Note that from a caller point of view, a computed property is indistinguishable from a defined property, so it's also possible to define a way to change it:

```
import Foundation

struct Player{
    var name: String
    var surname: String
    var age: Int
    var instrument: String
    var fullname: String {
        get { return "\(name) \(surname)" }
        set(newFullname) {
            let names = newFullname.componentsSeparatedByString(" ")
            name = names[0]
            surname = names[1]
        }
    }
}
var guitarPlayer = Player(name: "John", surname: "Lennon",
    age: 29,
    instrument: "guitar")

guitarPlayer.fullname = "Joe Satriani"
print(guitarPlayer.name)    //Joe
print(guitarPlayer.surname) //Satriani
```

There are a few things to talk about in this snippet.

First of all, we needed to use import Foundation to use the componentsSeparatedByString method, which creates an array of elements, splitting the string using the parameter string as a separator.

Inside the definition of the computed property, we defined two functions: a `getter` (get), which is the same code that we used in the previous example, and a `setter` (set), which accepts a string as a parameter. In the function body, split the parameter in tokens, separated by an empty space, and assign the first value to `name` and the second to `surname`.

As already mentioned, a `struct` is a value type in Swift, such as an integer, a string, an array, and so on. This means that an instance of a `struct` is copied when assigned to a new variable or passed as a parameter:

```
struct Player{
    var name: String
    var surname: String
    var age: Int
    var instrument: String
}

var originalPlayer = Player(name: "John", surname: "Lennon",
    age: 29,
    instrument: "guitar")

var newPlayer = originalPlayer
newPlayer.name = "Joe"
newPlayer.surname = "Satriani"

originalPlayer.surname // Lennon
newPlayer.surname      // Satriani
```

A `struct` is also copied when it is passed a parameter in a function:

```
var originalPlayer = Player(name: "John", surname: "Lennon",
    age: 29,
    instrument: "guitar")

func transformPlayer(var player: Player) -> Player {
    player.name = "Joe"
    player.surname = "Satriani"
    return player
}

var newPlayer = transformPlayer(originalPlayer)

originalPlayer.surname // Lennon
newPlayer.surname      // Satriani
```

This knowledge of `struct`s is enough to start using them efficiently.

Classes – common behavior objects

If you already know another object-oriented programming language, you might be wondering whether there are classes in Swift, and, if so, why we haven't introduced them earlier.

Of course there are! In the end, the main purpose of Swift is to create iOS or OS X apps using Cocoa, which is an object-oriented framework.

Nevertheless, with Swift being a multi-paradigm programming language, classes are no longer the central concepts around which everything is built, as in object-oriented languages. However, they are a way to encapsulate the business logic.

Let's explore classes by altering the previous example to use classes instead of structs:

```
class Player{
    var name: String
    var surname: String
    var age: Int
    var instrument: String
    init(name: String, surname: String, age: Int, instrument: String){
        self.name = name
        self.surname = surname
        self.age = age
        self.instrument = instrument
    }
}

var originalPlayer = Player(name: "John", surname: "Lennon", age:
29, instrument: "guitar")
```

Basically, instead of the `struct` keyword, we used `class`, and we also needed to provide an initializer with all the parameters to initialize the instance (a constructor is a method called when the object is instantiated and initialized).

At first sight, it seems that `class` and `struct` are the same construct, but, in reality, the difference is substantial and relative to the nature of the two constructs.

The main difference is that an instance of a class is copied by reference. This means that the object isn't copied, but the reference of the object is copied, so when we change the new object, we are changing the original object as well.

Let's convert the example of the structs using a class:

```
var originalPlayer = Player(name: "John", surname: "Lennon", age:
29, instrument: "guitar")
```

```
func transformPlayer(var player: Player) -> Player {
    player.name = "Joe"
    player.surname = "Satriani"
    return player
}

var newPlayer = transformPlayer(originalPlayer)

originalPlayer.surname // Satriani
newPlayer.surname      // Satriani
```

We can see in the log of the playground that the function changed originalPlayer as well.

The other main difference is that a class supports inheritance. This means that we can create a specialized version of a class, which is still of the same category as the original class but has more characteristics:

```
class Guitarist: Player{
    var guitarBrand: String
    init(name: String, surname: String, age: Int, guitarBrand: String)
{
        self.guitarBrand = guitarBrand
        super.init(name: name, surname: name, age: age,
instrument: "guitar")
    }
}

var alienGuitarist = Guitarist(name: "Joe", surname: "Satriani",
age: 31, guitarBrand: "guitar")
```

So, a guitarist is basically a player with a guitar.

Note that in the constructor, we need to initialize all the variables of our level (in our case, just one), and then call the parent initializer using the super keyword to continue the chain of initialization.

To help understand when to use a struct or a class, it is often stated to favor the use of structs over classes. When an object represents something concrete (for example, a view or a button), we must use a class. When we need to represent properties or values that don't exist as concrete real things, such as Coordinates or Rect, we must use structs.

Loose coupling with protocols

A good way to tame the complexity of code is to separate what an object does from how it does it.

This is accomplished by defining the `interface` of an object, namely the properties and the methods of a `class` or a `struct`.

If the `class` or `struct` adheres to a protocol, it must implement all the methods defined in the protocol:

```
protocol Playable {
    func play()
}

class Player: Playable{

    //...

    func play() {
        // use instrument to play
    }
}
```

This allows us to call the defined methods without knowing the actual value of an instance:

```
func concert(band: [Playable]){
    for player in band {
        player.play()
    }
}
```

The concept of protocols is widely used in Cocoa for loose coupling and permitting an object to interact without knowing which kind of implementation it has.

Composing objects using protocol extensions

In Swift 1.x, protocols just defined the `interface` that must be implemented, but from Swift 2.0, protocols can also have code than can be used in the implemented `class` or `struct`.

Let's see a simple example, implementing three different instrument players as a protocol:

```
protocol Guitarist {}
```

```
extension Guitarist {
    func playGuitar() {
        print("I'm playing a guitar")
    }
}

protocol BassPlayer {}
extension BassPlayer {
    func playBass() {
        print("I'm playing a bass guitar")
    }
}

protocol KeyboardPlayer {}
extension KeyboardPlayer {
    func playKeyboard() {
        print("I'm playing a keyboard")
    }
}
```

Given these, we can create a class that conforms to all of them:

```
class MultiInstrumentalist: Guitarist, BassPlayer, KeyboardPlayer{}
```

Finally, let's instantiate an object and call the `play` function:

```
let trent = MultiInstrumentalist()
trent.playBass()     // I'm playing a bass guitar
trent.playGuitar()   // I'm playing a guitar
trent.playKeyboard() // I'm playing a keyboard
```

As you can see, although the class doesn't have any defined functions, it exposes the functions implemented in the protocols.

What if we redefine one of the protocol functions inside the implemented class? As you can imagine, the class functions take the precedence:

```
class MultiInstrumentalist: Guitarist, BassPlayer, KeyboardPlayer{
    func playGuitar() {
        print("I'm playing an amazing guitar")
    }
}

let trent = MultiInstrumentalist()
trent.playBass()     // I'm playing a bass guitar
trent.playGuitar()   // I'm playing an amazing guitar
trent.playKeyboard() // I'm playing a keyboard
```

Probably this is one of the most important new features in Swift 2.0, which allows you to compound complex behavior without creating unnecessary complex object hierarchy.

The protocol extensions were introduced during the WWDC 2015 in a presentation called *Protocol Oriented Programming in Swift*. I strongly recommend you to watch it at https://developer.apple.com/videos/play/wwdc2015-408/.

Checking the existence of an optional value

We have already seen optional values when we discussed the `dictionary`.

The introduction of optional values is a radical, phenomenal change from Objective-C, where it is allowed to call a method on a `nil` object without crashing the app and the method call is silently discarded.

It might be handy in several occasions, but it can often create really subtle, difficult-to-track, bugs. For example, if some objects of the UI are not connected to the controller and we try to change their values, we send messages to `nil` and nothing happens, leaving us without a clue as to what happened.

On the other hand, when we try to insert a `nil` object into a collection such as `array` or `dictionary`, the app crashes at runtime.

Swift forces the developer to think of the nature of an element, whether it's always present or whether it could be `nil`.

An optional is declared using a question mark (?), and to make the code compile, the developer must check whether an optional value is `nil` before using it.

Also, an optional integer or optional string is not an ordinary integer or string; it's an integer or string wrapped in a container. To extract and evaluate the value inside the container, we must use the exclamation mark (!):

```
var optionalInt: Int?

if optionalInt != nil {
    let realInt = optionalInt!
    print("The value is [\(realInt)]")
} else {
    print("The value is nil!")
}
```

This pattern is so common that Swift allows us to create the unwrapped variable during the `nil` check:

```
var optionalInt: Int? = 3

if let realInt = optionalInt {
    print("The value is [\(realInt)]")
} else {
    print("The value is nil!")
}
```

As a good rule, it's recommended to use an optional as little as you can in your code, and to always check whether a variable is `nil` before using it.

Exploiting the fact that in Swift it is possible to define a non-optional variable from an option variable, with Swift 2.0 and the `guard` keyword, this is a very common patter to unwrap the optional:

```
var usefulValue: Int?
//….
guard let usefulValue = usefulValue else {
return
}
// Code that uses usefulValue
```

In this way the code is readable and safe.

Enumerations on steroids

Enumerations are common constructs in several programming languages, but in Swift they are really powerful.

They are used when we have a limited and well-defined set of possible values, for example, the code responses for HTTP or the suits of a card game.

While you can have only numeric-based enumerations in Objective-C, in Swift, enumerations can also be implemented with string:

```
enum Instrument: String {
    case Guitar = "guitar"
    case Bass = "bass"
    case Drums = "drums"
    case Sitar = "sitar"
    case Keyboard = "keyboard"
}
```

Using this enumeration, we can define a variable:

```
let instrument = Instrument.Drums
```

In this case, the constant infers the type from the initialization, but it is also possible to declare the type and use an abbreviated version of the value:

```
let instrument: Instrument = .Drums
```

Because the constant is an instrument, the compiler is expecting a value of the enumeration to assign to it, and it becomes superfluous when declaring the kind of enumerations on the right side.

We have already seen the switch construct, and it's really useful with enumeration, and in such a case, a statement contains a value of the enumeration:

```
let instrument: Instrument = .Drums

switch instrument {
case .Guitar:
    print("Let's play guitar")
case .Bass:
    print("Let's play bass")
case .Drums:
    print("Let's play drums")
case .Sitar:
    print("Let's play sitar")
case .Keyboard:
    print("Let's play keyboard")
}
// Let's play drums
```

As previously mentioned, the cases of a switch must be exhaustive and all possible values must have a case; this enforces Swift to eliminate, as much as it can, the chances of introducing bugs because of distraction or superficiality. For every case, as in optional values, the developer is forced to pay attention and make a decision, which can be wrong, of course, but at least it's not because he forgets to test a condition.

A really advanced feature of enumerations in Swift is the possibility to associate values with members. For example, we can add the number of strings for Guitar and the brand for Keyboard:

```
let keithEmersonInstrument: Instrument = .Keyboard("Hammond")
let steveVaiInstrument: Instrument = .Guitar(7)
let instrument = steveVaiInstrument
```

```
switch instrument {
case .Guitar(let numStrings):
    print("Let's play a \(numStrings) strings guitar")
case .Bass:
    print("Let's play bass")
case .Drums:
    print("Let's play drums")
case .Sitar:
    print("Let's play sitar")
case .Keyboard(let brand):
    print("Let's play a \(brand) keyboard")
}

// Let's play 7 strings guitar
```

Here, you can see that to extract the value from members, we need to use the binding inside the case.

Enumerations are more powerful than what we have seen in this section, but this is enough to understand their power, which, when linked with the features of switch statements, make them one of the most important additions to Swift.

Extended pattern matching

As seen in the previous paragraph, the switch statement is really useful to decide the logic given an input.

For example, a check can be added to a case statement having defined an enum with associated values:

```
enum Instrument{
    case Guitar(numStrings: Int)
    case Keyboard(brand: String)
}

let instrument = Instrument.Guitar(numStrings: 7)
```

We can extract the logic using these statements:

```
switch instrument {
case .Guitar(numStrings: let numStrings)
    where numStrings == 7:
    print("Let's play 'For the Love of God'")
case .Guitar(numStrings: let numStrings)
    where numStrings == 12:
```

```
        print("Let's play 'Stairway to Heaven'")
case .Keyboard(brand: let brand)
        where brand == "Hammond":
        print("Let's play 'Tarkus'")
case .Keyboard(brand: let brand)
        where brand == "Korg":
        print("Let's play 'The Show Must Go On'")
default:
        print("Sorry, I can't suggest any song")
}
```

Sometimes the logic resides in the composition of the input; for example, if we have two instruments and we want the first one to decide the kind of the songs, we can exploit the `switch` with a `tuple` to decide it:

```
let firstInstrument = Instrument.Keyboard(brand: "Hammond")
let secondInstrument = Instrument.Guitar(numStrings: 7)

switch (firstInstrument, secondInstrument) {
case (.Guitar, _):
        print("Let's play a guitar song")
case (.Keyboard, _):
        print("Let's play a keyboard song")
}
```

Because we don't care of the second instrument, which can be the same as the first, we use the wildcard character (_) that matches any value.

The final example I want to show is using the `switch` for a type casting pattern.

To define any possible type, `class`, `struct`, `protocol`, and so on, Swift provides the keyword `Any`.

```
import UIKit

var anUnknownObjct: Any?

anUnknownObjct = "Hello, World"

switch anUnknownObjct {
case nil:
        print("I cannot handle nil element")
case is UIView:
        print("I cannot handle graphic element")
case let value as String:
        print(value)
```

```
case let value as Int:
    print("The successor is \(value + 1)")
default:
    print("Unmatched object \(anUnknownObjct)")
}
```

Because we are not really interested in the value of the variable when the variable is a `UIView`, we just check is it is a `UIView`, whereas for the `String` and `Int`, we want to use that value so that we can bind it to a constant using `let`. If nothing matches, we just log the value.

Catching errors

To build the safest code possible, we must handle and manage errors in the most robust way possible.

Usually, each language has a particular way to handle the error, and Swift, as a successor of Objective-C, supports, and enhances, the Objective-C ways.

Historically, Objective-C did not have exception handling, which was added later through a class, `NSException`, and the **MACROs** `NS_DURING`, `NS_HANDLER`, and `NS_ENDHANDLER`.

This was the way to use them:

```
NS_DURING
{
    [obj riskyOperation];
    [safeObj safeOperation];
}
NS_HANDLER
    NSLog("Severe error happened!");
NS_ENDHANDLER
```

The code around the `NS_DURING` and `NS_HANDLER` ensures that if a exception is raised in the `riskyOperation` method, the execution is interrupted and the control is passed to the code inside `NS_HANDLER` and `NS_ENDHANDLER`.

This construct was very limited, for example it is impossible to define different exceptions to describe different error scenarios.

In OS X 10.3, native exception handling was added, basically importing the C++ mechanism.

It was then possible to write code like this:

```objc
@try {
    [obj riskyOperation];
    [safeObj safeOperation];
}
@catch (BadError *exception) {
    // Handle the exception…
}
@catch (TerribleError *exception) {
    // Handle the exception…
}
@catch (AwfulError *exception) {
    // Handle the exception…
}
@finally {
    // Clean up…
}
```

The pattern is similar to the implementation in other languages, like Java; the code in the @try block is guarded against any possible exception and if an exception is raised, the block related to that type of exception is executed.

The @finally block is executed regardless if an exception is raised or not.

Despite the fact that the implementation was seamlessly integrated with the rest of SDK, the Objective-C developers rarely used the exceptions as an error mechanism, and Apple itself suggested to use exceptions only for non recoverable errors.

The usual way to handle errors in Objective-C and Swift 1.x is through the use of a NSError variable passed as a parameter:

```objc
NSError *error;
BOOL success = [db saveData:data error:&error];
if (!success) {
    NSLog("Unexpected error [%@]", error);
} else {
    NSLog("Success");
}
```

This code is translated literally in Swift 1.x:

```swift
Var error: NSError?
let success = db.saveData(data, error:&error)
if!success {
    print("Unexpected error [\(error)]")
} else {
    print("Success")
}
```

Although the previous code is still valid in Swift 2.0, one of the biggest improvements in the new version of the language is the introduction of the exception handling mechanism.

The previous code could be rewritten as:

```
do {
try db.saveData(data)
}
catch ErrorType {
print("Unexpected error happened")
}
```

Although the syntax is similar to Objective-C, the exceptions in Swift are more lightweight: for example the stack is not unwind like in Objctive-C, which can lead to a memory leak, but it just exists from the scope.

Also, in Objective-C, all the exceptions are resolved at runtime, leading to some performance issues, but in Swift, part of those, mainly when there are concatenations of functions that can throw exceptions, can be optimized at compile time.

The exceptions must be defined as an `enum` implementing `ErrorType`.

Let's see a simple example where we implement a class, called `Vault`, and where we encrypt a string passing a password; the `Vault` uses exceptions to notify an invaded password.

First of all, it defines the possible exceptions:

```
enum VaultError: ErrorType {
    case Empty
    case Short
    case Invalid(String)
    case AlreadyEncrypted
}
```

These cases describe the scenario when a password is either too short, empty, or invalid, and also the case when we try to encrypt an already encrypted `Vault` class.

Then, we implement a simple `Vault` class:

```
class Vault {
    private let unencryptedData: String
    private var encryptedData: String?
    init(data: String){
        unencryptedData = data
    }
```

```
    func encryptWithPassword(password: String) throws {
        guard password.characters.count > 0 else {
            throw VaultError.Empty
        }
        guard password.characters.count >= 5 else {
            throw VaultError.Short
        }

        guard isValid(password) else {
            throw VaultError.Invalid("The password must contains
numbers and letters, lowercase and uppercase.")
        }

        guard encryptedData == nil else {
            throw VaultError.AlreadyEncrypted
        }

        encryptedData = encryptData(unencryptedData,
                        password: password)
    }
}
```

As you can see, the signature of encryptWithPassword() is decorated with the throws instruction so that the compile knows that the function can throw exceptions and force the use of the keyword try; a big difference with the Objective-C exceptions is that in Swift 2.0, the developer is forced to handle the exceptions, even with an empty implementation, but at least the compiler gives you an option to try to manage a possible error.

Going back to our example:

```
let dataToEncrypt = "Some super important stuff!"
let password = "23Hello_42"

let vault = Vault(data: dataToEncrypt)

do {
    try vault.encryptWithPassword(password)
}
catch VaultError.Empty {
    print("You should provide a password")
}
catch VaultError.Short {
    print("The password should be at least 5 characters")
```

```
}
catch VaultError.Invalid(let message) {
    print(message)
}
catch VaultError.AlreadyEncrypted {
    print("It's not possible to encrypt twice")
}
```

As you can see, all the case must be handled.

Sometime we are really sure that a function doesn't throw an exception and we have already checked the validity of the password before passing it to the `Vault`; for example, in this case we can use `try!`, whose behavior is similar to an implicitly unwrapped optional value with the risk of a crash if the function raises an exception:

```
try! vault.encryptWithPassword(password)
```

What if we need to clean up resources regardless if the encryption succeeds? Swift 2.0 implemented, and improved, the `@finally{}` pattern, calling it `defer`:

```
let vault = Vault(data: dataToEncrypt)
defer {
    vault.destroy()
}
```

Besides the fact that the `defer` block should be the last block of the exception handling, another interesting characteristic is that it is possible to define multiple `defers` for the same scope and Swift will call all of them in the same order it found was declared in the scope.

Swift functional programming patterns

One of the more exciting peculiarities of Swift is the introduction of functional programming patterns in the language.

As already mentioned, we can define functional programming as a paradigm where the focus, instead of steps of instructions to be executed, is on declaring the program as an evaluation of pure functions avoiding mutable state.

Although Swift cannot be considered a functional language, `http://robnapier.net/swift-is-not-functional`, it allows you to mix imperative and **Object-Oriented Programming (OOP)** concepts with functional patterns.

One important concept to include in Swift is that its functions are **High Order Functions** that means that they can accept functions as parameters and that can return functions as a `return value`.

Let's show the subject with an example.

Having defined two functions:

```
import Foundation

func square(value: Int) -> Int {
    return value * value
}

func cube(value: Int) -> Int {
    return value * value * value
}
```

Let's define a function that randomly returns one of those:

```
func randFunc() -> (Int) -> Int {
    if Int(arc4random_uniform(UInt32(100))) > 50 {
        return square
    } else {
        return cube
    }
}
```

Then, define a function that accepts another function as a parameter:

```
func average(v1: Int, v2: Int, f: (Int)->Int) -> Int {
    return (f(v1) + f(v2))/2
}
```

Finally, we can use them like this:

```
average(3, v2: 5, f: randFunc()) // 17 or 76
```

The collection category in Swift implements some High Order Functions that can be used to concatenate transformation.

Let's see the first one: `map()`.

This function is used when we want to transform an array of A elements to an array of B elements using a function that transforms A to B.

Giving, for example, an array of `double`, we want to map it to an array of `string`, prepending it the dollar symbol:

```
let notes = [5, 10, 20, 50, 20, 10]
notes.map { note in
    return "$\(note)"
}
// ["$5", "$10", "$20", "$50", "$20", "$10"]
```

Because the `transform` function is really simple, we can use the succinct form allowed by Swift, removing the input variable declaration and using the positional value ($) as the first parameter, $0 the third, and so on) and suppressing the return.

```
let notes = [5, 10, 20, 50, 20, 10]
notes.map { "$\($0)" }
// ["$5", "$10", "$20", "$50", "$20", "$10"]
```

The result is the same as the more conventional fast enumeration:

```
let notes = [5, 10, 20, 50, 20, 10]
var dollars = [String]()
for note in notes {
    dollars.append("$\(note)")
}
// ["$5", "$10", "$20", "$50", "$20", "$10"]
```

This way, though, avoids the creation of a temporary mutable structure and can be used to concatenate transformation. Moreover, the emphasis is on what to do instead of how to do it.

Another important function is the `filter()` function, which iterates on the array and checks if every element satisfies a `closure` passed as a parameter. Let's imagine wanting to filter out all the notes greater or equal to 50:

```
let notes = [5, 10, 20, 50, 20, 10]
notes.filter { note in
    return note < 50
}
// [5, 10, 20, 20, 10]
```

Again, we can use the succinct form:

```
let notes = [5, 10, 20, 50, 20, 10]
notes.filter { $0 < 50 }
// [5, 10, 20, 20, 10]
```

The third important High Order Function is `reduce()`, which accumulates the values in a variable, applying the passed `closure` to each element.

Let's assume we want to sum the notes:

```
let notes = [5, 10, 20, 50, 20, 10]
notes.reduce(0) { accumulator, element in
    return accumulator + element
}
// 115
```

We pass the first value and a function to apply to each value.

The closure can also be written like this:

```
let notes = [5, 10, 20, 50, 20, 10]
notes.reduce(0) { $0 + $1}
// 115
```

Because the operator + is a function that accepts two `Int` as parameters and returns the sum, the `reduce()` function can be even reduced like:

```
let notes = [5, 10, 20, 50, 20, 10]
notes.reduce(0, combine: +)
// 115
```

The power of these functions lies in the fact that we can *concatenate* them, and to sum the notes less than 50 we can write:

```
let notes = [5, 10, 20, 50, 20, 10]
notes.filter { $0 < 50 }.reduce(0, combine: +)
// 65
```

Swift 2.0 brought an alternative to fast enumeration to iterate on elements: `forEach()`.

The syntax is similar to `map()`, but the difference is that `forEach()` doesn't return any values but operates on the element.

For example, to print the dollar value of each note, we could write:

```
let notes = [5, 10, 20, 50, 20, 10]
notes.forEach { note in
    print("$\(note)")
}
// $5
// $10
// $20
// $50
// $20
// $10
```

Finally, the last High Order Function I want to present is the `flatMap()`, which flattens every contained element in the array:

```
let notes = [[5, 10, 20], [50, 20, 10]]
notes.flatMap { $0 }
// [5, 10, 20, 50, 20, 10]
```

Another valuable use of the `flatMap()` is to filter out the `nil` values:

```
func filterGreaterThan50(value: Int?) -> Int? {
    guard let value = value else {
        return nil
    }
    if value < 50 {
        return value
    }
    return nil
}
let notes: [Int?] = [5, nil, 10, 20, nil, 50, 20, 10]
let a = notes
        .map{filterGreaterThan50($0)}
        .flatMap { $0 }
// [5, 10, 20, 20, 10]
```

Summary

This was a really dense chapter because we squeezed in content that usually needs at least a book to explain properly in only tens of pages.

We took a quick look at Swift and its capabilities, starting from the definitions of variables and constants and then how to define the control flow. After that, we moved on to structs and classes, seeing how they are similar in some ways but profoundly different as philosophies. Finally, we explored the new features of Swift 2.0, how to create simple objects for complex problems, and how to exploit functional patterns to build more readable programs.

Of course, simply after reading this chapter, nobody can be considered an expert in Swift. However, the information here is enough to let you understand all of the code we'll be using in the upcoming chapters to build several kinds of apps.

In the next chapter, we'll continue to explore Swift and iOS, and, finally, we'll implement a simple iOS app to start to understand how the environment works.

2
Building a Guess the Number App

As mentioned in the previous chapter, learning a language is just half of the difficulty in building an app; the other half is the framework. This means that learning a language is not enough. In this chapter, we'll implement a simple *Guess the Number* app, just to become familiar with Xcode and part of the Cocoa Touch framework.

The app is…

Our first complete Swift program is a *Guess the Number* app, a classic educational game for children where the player must guess a number generated randomly.

For each guess, the game tells the player whether the guess is greater or lower than the generated number (also called the secret number).

It is worth to remember that the goal here is not to build an App Store ready app with a perfect software architecture, but to show how to use Xcode to build apps for the iOS platform, so forgive me if the code is not exactly *Clean Code*, and if the game is trivial.

Before diving into the code, we must define the interface of the app and the expected workflow.

This game presents only one screen, which is shown in the following screenshot:

At the top of the screen, a label reports the name of the app, **Guess a Number**.

In the next row, another static label with the word, **between**, connects the title with a dynamic label that reports the current range. The text inside the label must change every time a new number is inserted. A text field at the center of the screen is where the player will insert their guess.

A big button, with **OK** written on it, is the command that confirms that the player has inserted the chosen number.

The last two labels give feedback to the player:

- **Your last guess was too low** is displayed if the number inserted is lower than the secret number
- **Your last guess was too high** is displayed if it's greater than the secret number

The last label reports the current number of guesses. The workflow is straightforward:

1. The app selects a random number.
2. The player inserts their guess.
3. If the number is equal to the secret number, a popup tells the player that they have won, and shows them the number of guesses.

4. If the number is lower than the secret number but greater than the lower bound, it becomes the new lower bound. Otherwise, it is silently discarded.

5. If the number is greater and lower than the upper bound, it becomes the new upper bound. Otherwise, it's, again, silently discarded.

Building a skeleton app

Let's start building the app.

There are two different ways to create a new project in Xcode: using a wizard or selecting a new project from the menu.

When Xcode starts, it presents a wizard showing the recently used projects and a shortcut to create a new project, as shown in the following screenshot:

If you have already Xcode open, you can select a new project by going to **File** | **New** | **Project...**, as shown in this screenshot:

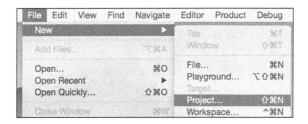

Either way you choose, Xcode will ask for the type of app to be created. Since our app is going to be really simple, let's choose the **Single View Application**:

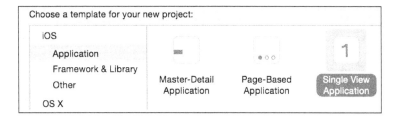

Before starting to write code, we need to complete the configuration by adding the **Organization Identifier**, using the reverse domain name notation like **co.uk. effectivecode**, and **Product Name**. Together, they produce a **Bundle Identifier**, which is the unique identifier of the app.

Pay attention to the selected language, which must obviously be **Swift**. Following is the screenshot that shows you how to fill in the form:

Once done with this data, we are ready to run the app by going to **Product | Run**, as shown in this screenshot:

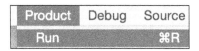

After the simulator finishes loading the app, we can see our magnificent creation, a shiny, brilliant white page!

We can stop the app by going to **Product** | **Stop**, as shown in the following screenshot:

Given that a white page is not what we want, let's fix that writing code and adding content.

Adding the graphics components

When we are developing an iOS app, it is good practice to implement the app outside-in, starting from the graphics.

By taking a look at the files generated by the Xcode template, we can identify the two files that we'll use to implement *Guess the Number* app:

- `Main.storyboard`: This contains the graphics components
- `ViewController.swift`: This handles all of the logic of the app

Here is a screenshot that presents the structure of the files in an Xcode project:

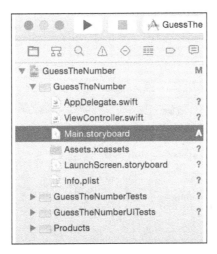

Let's start by selecting the storyboard file to add the labels.

The first thing we notice is that the canvas is not the same size or ratio as an iPhone and an iPad. To handle different sizes and different devices, Apple (since iOS 5) have added a constraints system, called **Auto Layout**, as a system to connect the graphics components in relative way, regardless of the actual size of the running device.

As Auto Layout is beyond the scope of this chapter, we'll implement the created app only for iPhone 6.

After deciding our target device, we need to resize the canvas as per the real size of the device. From the tree structure at the right, we select **View Controller**, as shown here:

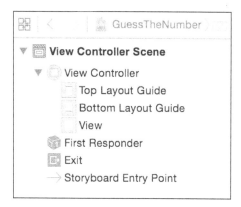

After having done that, we move to the right-hand side, where there are the properties of the **View Controller**. There, we select the tab containing **Simulated Metrics**, in which we can insert the requested size. The following screenshot will help you locate the correct tab:

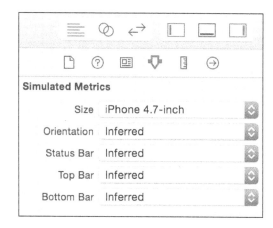

Selecting the **iPhone 4.7-inch** size, we selected the appropriate size for iPhone 6 and 6S; after implementing the app, you could run it in different simulators to understand what this means.

Now the size is the expected size, we can proceed to add labels, text fields, and the buttons from the list in the bottom-right corner of the screen.

To add a component, we must choose it from the list of components. Then, we drag it onto the screen, where we can place it at the expected coordinates.

This screenshot shows the list of UI components, called **Object library**:

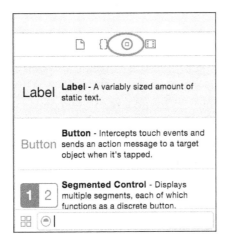

As it is usually difficult to find, it's worth mentioning that we select the circle icon with a square inside to select the **Object library**.

When you add the text field, pay attention to selecting **Number Pad** as the value for **Keyboard Type**, as illustrated in the following screenshot:

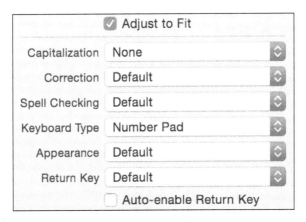

As mentioned, to add a component to the storyboard, it must be selected from the object library and with the left button of the mouse clicked and dragged onto the **View Controller**:

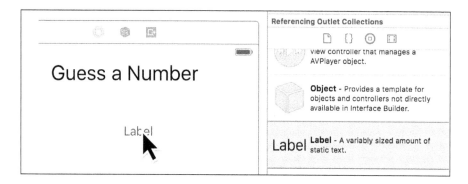

When the components are in the storyboard, you'll notice that moving the blue lines appear to help you to align them to the already set components:

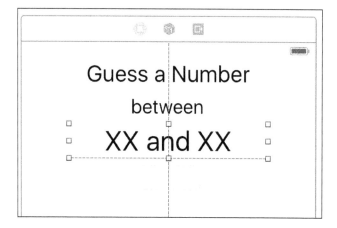

After selecting values for all the components, the app should appear as shown in the mockup we had drawn earlier, which this screenshot can confirm:

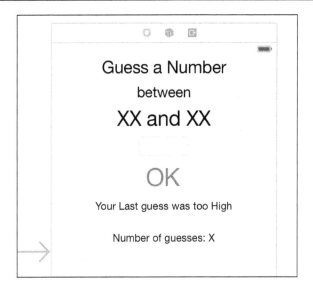

Connecting the dots

If we run the app, the screen is the same as the one in the storyboard, but if we try to insert a number into the text field and then press the button, nothing happens.

This is because the storyboard is still detached from the **View Controller**, which handles all of the logic.

To connect the labels to the **View Controller**, we need to create instances of a label prepended with the @IBOutlet keyword. Using this signature, **Interface Builder**, the graphic editor inside Xcode can recognize the instances available for connection to the components:

```
class ViewController: UIViewController {
    @IBOutlet weak var rangeLbl: UILabel!
    @IBOutlet weak var numberTxtField: UITextField!
    @IBOutlet weak var messageLbl: UILabel!
    @IBOutlet weak var numGuessesLbl: UILabel!

    @IBAction func onOkPressed(sender: AnyObject) {
    }
}
```

We have also added a method with the @IBAction prefix, which will be called when the button is pressed.

Now, let's move on to **Interface Builder** to connect the labels and outlets.

First of all, we need to select **View Controller** from the tree of components, as shown in this screenshot:

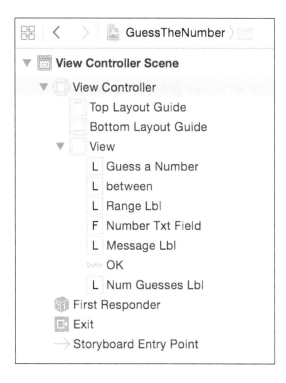

In the tabs to the right, select the outlet views, the last one with an arrow as a symbol. The following screenshot will help you find the correct symbol:

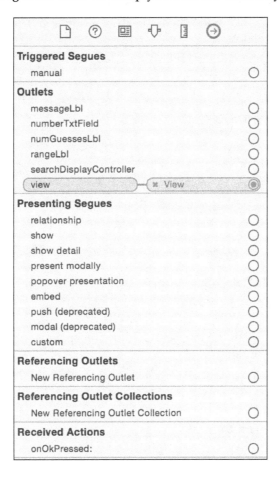

This shows all the possible outlets to which a component can be connected.

Upon moving the cursor onto the circle beside the **rangeLbl** label, we see that it changes to a cross. Now, we must click-and-drag a line to the label in the storyboard, as shown in this screenshot:

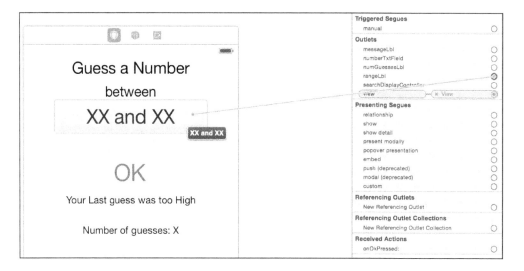

After doing the same for all the labels, the following screenshot shows the final configurations for the outlets:

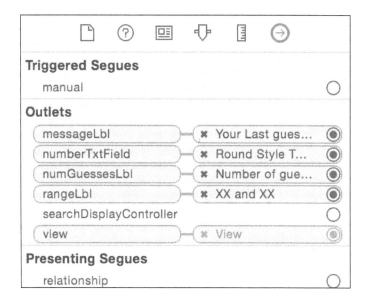

For the action of the button, the process is similar: select the circle close to the **onOkPressed** action, and drag a line to the **OK** button, as shown in this screenshot:

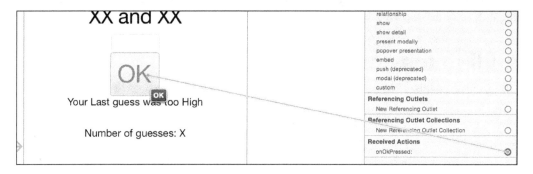

When the button is released, a popup appears with the list of possible events to connect the action to.

In our case, we connect the action to the **Touch Up Inside** event, which is triggered when we release the button without moving from its area. The following screenshot presents the list of the events raised by the `UIButton` component:

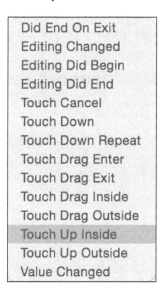

Now, suppose we added a `log` command like this one:

```
@IBAction func onOkPressed(sender: AnyObject) {
    print(numberTxtField.text)
}
```

Then, we can see the value of the text field we insert printed on the debug console.

Now that all the components are connected to their respective outlets, we can add the simple code required to create the app.

Adding the code

First of all, we need to add a few instance variables to handle the state:

```
private var lowerBound = 0
private var upperBound = 100
private var numGuesses = 0
private var secretNumber = 0
```

Just for the sake of clarity, and the separation of responsibilities, we create two extensions to the **View Controller**. An extension in Swift is similar to a category in Objective-C, a distinct data structure that adds a method to the class it extends.

Because we don't need the source of the class that the extension extends, we can use this mechanism to add features to third-party classes, or even to CocoaTouch classes.

Given this original purpose, extensions can also be used to organize the code inside a source file. This could seem a bit unorthodox, but if it doesn't hurt and is useful, why not use it?

The first extension contains the logic of the game:

```
private extension ViewController{
    enum Comparison{
        case Smaller
        case Greater
        case Equals
    }

    func selectedNumber(number: Int){
    }

    func compareNumber(number: Int, otherNumber: Int) -> Comparison {
    }
}
```

 The `private` keyword is added to the extension, making the methods inside private. This means that other classes that hold a reference to an instance of **View Controller** can't call these `private` methods.

Also, this piece of code shows that it is possible to create enumerations inside a `private` extension.

The second extension is for rendering all the labels:

```
private extension ViewController{
    func extractSecretNumber() {
    }

    func renderRange() {
    }

    func renderNumGuesses() {
    }
    func resetData() {
    }
    func resetMsg() {
    }
    func reset(){
        resetData()
        renderRange()
        renderNumGuesses()
        extractSecretNumber()
        resetMsg()
    }
}
```

Let's start from the beginning, which is the `viewDidLoad` method in the case of the **View Controller**:

```
override func viewDidLoad() {
    super.viewDidLoad()
    numberTxtField.becomeFirstResponder()
    reset()
}
```

When the `becomeFirstResponder` method is called, the component called is `numberTxtField`, in our case it gets the focus, and the keyboard appears.

After that, `reset()` is called:

```
func reset(){
    resetData()
    renderRange()
    renderNumGuesses()
    extractSecretNumber()
```

```
        resetMsg()
    }
```

This basically calls the `reset` method of each component:

```
func resetData() {
    lowerBound = 0
    upperBound = 100
    numGuesses = 0
}

func resetMsg() {
    messageLbl.text = ""
}
```

Then, the method is called and is used to render the two dynamic labels:

```
func renderRange() {
    rangeLbl.text = "\(lowerBound) and \(upperBound)"
}

func renderNumGuesses() {
    numGuessesLbl.text = "Number of Guesses: \(numGuesses)"
}
```

It also extracts the secret number using the `arc4random_uniform` function, and performs some typecast magic to align to the expected numeric type:

```
func extractSecretNumber() {
    let diff = upperBound - lowerBound
    let randomNumber = Int(arc4random_uniform(UInt32(diff)))
    secretNumber = randomNumber + Int(lowerBound)
}
```

Now, all the action is in the `onOkPressed` action (pun intended):

```
@IBAction func onOkPressed(sender: AnyObject) {
    guard let number = Int(numberTxtField.text!) else {
        let alert = UIAlertController(title: nil, message: "Enter a
number", preferredStyle: UIAlertControllerStyle.Alert)
        alert.addAction(UIAlertAction(title: "OK", style:
UIAlertActionStyle.Default, handler: nil))
        self.presentViewController(alert, animated: true, completion:
nil)
        return
    }
    selectedNumber(number)
}
```

Here, we retrieve the inserted number. Then, if it is valid (that is, it's not empty, not a word, and so on), we call the `selectedNumber` method. Otherwise, we present a popup asking for a number. This code uses the Swift 2.0 keyword guard that permits to create a really clear code flow; in this way, if the number is not a valid one, we return from the function and we don't need to check in the `selectecNumber()` function if the parameter is valid or not.

 The text property of a `UITextField` is an optional, but because we are certain that is present, we can safely unwrap it.

Also, the handy `Int(String)` constructor converts a string in a number only if the strings is a valid number.

All the juice is in `selectedNumber`, where there is a `switch` case:

```
func selectedNumber(number: Int){
    switch compareNumber(number, otherNumber: secretNumber){
//....
```

The `compareNumber` basically transforms a compare check into an enumeration:

```
func compareNumber(number: Int, otherNumber: Int) -> Comparison{
    if number < otherNumber {
        return .Smaller
    } else if number > otherNumber {
        return .Greater
    }

    return .Equals
}
```

Back to the `switch` statement of `selectedNumber`, it first checks whether the number inserted is the same as the secret number:

```
case .Equals:
    let alert = UIAlertController(title: nil, message: "You won in
\(numGuesses) guesses!", preferredStyle:
UIAlertControllerStyle.Alert)
    alert.addAction(UIAlertAction(title: "OK", style:
UIAlertActionStyle.Default,
        handler: { cmd in
            self.reset()
            self.numberTxtField.text = ""}))
            self.presentViewController(alert,
            animated: true, completion: nil)
```

If this is the case, a popup with the number of guesses is presented, and when it is dismissed, all of the data is cleaned and the game starts again.

If the number is smaller, we calculate the lower bound again, and then we render the feedback labels:

```
case .Smaller:
    lowerBound = max(lowerBound, number)
    messageLbl.text = "Your last guess was too low"
    numberTxtField.text = ""
    numGuesses++
    renderRange()
    renderNumGuesses()
```

If the number is greater, the code is similar, but instead of the lower bound, we calculate the upper bound:

```
case .Greater:
    upperBound = min(upperBound, number)
    messageLbl.text = "Your last guess was too high"
    numberTxtField.text = ""
    numGuesses++
    renderRange()
    renderNumGuesses()
}
```

Et voilà! With this simple code, we have implemented our app.

 You can download the code of the app from `https://github.com/gscalzo/Swift2ByExample/tree/1_GuessTheNumber`.

Summary

This chapter showed us, by exploiting the power of Xcode and Swift, we can create fully working app.

Depending on your level of iOS knowledge, you could have found this app either too hard or to simple to understand; for the former, don't loose your enthusiasm, read the code again, and try to execute the app adding few strategically placed `print()` instructions in the code to see the content of the various variables; for the latter's, I hope you have found at least some tricks you can start to use right now.

Of course, simply after reading this chapter, nobody can be considered an expert in Swift and Xcode. However, the information here is enough to let you understand all of the code we'll be using in the upcoming chapters to build several kinds of other interesting apps.

In the next chapter, we'll continue to explore Swift and iOS by implementing another game, a memory game that will let us make use of the power of `structs`. You will also learn about some new things in UIKit.

$\mathcal{3}$
A Memory Game in Swift

After learning the fundamental parts of the language and getting a basic introduction to creating a simple app with Xcode, it's now time to build something more complex, but still using the basics from the previous chapter. This chapter aims to show you how to structure an app, creating clean and simple code, and how to make it appealing to the user with nice colors and smooth animations.

Compared to the previous chapter, this chapter is more advanced because I think the best way to learn new concepts is to see them in a real, working app. One of the many ways to show content in an iOS app is using the UICollectionView class, which is a component that lays the subcomponents as a flow of cell. A good introduction to UICollectionView can be found at http://nshipster.com/uicollectionview/.

The app is...

The app we are going to implement is a UIKit implementation of a memory game: a solitaire version. A memory game, also known as **concentration**, is a card game where the player must match all the cards, which start reversed, turning up two of them in each turn. If the cards match, they are removed from the table. Otherwise, they are turned down again and the score increases. The goal is to clear the table with the lowest score possible.

In our implementation, we are going to use only standard UIKit components and look at another way of creating the interface in Xcode. We'll create all of our UI directly in the code without using **Interface Builder**.

Let's start prototyping the screens. Despite this being an educational app, we want it to be a pretty and fun app, so we need at least one option to decide the difficulty, selecting the quantity of cards laid on the table.

The following are the screens we'll implement for the app; the first is to select the difficulty — basically, selecting the number of the cards in the deck:

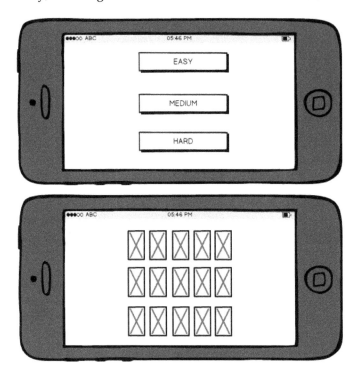

Building the skeleton of the app

As we have already seen in the previous chapter, we can create our app by going to **File | New | Project...**, and then selecting **Single View Application** from the list of templates.

To simplify the handling of different resolutions, our memory game is in the *landscape* mode only, so when the creation of the template has been completed, uncheck **Portrait** as the allowed **Device Orientation**, as shown in the following screenshot:

The menu screen

Let's start implementing the first view, in which we can select the level of the game.

Implementing the basic menu screen

As we have planned to implement all of the UI in the code itself, we won't bother to touch the storyboard. We will proceed to open the `View Controller` class in order to implement the menu screen.

From the mockup, we can observe that there are three difficulty levels, each represented by a horizontally centered and vertically equidistant button.

First of all, we will define an enumeration to describe the difficulty.

Then, we implement the setup for the layout:

```
enum Difficulty {
    case Easy, Medium, Hard
}
```

This `enum` must be defined outside the class so that it will be accessible by all classes.

Just for the sake of readability, we group the methods required in order to implement a feature in a separated extension, leaving only the public functions and the variable definition in the `main` class. Although extensions were born for a different goal, which is to extend classes we don't have the source for, I've found that grouping together methods in an extension helps describe the goals of those methods. Matt Thompson, the creator of *AFNetworking*, the most used network library for iOS, used this approach in Alamofire at `https://github.com/Alamofire/Alamofire`:

```
class ViewController: UIViewController {
    override func viewDidLoad() {
        super.viewDidLoad()
        setup()
    }
}

private extension ViewController {
    func setup() {
        view.backgroundColor = .whiteColor()

        buildButtonWithCenter(CGPoint(x: view.center.x,
y: view.center.y/2.0), title: "EASY", color:.greenColor(),
 action: "onEasyTapped:")
```

```
        buildButtonWithCenter(CGPoint(x: view.center.x, y:
    view.center.y), title: "MEDIUM", color:.yellowColor(),
      action: "onMediumTapped:")
            buildButtonWithCenter(CGPoint(x: view.center.x, y:
    view.center.y*3.0/2.0), title: "HARD", color:.redColor(),
      action: "onHardTapped:")
        }


        func buildButtonWithCenter(center: CGPoint,
        title: String, color: UIColor, action: Selector) {
        //
        }
    }
```

Again, we are not yet relying on Auto Layout to establish relations between the components, so we pass the coordinates of each button to the initializer method. In the same method, we also pass the text to be presented as a caption and the background color.

You may also notice that Swift 2.0 can understand the scope of a class function given the type of the receiver: if a variable is UIColor, it isn't necessary anymore to add the class name before the function, like this:

```
    let myColor: UIColor = UIColor.greenColor()
```

In Swift 2.0, you can just write it in this way:

```
    let myColor: UIColor = .greenColor()
```

This will apply for the parameters of a function as well, making the code really clean.

The last parameter, called action, contains the name of the method inside **View Controller** that the button must call when pressed. The following implementation of buildButtonCenter() shows you how to create a button programmatically:

```
    func buildButtonWithCenter(center: CGPoint, title: String, color:
    UIColor, action: Selector) {
        let button = UIButton()
        button.setTitle(title, forState: .Normal)
        button.setTitleColor(.blackColor(), forState: .Normal)

        button.frame = CGRect(origin: CGPoint(x: 0, y: 0), size:
    CGSize(width: 200, height: 50))
        button.center = center
        button.backgroundColor = color
```

```
        button.addTarget(self, action: action, forControlEvents:
    UIControlEvents.TouchUpInside)
        view.addSubview(button)
    }
```

The last statement before adding the button to the view is the way to connect a
callback to an event, the programmatic equivalent of creating a line connecting an
event of the button to @IBAction using **Interface Builder**. This is a technique we saw
in the previous chapter.

Because all the actions are logically tied together, we create another extension to
group them:

```
    extension ViewController {
        func onEasyTapped(sender: UIButton) {
            newGameDifficulty(.Easy)
        }

        func onMediumTapped(sender: UIButton) {
            newGameDifficulty(.Medium)
        }

        func onHardTapped(sender: UIButton) {
            newGameDifficulty(.Hard)
        }

        func newGameDifficulty(difficulty: Difficulty) {
            switch difficulty {
                case .Easy:
                    print("Easy")
                case .Medium:
                    print("Medium")
                case .Hard:
                    print("Hard")
            }
        }
    }
```

It is worth mentioning that this extension is not private, although it contains
functions that are used only internally; the reason here is because these are functions
called by the buttons when they are tapped, basically called by the **Cocoa Runtime**,
which can access the functions only if they are *internal* or *public*.

Now, if we run the app by going to **Product | Run**, we can see that we have almost implemented the screen in the mockup, as you can see in the following screenshot:

Also, by tapping the buttons, we can verify that the button calls the correct function. We must see the correct message in the console when we press a button.

Although the screen is how we expected to implement it, it isn't very appealing, so before proceeding to implement the game in **View Controller**, we customize the color palette to make the UI prettier.

Creating a nice menu screen

Because the flat design has become very fashionable lately, let's go to http://flatuicolors.com in order to choose a few colors to decorate our components.

After choosing the colors, we extend the UIColor class:

```
extension UIColor {
    class func greenSea() -> UIColor {
        return .colorComponents((22, 160, 133))
    }
    class func emerald() -> UIColor {
        return  .colorComponents((46, 204, 113))
    }
    class func sunflower() -> UIColor {
        return .colorComponents((241, 196, 15))
    }
    class func alizarin() -> UIColor {
        return  .colorComponents((231, 76, 60))
    }
}

private extension UIColor {
```

```
    class func colorComponents(components: (CGFloat, CGFloat,
CGFloat)) -> UIColor {
        return UIColor(red: components.0/255, green:
components.1/255, blue: components.2/255, alpha: 1)
    }
}
```

With this extended palette, we can change the setup of **View Controller**:

```
func setup() {
    view.backgroundColor =.greenSea()

    buildButtonWithCenter(CGPoint(x: view.center.x, y:
view.center.y/2.0), title: "EASY", color: .emerald(), action:
"onEasyTapped:")
    buildButtonWithCenter(CGPoint(x: view.center.x, y:
view.center.y), title: "MEDIUM", color:.sunflower(), action:
"onMediumTapped:")
    buildButtonWithCenter(CGPoint(x: view.center.x, y:
view.center.y*3.0/2.0), title: "HARD", color:.alizarin(), action:
"onHardTapped:")
}
```

Inside the builder, let's change the title color to white:

```
func buildButtonWithCenter(center: CGPoint, title: String, color:
UIColor, action: Selector) {
    //
    button.setTitleColor(.whiteColor(), forState: .Normal)
    //
}
```

The result, as shown in the following screenshot, is definitely prettier, reminding us of a real card table:

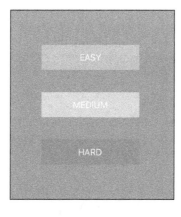

Now we can implement a proper `newGameDifficulty()` function for which we already wrote the empty implementation in the extension grouping the button callbacks:

```
func newGameDifficulty(difficulty: Difficulty) {
    let gameViewController = MemoryViewController(difficulty:
difficulty)
    presentViewController(gameViewController, animated: true,
completion: nil)
}
```

The function introduces a new **View Controller**, `MemoryViewController`, which will contain all the logic. Just to create the app build, let's make it empty.

 You can find the code at `https://github.com/gscalzo/Swift2ByExample/tree/2_Memory_1_menu`.

The game screen

Before implementing the game, let's proceed to build the layout of the cards on the table.

The structure

Now let's implement a new class called `MemoryViewController`, which extends the `UIVewController` class. This will be used to manage the actual view where the *Memory Game* will be played. The first thing we do is add the class life cycle functions:

```
class MemoryViewController: UIViewController {
    private let difficulty: Difficulty

    init(difficulty: Difficulty) {
        self.difficulty = difficulty
        super.init(nibName: nil, bundle: nil)
    }

    required init(coder aDecoder: NSCoder) {
        fatalError("init(coder:) has not been implemented")
    }

    deinit{
```

```
        print("deinit")
    }

    override func viewDidLoad() {
        super.viewDidLoad()
        setup()
    }
}
// MARK: Setup
private extension MemoryViewController {
    func setup() {
        view.backgroundColor = .greenSea()
    }
}
```

Besides the initializer that accepts the chosen difficulty, although it's not used, we need to add the required initializer with NSCoder. Moreover, you should note that we need to call the parent initializer with nibName and the bundle, used when UIViewController is built from an XIB file. If we call a plain super.init() function, we will receive a runtime error because the empty one is a convenience initializer, an initializer that calls a required initializer in the same class that, in our case, is not implemented.

Although not mandatory, we have implemented the deinitializer as well, inserting just a debug log statement to verify that the class is correctly removed from the memory when dismissed. Thus, a retain cycle is avoided.

Finally, we come to this comment:

```
// MARK: Setup
```

This is a special comment that tells Xcode to present the sentence in the structure of a class in order to facilitate navigation to a different part of the class.

The last element of the status bar of the code editor of Xcode must be selected.

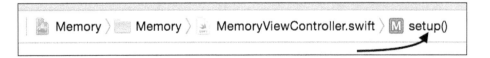

After this, a menu with all the functions appears, with a bold entry where we put the `//MARK:` comment.

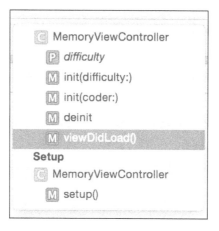

Adding a collection view

Let's move on to implementing the layout of the card. We'll use `UICollectionView` to lay the cards on the table. `UICollectionView` is a view that arranges the contained cells to follow a layout we set during the setup. In this case, we set a flow layout in which each card follows the previous one, and it creates a new row when the right border is reached.

We set the properties for the view and a model to fulfill the collection view:

```
private var collectionView: UICollectionView!
private var deck: Array<Int>!
```

Next, we write the function calls to set up everything in `viewDidLoad` so that the functions are called when the view is loaded:

```
override func viewDidLoad() {
    super.viewDidLoad()
    setup()
}
```

The `setup()` function basically creates and configures `CollectionView`:

```
// MARK: Setup
private extension MemoryViewController {
    func setup() {
        view.backgroundColor = .greenSea()

        let space: CGFloat = 5
```

```
        let (covWidth, covHeight) =
collectionViewSizeDifficulty(difficulty, space: space)
        let layout = layoutCardSize(cardSizeDifficulty(difficulty,
space: space), space: space)

        collectionView = UICollectionView(frame: CGRect(x: 0, y:
0, width: covWidth, height: covHeight),
        collectionViewLayout: layout)
        collectionView.center = view.center
        collectionView.dataSource = self
        collectionView.delegate = self
        collectionView.scrollEnabled = false
        collectionView.registerClass(UICollectionViewCell.self,
forCellWithReuseIdentifier: "cardCell")
        collectionView.backgroundColor = .clearColor()

        self.view.addSubview(collectionView)
    }
```

After setting the color of the collectionview, we define a constant, space, to set the space between every two cards.

Next, we calculate the size of the collectionview given the difficulty, and hence, the number of rows and columns; then, the layout. Finally, we put everything together to build the collectionview:

```
    func collectionViewSizeDifficulty(difficulty: Difficulty,
space: CGFloat) -> (CGFloat, CGFloat) {
        let (columns, rows) = sizeDifficulty(difficulty)
        let (cardWidth, cardHeight) = cardSizeDifficulty(difficulty,
space: space)

        let covWidth = columns*(cardWidth + 2*space)
        let covHeight = rows*(cardHeight + space)
        return (covWidth, covHeight)
    }
```

The cardSizeDifficulty() function calculates the size of the collection view by multiplying the size of each card by the number of rows or columns:

```
    func cardSizeDifficulty(difficulty: Difficulty, space: CGFloat) ->
(CGFloat, CGFloat) {
        let ratio: CGFloat = 1.452

        let (_, rows) = sizeDifficulty(difficulty)
        let cardHeight: CGFloat = view.frame.height/rows - 2*space
```

```
        let cardWidth: CGFloat = cardHeight/ratio
        return (cardWidth, cardHeight)
    }
```

The `sizeDifficulty()` function will be introduced later; just to make it buildable, let's implement it with only one hardcoded value:

```
    func sizeDifficulty(difficulty: Difficulty) -> (CGFloat,
CGFloat) {
        return (4,3)
    }
```

Because the column value returned by the `sizeDifficulty()` function is not used anywhere, we can safely associate it with the wildcard keyword _.

Sizing the components

As mentioned at the start of this chapter, we are not using Auto Layout, but we need to handle the issue of different screen sizes somehow. Hence, using basic math, we adapt the size of each card to the available size on the screen:

```
    func layoutCardSize(cardSize: (cardWidth: CGFloat, cardHeight:
CGFloat), space: CGFloat) -> UICollectionViewLayout {
        let layout: UICollectionViewFlowLayout =
UICollectionViewFlowLayout()
        layout.sectionInset = UIEdgeInsets(top: space, left:
space, bottom: space, right: space)
        layout.itemSize = CGSize(width: cardSize.cardWidth,
height: cardSize.cardHeight)
        layout.minimumLineSpacing = space
        return layout
    }
```

As mentioned earlier, the `UICollectionView` class shows a series of cells in its content view, but the way in which the cells are presented — as a grid or a vertical pile — the space between them is defined by an instance of `UICollectionViewFlowLayout`.

Finally, we set up the layout, defining the size of each cell and how they are separated and laid out.

We have seen that there is a connection between the difficulty setting and the size of the grid of the cards, and this relation is implemented simply using `switch` statements:

```
    // MARK: Difficulty
    private extension MemoryViewController {
```

```
func sizeDifficulty(difficulty: Difficulty) -> (CGFloat, CGFloat)
{
    switch difficulty {
        case .Easy:
            return (4,3)
        case .Medium:
            return (6,4)
        case .Hard:
            return (8,4)
    }
}

func numCardsNeededDifficulty(difficulty: Difficulty) -> Int {
    let (columns, rows) = sizeDifficulty(difficulty)
    return Int(columns * rows)
}
}
```

Connecting the dataSource and the delegate

You have probably noticed that when we created `collectionview`, we set **View Controller** itself as `dataSource` and `delegate`:

```
collectionView.dataSource = self
collectionView.delegate = self
```

A common pattern found in Cocoa in many components is the delegate pattern, where part of the behavior is delegated to another object, and that object must implement a particular protocol.

In the case of `UICollectionView`, and likewise for `UITableView`, we have to delegate one of the class references to provide the content for the view, `dataSource`, and the other to react to events from the view itself. In this way, the presentation level is completely decoupled from the data and the business logic, which reside in two specialized objects.

So, we need to implement the required methods of the protocols:

```
// MARK: UICollectionViewDataSource
extension MemoryViewController: UICollectionViewDataSource {
    func collectionView(collectionView: UICollectionView,
        numberOfItemsInSection section: Int) -> Int {
```

```
        return deck.count
    }

    func collectionView(collectionView: UICollectionView,
        cellForItemAtIndexPath indexPath: NSIndexPath) ->
UICollectionViewCell {
        let cell =
collectionView.dequeueReusableCellWithReuseIdentifier("cardCell",
forIndexPath: indexPath)

        cell.backgroundColor = .sunflower()
        return cell
    }
}
```

As you can see, in the method called for the cell at a certain position, we are calling a method to reuse a cell instead of creating a new one. This is a nifty feature of `UICollectionView` that saves all the cells in a cache and can reuse those outside the visible view. This not only saves a lot of memory, but it is also really efficient because creating new cells during scrolling could be CPU consumption and affect performance.

Because we want to see just the flow of the card, we use the default empty cell as the view cell, changing the color of the background:

```
// MARK: UICollectionViewDelegate
extension MemoryViewController: UICollectionViewDelegate {
    func collectionView(collectionView: UICollectionView,
didSelectItemAtIndexPath indexPath: NSIndexPath) {
    }
}
```

For the delegate, we simply prepare ourselves to handle a touch on the card. Because we don't need a real deck of cards, an array of integers is enough as a model:

```
override func viewDidLoad() {
    super.viewDidLoad()
    setup()
    start()
}

private func start() {
    deck = Array<Int>(count: numCardsNeededDifficulty(difficulty),
repeatedValue: 1)
    collectionView.reloadData()
}
```

Now, upon running the app and choosing a level, we will have all our empty cards laid out like this:

Using a different simulator and the iPhone 5 or 4S, we can see that our table adapts its size smoothly.

Implementing a deck of cards

So far, we have implemented a pretty generic app that lays out views inside a bigger view. Let's proceed to implement the foundation of the game: a deck of cards.

What we are expecting

Before implementing the classes for a deck of cards, we must define the behavior we are expecting, whereby we implement the calls in `MemoryViewController`, assuming that the `Deck` object already exists. First of all, we change the type in the definition of the property:

```
private var deck: Deck!
```

Then, we change the implementation of the `start()` function:

```
private func start() {
    deck = createDeck(numCardsNeededDifficulty(difficulty))
    collectionView.reloadData()
}
```

```swift
private func createDeck(numCards: Int) -> Deck {
    let fullDeck = Deck.full().shuffled()
    let halfDeck = fullDeck.deckOfNumberOfCards(numCards/2)
    return (halfDeck + halfDeck).shuffled()
}
```

We are saying that we want a deck to be able to return a shuffled version of itself and which can return a deck of a selected numbers of its cards. Also, it can be created using the plus operator (+) to join two decks. This is a lot of information, but it should help you learn a lot regarding `structs`.

The card entity

There hasn't been anything regarding the entities inside `Deck` so far, but we can assume that it is a `Card` struct and that it uses plain enumerations. A `Suit` and `Rank` parameter define a card, so we can write this code in a new file called `Deck.swift`:

```swift
enum Suit: CustomStringConvertible {
    case Spades, Hearts, Diamonds, Clubs
    var description: String {
        switch self {
            case .Spades:
                return "spades"
            case .Hearts:
                return "hearts"
            case .Diamonds:
                return "diamonds"
            case .Clubs:
                return "clubs"
        }
    }
}

enum Rank: Int, CustomStringConvertible {
    case Ace = 1
    case Two, Three, Four, Five, Six, Seven, Eight, Nine, Ten
    case Jack, Queen, King
    var description: String {
        switch self {
            case .Ace:
                return "ace"
            case .Jack:
                return "jack"
            case .Queen:
```

```
            return "queen"
        case .King:
            return "king"
        default:
            return String(self.rawValue)
    }
  }
}
```

Note that we have used an `integer` as a type in `Rank` but not in `Suit`. That's because we want the possibility of creating a `Rank` from an integer, its raw value, but not for `Suit`. This will soon become clearer.

We have implemented the `CustomStringConvertible` protocol, called `Printable` in Swift 1.x, in order to be able to print the enumeration. The `Card` parameter is nothing more than a pair of `Rank` and `Suit` cases:

```
struct Card: CustomStringConvertible, Equatable {
    private let rank: Rank
    private let suit: Suit

    var description: String {
        return "\(rank.description)_of_\(suit.description)"
    }
}
func ==(card1: Card, card2: Card) -> Bool {
    return card1.rank == card2.rank && card1.suit == card2.suit
}
```

Also, for `Card`, we have implemented the `CustomStringConvertible` protocol, basically joining the description of its `Rank` and `Suit` cases. We have also implemented the `Equatable` protocol to be able to check whether two cards are of the same value.

Crafting the deck

Now we can implement the constructor of a full deck, iterating through all the values of the `Rank` and `Suit` enumerations:

```
struct Deck {
    private var cards = [Card]()
    static func full() -> Deck {
        var deck = Deck()
        for i in Rank.Ace.rawValue...Rank.King.rawValue {
```

```
                for suit in [Suit.Spades, .Hearts,.Clubs,
.Diamonds] {
                        let card = Card(rank: Rank(rawValue: i)!, suit:
suit)
                        deck.cards.append(card)
                }
        }
        return deck
    }
}
```

Shuffling the deck

The next function we will implement is shuffled():

```
// Fisher-Yates (fast and uniform) shuffle
func shuffled() -> Deck {
    var list = cards
    for i in 0..<(list.count - 1) {
        let j = Int(arc4random_uniform(UInt32(list.count - i)))
+ i
        if i!= j {
            swap(&list[i], &list[j])
        }
    }
    return Deck(cards: list)
}
```

The usual way to shuffle a deck of cards in a computer program is to use the Fisher-Yates algorithm. Starting from the first card, we iterate until the very end, each time swapping the current card with a random card in the set with an index higher than the current one. A complete explanation of this can be found on Wikipedia at http://en.wikipedia.org/wiki/Fisher-Yates_shuffle.

If you look carefully at the swap() function, you will see an ampersand (&) symbol before the parameters. This means that the parameters are input and that they can be changed inside functions. We can consider input parameters as shared variables between the caller and the called.

Also, the swap() function needs two different variables to swap; it isn't possible to swap a variable with itself, so before swapping, we check whether the indices are different.

Finishing the deck

We are almost done with the expected behavior of Deck; we just need to add the creation of a subset of Deck:

```
func deckOfNumberOfCards(num: Int) -> Deck {
    return Deck(cards: Array(cards[0..<num]))
}
```

Note that using the notation for the [..<] range, the upper bound is not included in the range, whereas using [..], the upper bound is included. We can create this by exploiting the splicing feature of the Swift Array. Using this trick, we create the sum operator:

```
func +(deck1: Deck, deck2: Deck) -> Deck {
    return Deck(cards: deck1.cards + deck2.cards)
}
```

Note that this function must be defined outside the Deck struct.

The last function left is the count property, which we implement using a computed property:

```
var count: Int {
    get {
        return cards.count
    }
}
```

Before moving on to implementing the remainder of the game, we want to check whether everything works fine, so we add a log after creating Deck, like this:

```
init(difficulty: Difficulty) {
    self.difficulty = difficulty
    self.deck = Deck()
    super.init(nibName: nil, bundle: nil)
    self.deck = createDeck(numCardsNeededDifficulty(difficulty))
    for i in 0..<deck.count {
        print("The card at index [\(i)] is
[\(deck[i].description)]")
    }
}
```

Unfortunately, the compiler complains that it doesn't know how to retrieve the element at a specified index.

For the purpose of mimicking the accessor of an array, Swift provides a special computed property to add to the definition of our struct subscript. Implementing the subscript just involves forwarding the request to private property cards:

```
subscript(index: Int) -> Card {
    get {
        return cards[index]
    }
}
```

Now the app gets compiled. If we run it, we get a console output like this:

```
The card at index [0] is [8_of_clubs]
The card at index [1] is [ace_of_spades]
The card at index [2] is [ace_of_clubs]
The card at index [3] is [ace_of_hearts]
The card at index [4] is [9_of_hearts]
The card at index [5] is [ace_of_hearts]
The card at index [6] is [queen_of_clubs]
The card at index [7] is [ace_of_clubs]
The card at index [8] is [ace_of_spades]
The card at index [9] is [queen_of_clubs]
The card at index [10] is [9_of_hearts]
The card at index [11] is [8_of_clubs]
```

 The source code for this block can be downloaded from https://github.com/gscalzo/Swift2ByExample/tree/2_Memory_3_Cards_Foundation.

Put the cards on the table

Finally, let's add the card images and implement the entire game.

Adding the assets

Now that everything works, let's create a nice UI again.

First of all, let's import all the assets in the project. There are plenty of free card assets on the Internet, but if you are lazy, I've prepared a complete deck of images ready for this game for you, and you can download it from https://github.com/gscalzo/Swift2ByExample/raw/2_Memory_4_Complete/Memory/Assets/CardImages.zip.

The archive contains an image for the back of the cards and another image for the front. To include them in the app, select the image assets file from the project structure view, as shown in this screenshot:

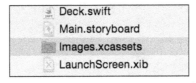

After selecting the catalog, the images can be dragged into Xcode, as shown in the following screenshot:

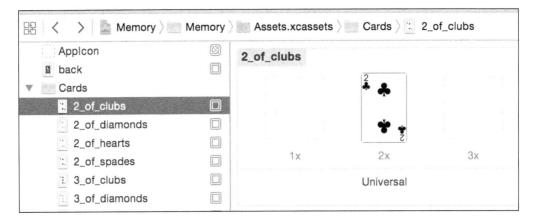

In this operation, you must pay attention and ensure that you move all the images from **1x** to **2x** as shown in this screenshot. Otherwise, when you run the app, you will see them pixelate.

The CardCell structure

Let's go ahead and implement our `CardCell` structure. Again, we pretend that we already have the class, so we register that class during the setup of **Collection View**:

```
func setup() {
    //
    collectionView.registerClass(CardCell.self,
    forCellWithReuseIdentifier: "cardCell")
    //
}
```

Then, we implement the rendering of the class when the data source protocol asks for a cell given an index:

```
func collectionView(collectionView: UICollectionView,
cellForItemAtIndexPath indexPath: NSIndexPath) ->
UICollectionViewCell {
    let cell =
collectionView.dequeueReusableCellWithReuseIdentifier("cardCell",
forIndexPath: indexPath) as! CardCell
    let card = deck[indexPath.row]
    cell.renderCardName(card.description, backImageName: "back")
    return cell
}
```

We are trying to push as much presentation code as we can into the new class in order to decouple the responsibilities of Cell and controller, which hold the model.

So, let's implement a new class called CardCell, which inherits from UICollectionViewCell, so don't forget to select that class in the Xcode wizard.

CardCell contains only UIImageView to present the card images and two properties to hold the names of the front and back images:

```
class CardCell: UICollectionViewCell {
    private let frontImageView: UIImageView!
    private var cardImageName: String!
    private var backImageName: String!

    override init(frame: CGRect) {
        frontImageView = UIImageView(frame: CGRect(
            origin: CGPointZero,
            size: frame.size))
        super.init(frame: frame)
        contentView.addSubview(frontImageView)
        contentView.backgroundColor = UIColor.clearColor()
    }

    required init(coder aDecoder: NSCoder) {
        fatalError("init(coder:) has not been implemented")
    }

    func renderCardName(cardImageName: String, backImageName:
String){
        self.cardImageName = cardImageName
        self.backImageName = backImageName
```

```
frontImageView.image = UIImage(named: self.backImageName)
    }
}
```

If you run the app now, you should see some nice cards face down.

Handling touches

Now, let's get the cards face up!

This code is part of the UICollectionViewDelegate protocol, so it must be implemented inside the MemoryViewController class:

```
func collectionView(collectionView: UICollectionView,
didSelectItemAtIndexPath indexPath: NSIndexPath) {
    let cell = collectionView.cellForItemAtIndexPath(indexPath)
    as! CardCell
    cell.upturn()
}
```

This code is pretty clear, and now we only need to implement the upturn() function inside CardCell:

```
func upturn() {
    UIView.transitionWithView(contentView, duration: 1, options:
.TransitionFlipFromRight, animations: {
        self.frontImageView.image =UIImage(named:
self.cardImageName)
    },
    completion: nil)
}
```

By leveraging a handy function inside the UIView class, we have created a nice transition from the back image to the front image, simulating the flip of a card.

To complete the functions required to manage the card from a visual point of view, we implement the downturn() function in a similar way:

```
func downturn() {
    UIView.transitionWithView(contentView, duration: 1, options:
.TransitionFlipFromLeft,
    animations: { self.frontImageView.image = UIImage(named:
self.backImageName)
    },completion: nil)
}
```

To test all the functions, we turn down the card for 2 seconds after we have turned it up. To run a delayed function, we use the `dispatch_after` function, but to remove the boilerplate call, we wrap it in a smaller common function, added as an extension of `UIViewController`:

```
extension UIViewController {
    func execAfter(delay: Double, block: () -> Void) {
        dispatch_after(
            dispatch_time(
                DISPATCH_TIME_NOW,
                Int64(delay * Double(NSEC_PER_SEC))
            ),
            dispatch_get_main_queue(), block)
    }
}
```

So, after having the card turned up, we turn it down using this newly implemented function:

```
func collectionView(collectionView: UICollectionView,
    didSelectItemAtIndexPath indexPath: NSIndexPath) {
        //...
        cell.upturn()
        execAfter(2) {
            cell.downturn()
        }
}
```

By running the app, we now see the cards turning up and down with a smooth and nice animation.

Finishing the game

In this section, we will finally be able to play the game.

Implementing the game logic

After having all the required functions in place, it's now a straightforward task to complete the game. First of all, we add the instance variables to hold the number of the pairs already created, the current score, and the list of selected cards turned up:

```
private var selectedIndexes = Array<NSIndexPath>()
private var numberOfPairs = 0
private var score = 0
```

Then, we apply the logic when a card is selected:

```
func collectionView(collectionView: UICollectionView,
didSelectItemAtIndexPath indexPath: NSIndexPath) {
      if selectedIndexes.count == 2 || selectedIndexes
.contains(indexPath) {
            return
      }
      selectedIndexes.append(indexPath)

      let cell =
collectionView.cellForItemAtIndexPath(indexPath)
      as! CardCell
      cell.upturn()

      if selectedIndexes.count < 2 {
          return
      }

      let card1 = deck[selectedIndexes[0].row]
      let card2 = deck[selectedIndexes[1].row]

      if card1 == card2 {
          numberOfPairs++
          checkIfFinished()
          removeCards()
      } else {
          score++
          turnCardsFaceDown()
      }
}
```

We first check whether we have touched an already turned-up card or whether we have two cards turned up. If not, we save the index. Then, we check whether we have flipped the first card, and if not, we proceed to check the values of the cards.

The pattern of checking a condition and leaving the current function if the condition is true is called **Guard**. It helps make the code more readable by avoiding the use of the `else` clause and the nesting of curly braces.

We got a pair

As shown in the previous part of the source, we implement the missing actions in a `private` extension:

```
// MARK: Actions
private extension MemoryViewController {
    func checkIfFinished(){
    }
    func removeCards(){
    }
    func turnCardsFaceDown(){
    }
}
```

The first one checks whether we have completed all the pairs, and if so, it presents a popup with the score and returns to the `main` menu:

```
func checkIfFinished(){
    if numberOfPairs == deck.count/2 {
        showFinalPopUp()
    }
}
func showFinalPopUp() {
    let alert = UIAlertController(title: "Great!", message: "You
won with score: \(score)!", preferredStyle:
UIAlertControllerStyle.Alert)
    alert.addAction(UIAlertAction(title: "Ok", style: .Default,
handler: { action in self.dismissViewControllerAnimated(true,
completion: nil)}))

    self.presentViewController(alert, animated: true, completion:
nil)
}
```

Note that in iOS 8, `UIAlertController` is slightly different from that in the previous version. In our case, a simple dialog box with an OK button is enough.

If the cards are equal, we need to remove them:

```
func removeCards(){
    execAfter(1.0) {
        self.removeCardsAtPlaces(self.selectedIndexes)
        self.selectedIndexes = []
    }
}
```

```
func removeCardsAtPlaces(places: Array<NSIndexPath>){
    for index in selectedIndexes {
        let cardCell =
collectionView.cellForItemAtIndexPath(index)
        as! CardCell
        cardCell.remove()
    }
}
```

The `remove()` function in `CardCell` is similar to `turnUp()` and `turnDown()`, but instead of making a transition, it just performs an animation before hiding the cell:

```
func remove() {
    UIView.animateWithDuration(1,
        animations: {
            self.alpha = 0
        },
        completion: { completed in
        self.hidden = true
    })
}
```

We made the wrong move

Finally, if the cards are different, we need to turn them down:

```
func turnCardsFaceDown(){
    execAfter(2.0) {
        self.downturnCardsAtPlaces(self.selectedIndexes)
        self.selectedIndexes = []
    }
}
```

```
func downturnCardsAtPlaces(places: Array<NSIndexPath>){
    for index in selectedIndexes {
        let cardCell =
collectionView.cellForItemAtIndexPath(index)
        as! CardCell
        cardCell.downturn()
    }
}
```

Et voilà! The game is completed

As you can see in the following screenshot, the game presents a smooth animation and nice images:

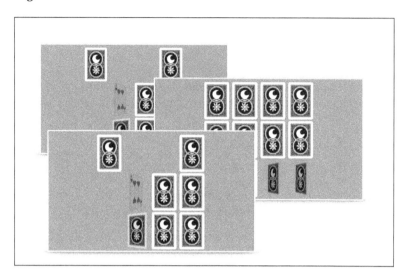

 The complete source can be downloaded from https://github.com/ gscalzo/Swift2ByExample/tree/2_Memory_4_Complete.

Summary

In this chapter, we implemented our first complete app, beginning with using basic components and then moving on to using more advanced techniques to create a smooth animation without relying on game frameworks such as Cocos2d or SpriteKit.

We saw when, and how, to use structs in an effective way and how to split responsibilities among different classes. Moreover, we experimented and saw how to separate different parts of the same class using extensions and how to design an interface of a class or struct, pretending we have already implemented it.

You learned a few things about puzzle games, and now it's time to move on to something different but more similar to a normal app; we'll have a chance to work on a *TodoList* app.

4
A TodoList App in Swift

After playing in the first two chapters, it's now time to move on to something different: exploring how to implement a utility app and solving the most common problems you face during the development of an iOS app.

This will be a really dense chapter because we'll cover several problems, such as Auto Layout, interactions between View Controllers, using third-party libraries without getting mad, configuring the project, and handling library dependencies.

The app is...

The most common, and perhaps the simplest, way to learn how to develop an iOS app is by starting with a to-do list, where the user can add tasks, show them, and change their status.

You need to be aware that a generic utility app for iOS must handle the following:

- Getting data from the user
- Presenting data obtained from the user
- Manipulating data
- Somehow saving data
- Synchronizing data with a server

Our *TodoList* app has all of these features except the last one, and it can be considered the prototype of all utility apps. Let's define the specifications of our app. The first, and the most useful, screen must present the list of **Todos**, as shown in the following screenshot:

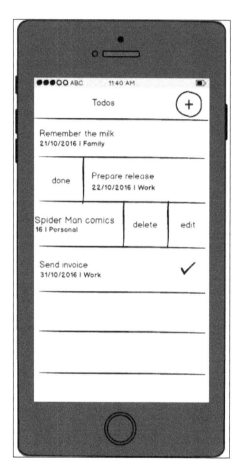

Each one in the list of **Todos** has a description, due date, and category (**Family**, **Personal**, **Work**, and so on), which can be used to filter and catalog tasks. A checkbox indicates whether the corresponding task is done or still open.

The user can perform three different actions: edit, delete, or set a particular **Todo** task as done. The action buttons are normally hidden, but the user can see them by sliding the **Todo** cell either to the right or to the left.

A single button in the top-right corner allows the creation of a new **Todo** task. When this button is pressed, a new view slides in from the right, with a back button in the top-left corner that allows you to go back to the main view. This is a common UI pattern, which is used when screens are related in a sort of master-detail relationship.

The following screenshot shows the screen where the user can create a **Todo** task:

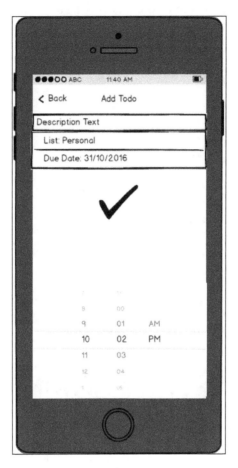

The user can add a description using Text Field. They can define the containing list and the due date by selecting their buttons. However, both the fields have default values: **Personal** for the former, and the date of the next day for **Due Date**.

When the **Due Date** button is selected, the keyboard slides down, and a time picker allows the user to select the due date. When the **List** button is selected, a new controller appears. When the user is satisfied with the content, they can click on the checkmark button to save the **Todo** task and to go back to the main controller.

As we saw in the previous screenshot, the user can edit the **Todo** task. This operation is similar to the creation of the **Todo** task, so it makes sense to use the same screen. In it, instead of getting the default values, all the fields will be prepopulated with the values of the **Todo** task to be edited.

As mentioned earlier, by pressing the **List** button, the screen changes to a new one, allowing us to select a list or create a new list, as shown in this screenshot:

Building a skeleton app

Let's start implementing the base structure on top of which we'll implement the entire app.

Implementing an empty app

Let's start creating a new app called *Todolist* using the **Single View Application** template in Xcode. The app will be in portrait mode only, so you must uncheck **Landscape** from the allowed device orientations:

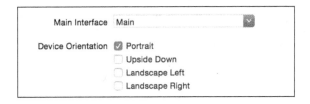

Although Apple has improved **Interface Builder** in Xcode 7, most developers still favor writing the layout in code instead of using **Interface Builder**. The common reasons are that with **Interface Builder**, it is more difficult to create reusable views, which makes working in a team difficult because of merging of the storyboard files; in general, it is more difficult to debug a complex layout.

However, Apple strongly encourages that you use **Interface Builder** to build **User Interface** and we will use it to build our first complex app. To show the difference, the app in the next chapter will be built using Auto Layout by code, helped by a third-party library called **Cartography**.

To manage a table view, iOS provides a class called `UITableViewController`.

First of all, we create a subclass of `UITableViewController`, calling it `TodoTableViewController`.

To do this, select a new `CocoaTouch` class:

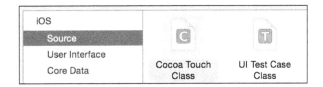

Then, select the correct subclass for `TodoTableViewController`:

If you look at the generated code now, you can see some already implemented functions and several other commented out functions if you want to have a template to add complex behavior to your **Table View**.

Now we'll move on to the storyboard to create the interface.

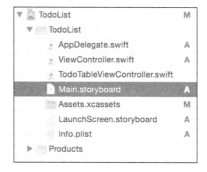

From the components palette, select **TableViewController** and drag it onto the storyboard, as shown in the following screenshot:

The component presents **Table View** with a prototype for each cell that can be customized in **Interface Builder**.

Now, we must associate the generic `UITableViewController` class with the subclass we created, as shown in the following screenshot:

Selecting the last tab with the arrow, we can see that **Interface Builder** has automatically connected the **Table View** with the parts of our class, notably setting it as `dataSource`, the providers of the data **Todos** in our case, and delegate what will receive the selecting event.

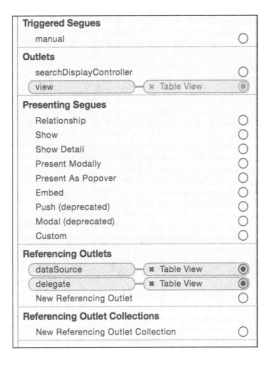

If we run the app now, we should see an empty view.

This is because the app presents **View Controller** set as **Initial View Controller**, which is still the original empty app.

So, we must set **TableView** as **Initial View Controller**.

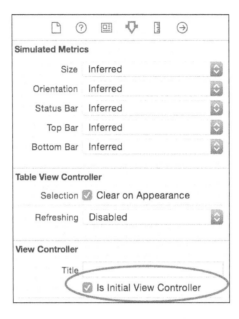

Now it's time to customize the cells. Let's select the cell prototype in the tree hierarchy:

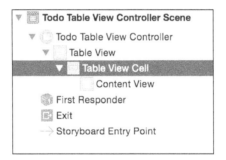

For the sake of simplicity, we'll use one of the predefined cell types provided by iOS, but obviously, we can create custom ones as well.

An important parameter to set is **Cell Identifier**. To save on memory and improve the performance, the table view doesn't recreate a new cell for every new content to show, but it reuses an already created cell that is outside the viewport. **Table View** can have different kinds of presented cells; each type must be identified using a parameter called **Cell Identifier**. Make sure to put the same value in **Interface Builder** and the code in order to reuse the cell:

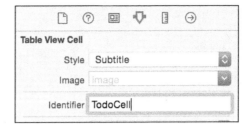

Finally, let's add the code to present some data in **Table View**:

```swift
import UIKit

@objc(TodoTableViewController)
class TodoTableViewController: UITableViewController {

    override func viewDidLoad() {
        super.viewDidLoad()
    }

    // MARK: - Table view data source

    override func tableView(tableView: UITableView,
numberOfRowsInSection section: Int) -> Int {
        return 10
    }
    override func tableView(tableView: UITableView,
cellForRowAtIndexPath indexPath: NSIndexPath) -> UITableViewCell {
        let cell =
tableView.dequeueReusableCellWithIdentifier("TodoCell",
forIndexPath: indexPath)

        cell.textLabel?.text = "Todo number \(indexPath.row)"

        return cell
    }
}
```

Note the first instruction, `@objc(TodoTableViewController)`, that exposes the class to the Objective-C runtime; otherwise, the app cannot bind the storyboard to the class.

Running the app, we can finally view **Table View**:

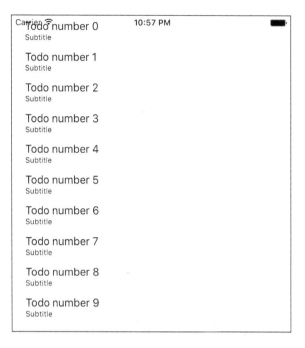

You've probably noticed that the app is missing a navigation bar; to add this, we must embed **View Controller** into `UINavigationController`.

`UINavigationController` is the base class for one of the most widely used types of navigation in iOS, where each new view is pushed on top of the current view, appearing from the right. When the new screen is dismissed, which is popped from the stack of views, it disappears by sliding to the right.

To embed it, select **View Controller** in the storyboard, and then from the menu, navigate to **Editor | Embed In | Navigation Controller**:

Now, **Storyboard** presents two connected screens:

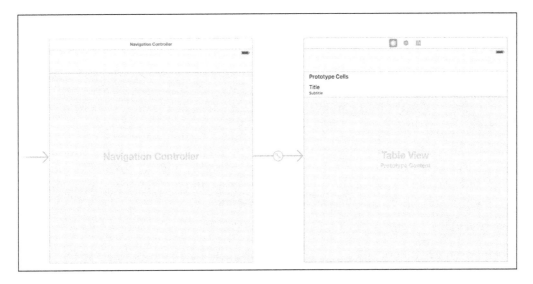

If you run the app now, **Table View** appears with a navigation bar. Before moving on, we add assets to the app.

 Assets can be downloaded from `https://github.com/gscalzo/Swift2ByExample/raw/3_Todolist_1_Skeleton/TodoList/Assets/Images.zip`.

Adding third-party libraries with CocoaPods

Before starting to implement the app, I want to introduce the secret weapon of productive iOS developers, *CocoaPods*.

CocoaPods (`http://cocoapods.org`) is the dependency manager for Cocoa projects that allows you to add a thousand libraries to your project by adding just one line of code to a configuration file. To add CocoaPods using Ruby, which is installed by default, you can type the following command in a terminal:

```
sudo gem install cocoapods
```

Then, we need to create `Podfile`, where we will add the required libraries. Consider this command:

```
pod init
```

It creates an empty `Podfile` file which is preconfigured to match our targets. We can now add the libraries to `Podfile`:

```
use_frameworks!
target 'TodoList' do
    pod 'LatoFont', :git => "https://github.com/gscalzo/LatoFont.git"
    pod 'MGSwipeTableCell', '~> 1.5.1'
end
```

You will notice that you can select either the version of the library or the GitHub path. This is really convenient when you need to modify a library to match your needs but you can't wait for the maintainer to merge the pull request and publish the new version. Now, run the `install` command:

```
pod install
```

The libraries are downloaded and added as frameworks to your project without the need to touch any of the project settings. Neat, isn't it?

Pay attention to this: sometimes, Xcode doesn't like the fact that an external app changes a project while it is open in Xcode. So, before running the pod, you must close Xcode.

As the `pod` command says at the end of the installation, we should now use `TodoList.xcworkspace` instead of `TodoList.xcodeproj`.

By opening the workspace, we can see that we now have a **Pods** project, with all the libraries as subdirectories, as shown in the following screenshot:

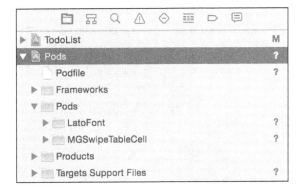

It is worth noting that pods are added as subprojects for this app, and if you need the same pods in a different app, you need to write or copy the `Podfile` in the folder of the other app and run `pod install` there.

Performing configuration via files is really handy, and if you need to remove a pod from your project, just delete the entry in `Podfile` and run `pod install` again.

Implementing the Todos view controller

We want to separate different responsibilities into different classes, so we are going to implement two classes: `TodosViewController` to handle the UI and the commands received from the user, and `TodosDatastore` to handle the creation and changes in the entities.

These classes manipulate two entities: **Todo** and **List**. As already experimented, we implement these classes in a top-down fashion, starting from **View Controller**, which basically presents just a button and a table view.

Let's add the button in the navigation bar using the storyboard. Select **Bar Button Item**, as shown in the following screenshot:

Drag **barbuttonitem** to the left of **Navigation Bar**.

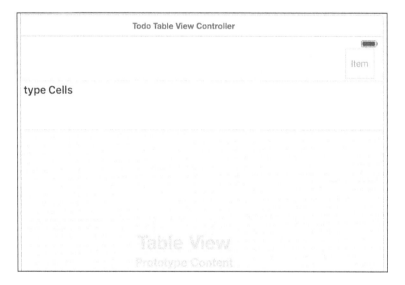

Now, select the button to configure it, setting the `tint` color and the image of the cross:

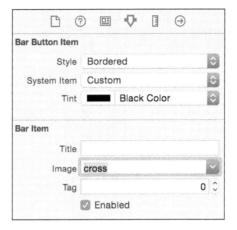

Let's add the title to **View Controller** in `viewDidLoad`:

```
override func viewDidLoad() {
    super.viewDidLoad()

    title = "Todos"
}
```

Just to make the cell prettier, we'll use the open source font **Lato** (`https://www.google.com/fonts/specimen/Lato`), which we added using CocoaPods.

Select the two labels inside the cell:

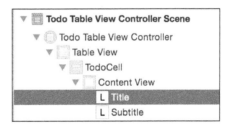

Then, change the font of **Title**:

Finally, change the **Font** of **Subtitle**:

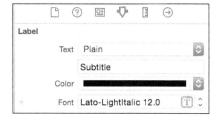

When you run the app, it looks really nice, as shown in this screenshot:

You can find the code for this version at `https://github.com/gscalzo/Swift2ByExample/tree/3_Todolist_1_Skeleton`.

Building the Todos screen

Let's move on to populating the **View Controller** we just created with the proper entities.

Adding entities

The first thing we need to do is create entities, which is really straightforward. Basically, we just need to map the requested fields in `struct`:

```
import Foundation

struct Todo: Equatable {
    let description: String
    let list: List
    let dueDate: NSDate
    let done: Bool
    let doneDate: NSDate?
}

func ==(todo1: Todo, todo2: Todo) -> Bool {
    return todo1.description == todo2.description
    && todo1.dueDate == todo2.dueDate
}

struct List {
    let description: String
}
```

`Foundation` is the core module in Swift, and it contains fundamental objects, for example, `NSDate`, which is required to implement every kind of app.

Implementing datastore

Next, we create `datastore` to handle all the operations of entities.

For now, we only return two lists of entities:

```swift
import Foundation

class TodosDatastore {
    private var savedLists = [List]()
    private var savedTodos = [Todo]()

    init(){
        savedLists = [
            List(description: "Personal"),
            List(description: "Work"),
            List(description: "Family")
        ]
        savedTodos = [
            Todo(description: "Remember the Milk",
                list: List(description: "Family") ,
                dueDate: NSDate(),
                done: false,
                doneDate: nil),
            Todo(description: "Buy Spider Man Comics",
                list: List(description: "Personal") ,
                dueDate: NSDate(),
                done: true,
                doneDate: NSDate()
            ),
            Todo(description: "Release build",
                list: List(description: "Work") ,
                dueDate: NSDate(),
                done: false,
                doneDate: nil)
            ]
    }

    func todos() -> [Todo] {
        return savedTodos
    }

    func lists() -> [List] {
        return savedLists
    }
}
```

Connecting datastore and View Controller

Then, we need to inject this `datastore` repository into `TodoTableViewController`.

To do that, we create a couple of properties and we implement a `configure()` function that accepts `datastore` as a parameter:

```
private var todosDatastore: TodosDatastore?
private var todos: [Todo]?

// MARK: - ViewController View Life Cycle

override func viewDidLoad() {
    super.viewDidLoad()

    title = "Todos"
}

required init?(coder aDecoder: NSCoder) {
    super.init(coder: aDecoder)
}

// MARK: - Configure

func configure(todosDatastore: TodosDatastore) {
    self.todosDatastore = todosDatastore
}
```

Up until now, App presents view controller because it is defined as initial **View Controller** in the storyboard; this works perfectly if **View Controller** doesn't need any parameters from the caller because now, we need to inject the `datastore` repository we need to find a way to intercept `TodoTableViewController` before it appears.

To do this, we add a fetch in `AppDelegate`:

```
func application(application: UIApplication,
didFinishLaunchingWithOptions launchOptions: [NSObject:
AnyObject]?) -> Bool {
    if let navigationController = window?.rootViewController
        as? UINavigationController,
        todoTableViewController = navigationController.
viewControllers.first
        as? TodoTableViewController
    {
        todoTableViewController.configure(TodosDatastore())
    }
    return true
}
```

This code could look a bit cumbersome, but in reality, it is just retrieving the expected view controller from the hierarchy of the screen.

The **Todo** tasks must be sorted by the date crescent, so we add a function to refresh the order of the **Todo** tasks:

```
override func viewWillAppear(animated: Bool) {
    super.viewWillAppear(animated)
    refresh()
}

// MARK: - Internal Functions
private func refresh() {
    if let todosDatastore = todosDatastore {
        todos = todosDatastore.todos().sort{
            $0.dueDate.compare($1.dueDate) ==
NSComparisonResult.OrderedAscending
        }
        tableView.reloadData()
    }
}
```

A closure may omit the names of its parameters. In this case, its parameters are implicitly named, starting with $, followed by their position, such as: $0, $1, and so on.

Actually, we could have implemented the sort inside `datastore`, but the sorting is presentation logic, hence it is a **View Controller** responsibility.

Configuring tableView

Primarily, we must replace the hardcoded value with the number of rows in the table we added, implementing the skeleton with the number of elements in the sorted **Todos** array:

```
override func tableView(tableView: UITableView,
    numberOfRowsInSection section: Int) -> Int {
        return todos?.count ?? 0
}
```

Because the array is optional, we must assure that it is not `nil` and then get the count like this:

```
if let todos = todos {
    return todos.count
} else {
    return 0
}
```

Because this check is really common, Swift supports the null coalescing `?` operator that implements the three preceding lines in one line.

Then, we change `dataSource`:

```
override func tableView(tableView: UITableView, cellForRowAtIndexPath
indexPath: NSIndexPath) -> UITableViewCell {
    let cell =
tableView.dequeueReusableCellWithIdentifier("TodoCell",
forIndexPath: indexPath)

    if let todo = todos?[indexPath.row] {
        renderCell(cell, todo: todo)
    }

    return cell
}
```

Basically, we retrieve the correct `todo` task and we render it into a cell:

```
private func renderCell(cell:UITableViewCell, todo: Todo){
    let dateFormatter:NSDateFormatter = NSDateFormatter()
    dateFormatter.dateFormat = "HH:mm dd-MM-YY"
    let dueDate = dateFormatter.stringFromDate(todo.dueDate)
    cell.detailTextLabel?.text = "\(dueDate) | \(todo.list.
description)"
    cell.textLabel?.text = todo.description

    cell.accessoryType = todo.done ? .Checkmark : .None
}
```

Finishing touches

If we run the app, we can see that the **Todos** are correctly rendered, but the rows are too short and the checkmark is blue, while everything else is black.

Let's go to the storyboard to fix these things.

1. First, select **Table View**:

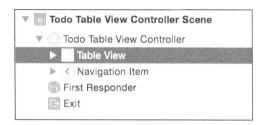

2. In the metrics tab, let's increase the height of the cell:

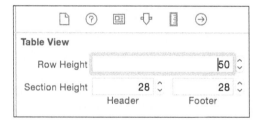

3. To change the checkmark, select the cell and then change the `tint` color from blue to black:

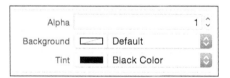

4. Now, if we run the app, we can see how gorgeous it is, as shown in the following screenshot:

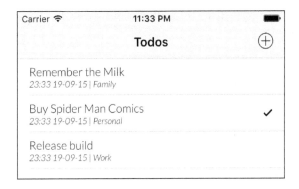

Swipe that cell!

The last thing missing in this screen is swappable cells.

Guess what? We are going to solve this problem using a pod, MGSwipeTableCell.

Note that CocoaPods makes integrating Objective-C and Swift libraries really straightforward. It basically creates frameworks, and the client app can simply import them without worrying about which language was used to create them.

The MGSwipeTableCell (https://github.com/MortimerGoro/MGSwipeTableCell) pod is a really powerful and flexible add-on for UITableViewCell.

First of all, we must change the type of cell in the storyboard.

In TodoTableViewController, we import MGSwipeTableCell:

```
import UIKit
import MGSwipeTableCell

@objc(TodoTableViewController)
class TodoTableViewController: UITableViewController {
```

Given that we changed the type of the cell, we must cast the type in the `datastore` function implementation:

```
    let cell = tableView.dequeueReusableCellWithIdentifier("TodoCell",
forIndexPath: indexPath) as! MGSwipeTableCell

    if let todo = todos?[indexPath.row] {
        renderCell(cell, todo: todo)
        setupButtonsForCell(cell, todo: todo)
    }
```

Also, we call a function to set up the buttons:

```
    private func setupButtonsForCell(cell: MGSwipeTableCell, todo:
Todo) {
        cell.rightButtons = [
            MGSwipeButton(title: "Edit",
                backgroundColor: UIColor.blueColor(),
                padding: 30) {
                    [weak self] sender in
                    self?.editButtonPressed(todo)
                    return true
            },
            MGSwipeButton(title: "Delete",
                backgroundColor: UIColor.redColor(),
                padding: 30) {
                    [weak self] sender in
                    self?.deleteButtonPressed(todo)
                    return true
            }
        ]

        cell.rightExpansion.buttonIndex = 0
        cell.leftButtons = [
            MGSwipeButton(title: "Done",
                backgroundColor: UIColor.greenColor(),
                padding: 30) {
                    [weak self] sender in
                    self?.doneButtonPressed(todo)
                    return true
            } ]
        cell.leftExpansion.buttonIndex = 0
    }
```

One of the problems that can appear while using blocks in ARC is the creation of a strong retain cycle. If we remove `[weak self]` from the implementation of the code blocks, this is what will happen:

- The cell will own the button
- The button will own the block
- The block will own the cell

This means that none of these objects will be removed from the memory when the cell is released by all of its clients.

Using `[weak self]`, the cell is just assigned to the block instead of being passed with a strong reference (thus incrementing the reference counter for the cell), without incrementing the reference counter. In this way, the cycle is not completed.

As the `weak` reference creates an optional variable, to use `self`, we must use the question mark, which doesn't call the method if the variable is `nil`.

Then, we implement the three skeleton callbacks bounded to the three buttons:

```
// MARK: Actions
extension TodoTableViewController {
    func addTodoButtonPressed(sender: UIButton!){
        print("addTodoButtonPressed")
    }

    func editButtonPressed(todo: Todo){
        print("editButtonPressed")
    }

    func deleteButtonPressed(todo: Todo){
        todosDatastore?.deleteTodo(todo)
        refresh()
    }

    func doneButtonPressed(todo: Todo){
        todosDatastore?.doneTodo(todo)
        refresh()
    }
}
```

Finally, we create the empty methods inside `datastore`:

```
// MARK: Actions
extension TodosDatastore {
    func addTodo(todo: Todo) {
        print("addTodo")
    }
    func deleteTodo(todo: Todo?) {
        print("deleteTodo")
    }
    func doneTodo(todo: Todo) {
        print("doneTodo")
    }
}
```

By running the app, we can see that we have implemented all of the requested features for the first screen:

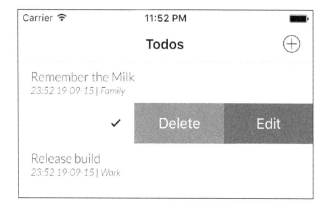

 You can find the the code that implements the app is now up to date at `https://github.com/gscalzo/Swift2ByExample/tree/3_Todolist_2_TodoScreen`.

Adding a Todo task

So far, the app works very well, presenting all the **Todo** tasks, but we need to allow the user to create their own **Todo** task.

The add a Todo view

As the specifications require that a **Todo** task is editable, it makes sense to use the same **View Controller** either to create a new **Todo** task, or to edit an already existing **Todo** task.

To implement the desired layout, we are going to use a `TableViewController` class again using static cells so that we can configure and lay it out directly in **Interface Builder**.

Add another `TableViewController` class close to `TodoTableViewController`, and after selecting the **Table View** inside, set the content as **Static Cells** instead of **Dynamic Cells**.

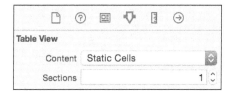

Then, select the first and only section, that is, **Table View Section**.

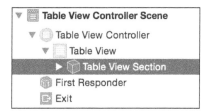

Now set the number of **Rows** to **5**.

Before implementing the cells, select **Table View** and set the height of each cell to **50**.

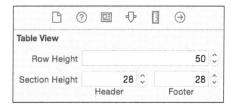

The first row must contain the description of **Todo**, so we use `UITextField` to handle this.

Select the `UITextField` component and drag it onto the **Content View** of the first cell.

Now you may surely notice that the field is neither centered nor filling the parent; it's time to add constraints.

To do that, while selecting **Text Field**, select the penultimate button in bottom-left corner, the square between two pipes; it will permit us to add constraints based on the relation with the parent container.

A pop-up will appear, and after deselecting the **Constrain to Margin** checkbox, add the value indicated in the following screenshot:

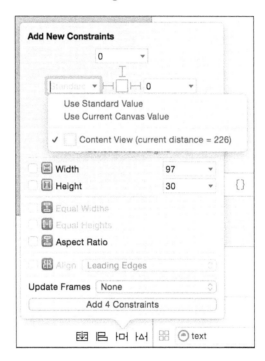

After that, press the **Add 4 Constrains** button. The screen now will present some warnings.

This is because the actual layout is different than the one that will be presented at runtime. To remove them, select the yellow arrow in the controller tree view:

Then, select the yellow triangle:

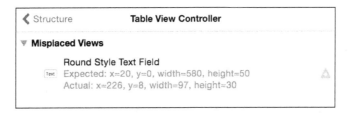

Finally, fix the misplacement, updating the frames:

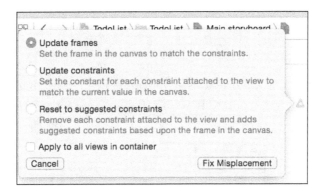

Now, configure the look of **Text Field**, setting the placeholder text, removing the text and the border, and setting the correct font:

The next cell will contain a label for a list, and we'll follow the same path: add **Label**, add constraints, and customize the appearance:

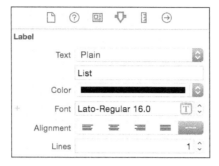

The third cell is the **Due Date** label, which is exactly the same as the previous label. The fourth is still a label, but it's a bit more interesting. First, set the height of the cell to **120**:

To add a label, we follow the previous steps, but instead of plain text, we are going to add a checkmark using a special character; from the edit menu, select **Emoji & Symbols**:

Then, look for the checkmark symbol:

Then, copy the character information and copy it as the text of the label, changing the size of the font to **160**:

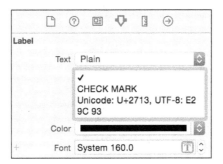

The last cell will contain a date picker, which is a big component, so we set the height of the cell to **300**. Don't forget to set the constraints to fill the cell after dragging it into **Content View**. Now, it's time to create the segues to the present **View Controller**.

A segue is a sort of link between **View Controllers** that have an identifier and that I use to move from one controller to another. Select the yellow icon in `TodoTableViewController`:

Then, from the outlet, drag from the bullet of **Manual Segue** to the new **View Controller** twice:

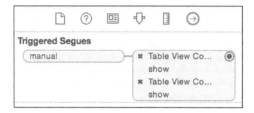

You should see two lines connecting the View Controllers.

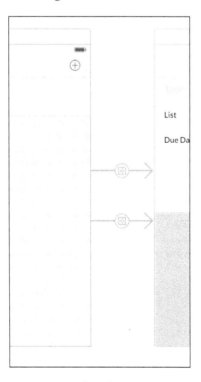

Select each of them to give them an identifier; one must be **addTodo**, and the other must be **Edit Todo**.

To test the connection, we add an action trigger with the **Add** button:

```
@IBAction func addTodoButtonPressed(sender: AnyObject){
    print("addTodoButtonPressed")
    performSegueWithIdentifier("addTodo", sender: self)
}
```

Connect the **Bar** button to this action:

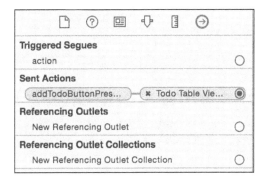

Running the app, we can see that the screen is exactly how we expected it to be:

The add a Todo View Controller

After finishing view, let's create another `TableViewController` to manage that view; it will be called `EditTodoTableViewController`:

```
import UIKit

class EditTodoTableViewController: UITableViewController {
    @IBOutlet var descriptionTextField: UITextField!
    @IBOutlet var listLabel: UILabel!
    @IBOutlet var dueDateLabel: UILabel!
    @IBOutlet var dueDatePicker: UIDatePicker!

    var todoToEdit: Todo?
    var todosDatastore: TodosDatastore?
```

```
    private var list: List?
    private var dueDate: NSDate?
}
```

We defined IBOutlets to connect the components, the eventual todo to edit, the datastore repository to update the data and finally, the list and the due date of **Todo**.

After setting the class as **Custom Class** for view controller, we must connect the outlets in **Interface Builder**, as shown in the following two screenshots:

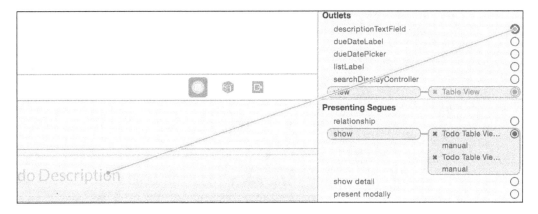

After connecting all the outlets, this is how the view controller should appear:

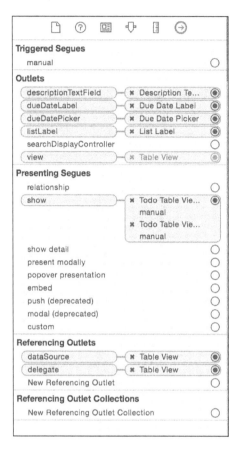

In `viewDidLoad()`, we add the calls to initialization functions:

```
override func viewDidLoad() {
    super.viewDidLoad()

    setup()
    refresh()
    descriptionTextField.becomeFirstResponder()
}
```

The `setup` function sets the original `dueDate` function and the description of the todo to edit if it exists; otherwise, ask the defaults values to the store:

```
private extension EditTodoTableViewController {
    func setup(){
```

```
        if let todo = todoToEdit {
            descriptionTextField.text = todo.description
            list = todo.list
            dueDate = todo.dueDate
        } else if let todosDatastore = todosDatastore{
            list = todosDatastore.defaultList()
            dueDate = todosDatastore.defaultDueDate()
        }
        datePickerSetup()
    }

    func datePickerSetup() {
        dueDatePicker.datePickerMode = .DateAndTime
        dueDatePicker.minimumDate = NSDate()
        dueDatePicker.date = dueDate!
        dueDatePicker.addTarget(self, action: "dueDateChanged:",
            forControlEvents: .ValueChanged)
    }
}
```

When the optional **Todo** contains an actual value, the fields from that value are extracted to initialize the fields. Otherwise, the default values are provided.

As you can see, the default values aren't set directly in the **View Controller** code. Instead, **View Controller** asks for the default values of lists and dueDate from the datastore, giving it the responsibility of handling them.

This distinction, which can seem confusing, is really important. The default values are from the domain of the data and not from the domain of the presentation, and the proper place is in datastore.

Let's implement them in TodosDatastore:

```
// MARK: Defaults
extension TodosDatastore {
    func defaultList() -> List {
        return List(description: "Personal")
    }

    func defaultDueDate() -> NSDate {
        let now = NSDate()
        let secondsInADay = NSTimeInterval(24 * 60 * 60)
        return now.dateByAddingTimeInterval(secondsInADay)
    }
}
```

Because the default list is always present, we change the `lists()` function accordingly:

```
func lists() -> [List] {
    return [defaultList()] + savedLists
}
```

The callback connected to the picker just grabs the date and sets it in the `dueDate` property:

```
@objc func dueDateChanged(sender: UIButton!) {
    dueDate = dueDatePicker.date
    refresh()
}
```

As usual, because the callback must be visible for the Objective-C runtime, the `@objc` keyword must be present:

```
func refresh(){
    listLabel.text = "List: \(list!.description)"
    let dateFormatter:NSDateFormatter = NSDateFormatter()
    dateFormatter.dateFormat = "HH:mm dd-MM-YY"
    if let dueDate = dueDate {
        let formattedDueDate =
dateFormatter.stringFromDate(dueDate)
        dueDateLabel.text = "Due date: \(formattedDueDate)"
    }
}
```

The `refresh()` function updates the view based on the value of the properties.

Finally, we add two functions to be called when the **Done** button and the **Due Date** row are selected:

```
func doneSelected() {
    if let descriptionText = descriptionTextField.text,
        list = list,
        dueDate = dueDate
        where !descriptionText.isEmpty {
            let newTodo = Todo(description: descriptionText,
                list: list,
                dueDate: dueDate,
                done: false,
                doneDate: nil)
            todosDatastore?.addTodo(newTodo)
            todosDatastore?.deleteTodo(todoToEdit)
```

```
                navigationController!.popViewControllerAnimated(true)
        }
    }

    func showAddList() {
        performSegueWithIdentifier("addList", sender: self)
    }
```

The former creates a new **Todo** based on the inserted properties, and the latter goes to a new **View Controller** to insert and select a new **List**.

To select the table rows, we implement `tableViewDelegate` using a custom `enum` to define the sections:

```
enum EditTableViewRow : Int {
    case Description
    case List
    case DueDate
    case Done
    case DatePicker
}
```

In this way, we can access the different parts of **Table View** without relying on magic numbers in our code:

```
// MARK: UITableViewDelegate
extension EditTodoViewController {
    override func tableView(tableView: UITableView,
didSelectRowAtIndexPath indexPath: NSIndexPath) {
        switch EditTableViewRow(rawValue: indexPath.row)! {
        case .List:
            showAddList()
        case .DueDate:
            descriptionTextField.resignFirstResponder()
        case .Done:
            doneSelected()
        default:
            break
        }
    }
}
```

If you run the app now, it will crash because the `dueDate` property is `nil` and is unwrapped in order to set it to `date picker`.

This happens because we need to complete the code in order to move it from `TodoTableViewController` to `EditTodoTableViewController`.

Let's go back to the former and add a new property for the eventually selected `Todo`:

```
private var selectedTodo: Todo?
```

This value will be set when we want to edit `Todo`:

```
func editButtonPressed(todo: Todo){
    selectedTodo = todo
    performSegueWithIdentifier("editTodo", sender: self)
}
```

Finally, we add the configuration code in the `prepareForSegue()` function; this is a function called by **View Controller** just before presenting a new **View Controller**, and it is the place where the configuration code usually is put for the **View Controller** destination:

```
// MARK: Segue
extension TodoTableViewController {
    override func prepareForSegue(segue: UIStoryboardSegue, sender:
AnyObject?) {
        guard let identifier = segue.identifier,
        destinationViewController = segue.destinationViewController
as? EditTodoTableViewController
        else {
            return
        }

        destinationViewController.todosDatastore = todosDatastore
        destinationViewController.todoToEdit = selectedTodo

        switch identifier {
        case "addTodo":
                destinationViewController.title = "New Todo"
        case "editTodo":
                destinationViewController.title = "Edit Todo"
        default:
            break
        }
    }
}
```

As you can see, the only difference based on the `segue` identifier is the title.

Finishing TodoDatastore

Before implementing the last `TableViewController` for this app, let's implement all the missing functions of `datastore`.

Let's begin with the actions:

```
// MARK: Actions
extension TodosDatastore {
    func addTodo(todo: Todo) {
        savedTodos = savedTodos + [todo]
    }
    func deleteTodo(todo: Todo?) {
        if let todo = todo {
            savedTodos = savedTodos.filter({$0 != todo})
        }
    }

    func doneTodo(todo: Todo) {
        deleteTodo(todo)
        let doneTodo = Todo(description: todo.description,
                            list: todo.list,
                            dueDate: todo.dueDate,
                            done: true,
                            doneDate: NSDate())
        addTodo(doneTodo)
    }

    func addListDescription(description: String) {
        if !description.isEmpty {
            savedLists = savedLists + [List(description: description)]
        }
    }
}
```

Note that in order to update **Todo**, because all **Todos** are an immutable `struct`, we delete the previous one, and then we add a copy of it with the Boolean set to `true` and with `doneDate` set to now.

The last thing we do is we delete the hardcoded values for **Todos** and the lists we added in the initializer:

```
    init(){

    }
```

List View Controller

This **List View Controller** will permit us to add and select a **List** for the current **Todo**.

Let's add a `TableViewController`, and a `ListTableViewController` class with the plus button in the top-right corner, as shown in the following screenshot:

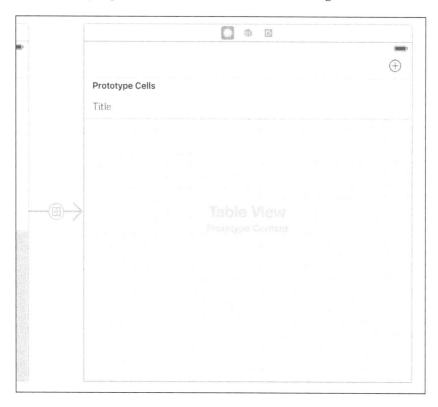

The identifier of the segue is `addList`. Set the height of the cell to `50` and the font for the **Basic** `UITableViewCell` class to **Lato Light** size `18`.

As mentioned already, the name of the controller is `ListTableViewController`, and along with the usual `TodoDatastore` class, it expects a property with a block to be called when a list is selected:

```swift
import UIKit

class ListTableViewController: UITableViewController {
    var onListSelected: ((list: List) -> Void)?
    var todosDatastore: TodosDatastore?
```

```
override func viewDidLoad() {
    super.viewDidLoad()
    title = "Lists"
}
```

`TableViewDataSource` basically renders the saved **List**:

```
// MARK: - Table view data source
override func tableView(tableView: UITableView, numberOfRowsInSection
section: Int) -> Int {
    return todosDatastore?.lists().count ?? 0
}

override func tableView(tableView: UITableView, cellForRowAtIndexPath
indexPath: NSIndexPath) -> UITableViewCell {
    let cell = tableView.dequeueReusableCellWithIdentifier("Cell",
forIndexPath: indexPath)

    if let list = todosDatastore?.lists()[indexPath.row] {
        cell.textLabel?.text = list.description
    }
    cell.selectionStyle = .None
    return cell
}
```

The **Table View** delegate calls the closure mentioned earlier, when a row is selected:

```
// MARK: - Table view delegate
override func tableView(tableView: UITableView,
didSelectRowAtIndexPath indexPath: NSIndexPath) {
    let list = todosDatastore?.lists()[indexPath.row]
    if let list = list, onListSelected = onListSelected {
        onListSelected(list: list)
    }
    navigationController?.popViewControllerAnimated(true)
}
```

Finally, an action is implemented in order to permit the creation of a new list:

```
// MARK: Actions
extension ListTableViewController {
    @IBAction func addListButtonTapped(sender: AnyObject) {
        let alert = UIAlertController(title: "Enter list name",
                        message: "To create a new list, please enter the
name of the list",
                        preferredStyle: .Alert)
```

```
        let okAction = UIAlertAction(title: "OK",
        style: .Default) { (action: UIAlertAction!) -> Void in
                            let textField = alert.textFields?.first
                            self.addList(textField?.text ?? "")
                    }
        let cancelAction = UIAlertAction(title: "Cancel",
        style: .Default, handler: nil)
        alert.addAction(okAction)
        alert.addAction(cancelAction)
        alert.addTextFieldWithConfigurationHandler(nil)
        presentViewController(alert,
                animated: true,
                completion: nil)
    }

    func addList(description: NSString) {
        todosDatastore?.addListDescription(description as String)
        tableView.reloadData()
    }
}
```

With the new `UIAlertController` class introduced in iOS 8, it is just a matter of
defining two `UIAlertAction` components, where the **Cancel** button has an empty
handler because it must only dismiss the alert view, and a `textfield` class without
any handler because the inserted value has already been retrieved by the handler of
the **OK** button.

This function must be connected as an action to the button in the top-right corner:

The very last thing we do is set `datastore` and the closure to **View Controller**.

Because we already implemented `performSegue()` in
`EditTodoTableViewController`, we just need to add the `prepareForSegue()` block:

```
// MARK: Segue
extension EditTodoTableViewController {
```

```
        override func prepareForSegue(segue: UIStoryboardSegue, sender:
    AnyObject?) {
            guard let identifier = segue.identifier,
                destinationViewController = segue.
        destinationViewController as? ListTableViewController
                else {
                return
            }
            if identifier == "addList" {
                destinationViewController.title = "Lists"
                destinationViewController.todosDatastore = todosDatastore
                destinationViewController.onListSelected = { list in
                    self.list = list
                    self.refresh()
                }
            }
        }
    }
```

With this, we finish our **Todo** app. As you may have experienced that the simplest app too needs a lot of work in order to make it flexible and ready to be extended; however, to keep the architecture clean and the responsibilities split in well-defined components pay in the long term, we need to add or modify features.

Where do we go from here?

The app looks nice, but there is a lot to improve, starting with the persistence layer.

There are several ways to save data in an iOS app. None of them are straightforward, so they are beyond the scope of this book. Yet, you can find two different ways to make the data persist in the master branch (one method uses a file to persist the data and the other uses CoreData, a library to manage data in a database).

 You can find the complete source code of the app at https://github.com/gscalzo/Swift2ByExample/tree/3_Todolist_3_Complete.

Another cool thing to implement is adding local notifications when the **Todo** task reaches the due date. Adding is also a quick way to increase the due date; you can add 10 minutes, 1 hour, or 1 day.

Summary

You must have thought that developing with Swift makes creating an app straightforward, right? Unfortunately, it does not. This long chapter showed that most of the coding is devoted to configuring components of the SDK and creating connections between the classes of our app instead of using cool functional programming tricks.

However, in this chapter, we covered most of the aspects that an iOS developer must know, starting with CocoaPods to laying out the components of the views and differentiating responsibilities between the different layers of an app.

Another important skill you need to learn is how to connect to a server in order to retrieve data, a server that could be either under our control, or a third-party server, such as a service.

In the next chapter, you'll learn how to exploit external servers to add content to an app and how to retrieve and send JSON data. We'll pack this technique to create a pretty weather app.

5

A Pretty Weather App

In the previous chapter, when we developed the *TodoList* app, we mentioned that a connection with a remote server was the tool that was missing from the common iOS developer tool set we were covering.

In this chapter, we are going to fill this gap, showing you how to retrieve data from two different remote services.

We'll also implement an app that solves a real problem using most of the techniques that we have already seen in the previous chapter.

The app is...

One of the key facts of the mobile revolution is that we always have a computer that constantly uses GPS in our pocket, to which we can ask anything regarding everything around us.

As we can see by searching the App Store, forecasting weather is a common problem that apps try to solve, often using stunning designs but sometimes using a basic design with a lot a features. This confuses the user.

If we look carefully at the nicest, and most famous, weather apps, we realize that the structures are really similar, and this is the kind of app we want to build.

Although a few apps allow you to check the weather of several cities at a time, for simplicity, we'll implement an app that shows only the weather of your current city.

That said, the aim of the app is:

- To show the current weather for the current location
- To show the forecast for the upcoming hours and days

To make the app more appealing, we'll add a nice photo of the current city as the background. The following screenshot shows the wireframe of the first page:

Basically, the information required for this view includes the temperature (current, maximum, and minimum) and a description of the current weather.

When we slide the scroll view up, the forecasts appear. At the top, in a horizontal scroll view, there is an hourly forecast for the current day. Next, it shows a list of the forecast for the days in the following week, showing the temperature and weather icons, as shown next:

Because the scroll view is transparent, in order to increase the contrast with the underlying image, we will add a blur effect to the image itself.

Building the skeleton

Having defined the requirements, let's start implementing them, splitting the implementation into auto-conclusive phases.

In the previous chapter, we implemented the app using **Interface Builder** to create the UI, but we mentioned that it is definitely possible to do that entirely by code.

Although Apple provides two ways to do this, either via NSLayoutConstraintss or Visual Format Language, both are really verbose and error-prone; hence, we'll use a nice Cartography library, which permits us to set up constraints in a declarative way without using any hardcoded strings.

 A description of Cartography can be found here: https://github. com/robb/Cartography.

Creating the project

In the same way we did for the previous apps, we create an empty **Single View** app, from which we remove the reference to the main storyboard and the **View Controller** template.

Just for the sake of a quick test, we create `PrettyWeatherViewController`, showing a red background:

```
class PrettyWeatherViewController: UIViewController {
    override func viewDidLoad() {
        super.viewDidLoad()
        view.backgroundColor = UIColor.redColor()
    }
}
```

Also, we add the creation of **View Controller** in `AppDelegate`:

```
func application(application: UIApplication,
didFinishLaunchingWithOptions launchOptions: [NSObject:
AnyObject]?) -> Bool {
    let viewController = PrettyWeatherViewController()

    let mainWindow = UIWindow(frame: UIScreen.mainScreen().bounds)
    mainWindow.backgroundColor = UIColor.whiteColor()
    mainWindow.rootViewController = viewController
    mainWindow.makeKeyAndVisible()
    window = mainWindow

    return true
}
```

A newly generated app runs the first view controller set in `Main.storyboard`; because we want to set up the layout without using storyboards, we override this behavior, setting the first view controller to be displayed manually in `AppDelegate`.

If we run the app, a red background is the only thing we see. Now let's install CocoaPods, creating `Podfile` with these pods:

```
use_frameworks!
inhibit_all_warnings!

target 'PrettyWeatherApp' do
    pod 'Cartography', :git => "https://github.com/robb/Cartography.
git", :tag => '0.6.0'
    pod 'Alamofire', '~> 2.0'
    pod 'SwiftyJSON', '~> 2.3.0'
```

```
    pod 'WeatherIconsKit', :git => 'git@github.com:gscalzo/
WeatherIconsKit.git'
    pod 'FlickrKit', '~> 1.0.5'
    pod 'FXBlurView', '~> 1.6.4'
    pod 'LatoFont', :git => "https://github.com/gscalzo/LatoFont.git"
end
```

After running the `pod` installation, we have all the required libraries.

We recommend that you install all the libraries at the beginning instead of when each of them is introduced in the app; I think that this approach will reduce the time jumping from the code to `Podfile`.

Let me just briefly summarize the libraries:

- **Cartography** is a pod to simplify Auto Layout by code
- **Alamofire** will help us to make network requests
- **SwiftyJSON** is a helper for the serialization and deserialization of JSON values
- **WeatherIconsKit** is a collection of weather images of the weather
- **FlickrKit** is the Flickr SDK API, which will help us get images from Flickr
- **FXBlurView** is a blurring image view
- **LatoFont** is a nice custom font we already used in the previous chapter

Adding assets

Before moving onto implement the scaffold of the UI, we add the icon and the default background image that is presented while we are downloading the one relative to the current location.

 The assets can be downloaded from `https://github.com/gscalzo/Swift2ByExample/raw/4_PrettyWeather_1_Skeleton/PrettyWeatherApp/assets/assets.zip`.

Insert the icon and the default image into **Asset Catalogue**, and then move on to implementing `PrettyWeatherViewController`:

```
import UIKit
import Cartography

class PrettyWeatherViewController: UIViewController {
```

```
private let backgroundView = UIImageView()

override func viewDidLoad() {
    super.viewDidLoad()
    setup()
    layoutView()
    style()
    render(UIImage(named: "DefaultImage"))
}
}
```

The top part of the controller just builds all the structure components when
View Controller has loaded:

```
// MARK: Setup
private extension PrettyWeatherViewController{
    func setup(){
        backgroundView.contentMode = .ScaleAspectFill
        backgroundView.clipsToBounds = true
        view.addSubview(backgroundView)
    }
}
```

The only graphic component of **View Controller** is the background image view,
which is configured to contain the image to fulfill it completely:

```
// MARK: Layout
extension PrettyWeatherViewController{
    func layoutView() {
        layout(backgroundView) { view in
            view.top == view.superview!.top
            view.bottom == view.superview!.bottom
            view.left == view.superview!.left
            view.right == view.superview!.right
        }
    }
}
```

As the background, the image view must occupy the entire screen. For the time
being, the render just puts the image inside the image view:

```
// MARK: Render
private extension PrettyWeatherViewController{
    func render(image: UIImage?){
        if let image = image {
```

```
            backgroundView.image = image
        }
    }
}
```

Finally, an empty style function is added for uniformity with our structure:

```
// MARK: Style
private extension PrettyWeatherViewController{
    func style(){
    }
}
```

Now, on running the app, the interface is what we expected, as shown in the following screenshot:

 You can find the code for this version at https://github.com/ gscalzo/Swift2ByExample/tree/4_PrettyWeather_1_ Skeleton.

Implementing the UI

A UI that is as complicated as the one required can be really difficult to implement if we don't take the correct precautions.

A good way to minimize the complexity is to split the problem into more manageable sub-problems, so we'll define three sub-views: **CurrentWeatherView**, **HourlyForecastView**, and **DailyForecastView**. We'll implement them as separate entities. The following screenshot shows the view's structure:

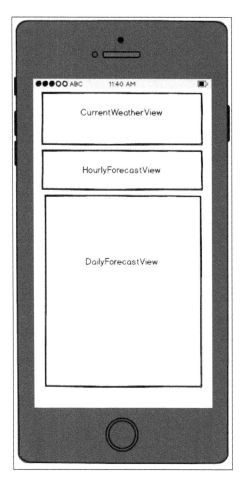

The UI in blocks

As we just said, we implement the UI by creating three custom views, whose size and position we are temporarily hardcoding.

Let's start with **CurrentWeatherView**, adding it to `PrettyWeatherViewController`:

```
    private let scrollView = UIScrollView()
private let currentWeatherView = CurrentWeatherView(frame:
CGRectZero)
```

As the height of the three elements is more than the height of the view, we create a scroll view to contain them:

```
func setup(){
    //...
    scrollView.showsVerticalScrollIndicator = false
    scrollView.addSubview(currentWeatherView)
    view.addSubview(scrollView)
}
```

The `setup()` function just adds the components to the views hierarchy:

```
func layoutView() {
    //...
    constrain(backgroundView) {
        $0.edges ==  $0.superview!.edges
    }

    constrain(scrollView) {
        $0.edges ==  $0.superview!.edges
    }

    constrain(currentWeatherView) {
        $0.width == $0.superview!.width
        $0.centerX == $0.superview!.centerX
    }
```

The layout basically centers `subview` in the scroll view; to do this, we use this useful construct of Cartography that permits you to bind the edges of a view to those of another view.

Let's move on to **Custom View**:

```
class CurrentWeatherView: UIView {
    static var HEIGHT: CGFloat { get { return 160 } }
    private var didSetupConstraints = false
    override init(frame: CGRect) {
        super.init(frame: frame)
        setup()
        style()
    }
```

```swift
required init(coder aDecoder: NSCoder) {
    fatalError("init(coder:) has not been implemented")
}

override func updateConstraints() {
    if didSetupConstraints {
        super.updateConstraints()
        return
    }
    layoutView()
    super.updateConstraints()
    didSetupConstraints = true
}
}
```

Here, the only difference from the usual structure is that `layoutView()` is not called during the initialization but in the overridden method, which is `updateConstraints()`. This method is called by the framework when all other constraints are set and the view needs to be laid out. If you try to move the `layoutView()` call into the `init` method, you will see that the constraints will conflict.

Also, because `updateConstraints()` can be called more than once, we need to ensure that the constraints are not added multiple times:

```swift
// MARK: Setup
private extension CurrentWeatherView{
    func setup(){
    }
}

// MARK: Layout
private extension CurrentWeatherView{
    func layoutView(){
        constrain(self) {
            $0.height == CurrentWeatherView.HEIGHT
        }
    }
}

// MARK: Style
private extension CurrentWeatherView{
    func style(){
```

```
backgroundColor = UIColor.redColor()
   }
}
```

The `setup()` function is just an empty method; `layoutView()` defines the height, and `style()` paints the view red. If you run the app now, you will see a red rectangle at the top of the view. However, we want the view at the bottom. Also, the scroll view is not scrollable.

Before fixing this issue, here's a quick note on how `scrollView` works: the frame of `scrollView` is the frame of the viewport that makes the content visible. Inside `scrollView`, there is another view that contains the actual sub views. If `contentView` is smaller than `scrollView`, it is not scrollable.

So, if we want to change the position of `currentWeatherView`, we need to lay it out inside **Content View**. To do this, we add the following code to `layoutView()` in `PrettyWeatherViewController`:

```
let currentWeatherInsect: CGFloat = view.frame.height -
CurrentWeatherView.HEIGHT - PrettyWeatherViewController.INSET

constrain(currentWeatherView) {
$0.top == $0.superview!.top + currentWeatherInsect
}
```

As you can see, we have defined a new constant, other than the height of `CurrentWeatherView`:

```
class PrettyWeatherViewController: UIViewController {
    static var INSET: CGFloat { get { return 20 } }
```

When we run the app now, we can see that the view is in the correct position.

Implementing the two missing views is straightforward. First of all, we add the instances:

```
private let hourlyForecastView = WeatherHourlyForecastView(frame:
CGRectZero)
private let daysForecastView = WeatherDaysForecastView(frame:
CGRectZero)
```

Then, we add the views to `scrollView`:

```
scrollView.addSubview(hourlyForecastView)
scrollView.addSubview(daysForecastView)
```

Finally, we lay them out:

```
constrain(hourlyForecastView, currentWeatherView) {
    $0.top == $1.bottom + PrettyWeatherViewController.INSET
    $0.width == $0.superview!.width
    $0.centerX == $0.superview!.centerX
}

constrain(daysForecastView, hourlyForecastView) {
    $0.top == $1.bottom
    $0.width == $1.width
    $0.bottom == $0.superview!.bottom -
PrettyWeatherViewController.INSET
    $0.centerX == $0.superview!.centerX
}
```

The three views are stacked on top of each other. The only thing to note is that the bottom of `daysForecastView` is connected to the bottom of `scrollView`; as a result, it enlarges **Content View** and makes the view scrollable.

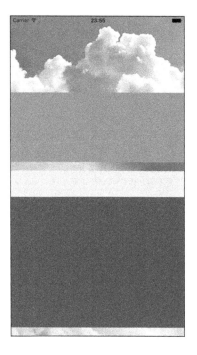

 You can find the code for this version at https://github.com/ gscalzo/Swift2ByExample/tree/4_PrettyWeather_2_ UIInBlocks.

Completing the UI

Although the views are in the correct place, we need to implement all the components.

Implementing CurrentWeatherView

First of all, we need to import the fonts' frameworks:

```
import LatoFont
import WeatherIconsKit
```

Former Airlines is the font we've already used in the *TodoList* app; the latter is similar to Awesome Kit, and it contains a series of icons related to the weather:

```
private let cityLbl = UILabel()
private let maxTempLbl = UILabel()
private let minTempLbl = UILabel()
private let iconLbl = UILabel()
private let weatherLbl = UILabel()
private let currentTempLbl = UILabel()
```

We simply add all the labels and lay them out:

```
func layoutView(){
    constrain(self) {
        $0.height == CurrentWeatherView.HEIGHT
    }
    constrain(iconLbl) {
        $0.top == $0.superview!.top
        $0.left == $0.superview!.left + 20
        $0.width == 30
        $0.width == $0.height
    }
    constrain(weatherLbl, iconLbl) {
        $0.top == $1.top
        $0.left == $1.right + 10
        $0.height == $1.height
        $0.width == 200
    }

    constrain(currentTempLbl, iconLbl) {
        $0.top == $1.bottom
        $0.left == $1.left
    }
```

```
        constrain(currentTempLbl, minTempLbl) {
            $0.bottom == $1.top
            $0.left == $1.left
        }

        constrain(minTempLbl) {
            $0.bottom == $0.superview!.bottom
            $0.height == 30
        }

        constrain(maxTempLbl, minTempLbl) {
            $0.top == $1.top
            $0.height == $1.height
            $0.left == $1.right + 10
        }
        constrain(cityLbl) {
            $0.bottom == $0.superview!.bottom
            $0.right == $0.superview!.right - 10
            $0.height == 30
            $0.width == 200
        }
    }
```

As usual, the layout part is the longest and is full of **boilerplate** code:

```
func style(){
    iconLbl.textColor = UIColor.whiteColor()
    weatherLbl.font = UIFont.latoLightFontOfSize(20)
    weatherLbl.textColor = UIColor.whiteColor()

    currentTempLbl.font = UIFont.latoLightFontOfSize(96)
    currentTempLbl.textColor = UIColor.whiteColor()

    maxTempLbl.font = UIFont.latoLightFontOfSize(18)
    maxTempLbl.textColor = UIColor.whiteColor()

    minTempLbl.font = UIFont.latoLightFontOfSize(18)
    minTempLbl.textColor = UIColor.whiteColor()

    cityLbl.font = UIFont.latoLightFontOfSize(18)
    cityLbl.textColor = UIColor.whiteColor()
    cityLbl.textAlignment = .Right
}
```

In the `style()` function, we set the correct font and color, and finally we set a `render()` function with dummy values:

```
// MARK: Render
extension CurrentWeatherView{
    func render(){
        iconLbl.attributedText = WIKFontIcon.
wiDaySunnyIconWithSize(20).attributedString()
        weatherLbl.text = "Sunny"

        minTempLbl.text = "4°"
        maxTempLbl.text = "10°"
        currentTempLbl.text = "6°"

        cityLbl.text = "London"
    }
}
```

Don't forget to call the render in `PrettyWeatherViewController`:

```
// MARK: Render
private extension PrettyWeatherViewController{
    func renderSubviews() {
        currentWeatherView.render()
    }
}
```

When we run the app, we can see that the view is shown in the correct place with the correct info and style. However, because of the color, the label is not contrasting enough with the background, and it's difficult to read the data.

To solve this problem, we add a semitransparent view between the background and `scrollView`, with a dark gradient that fades to completely transparent at the top.

To do this, we create an instance of `UIView`:

```
private let gradientView = UIView()
```

Next, we add it to the view in `setup()`:

```
view.addSubview(gradientView)
```

Then, we set the constraints:

```
constrain(gradientView) {
    $0.edges ==  $0.superview!.edges
}
```

In the `style` function, we set `gradient`:

```
func style(){
    gradientView.backgroundColor = UIColor(white: 0, alpha: 0.7)
    let gradientLayer = CAGradientLayer()
    gradientLayer.frame = gradientView.bounds

    let blackColor = UIColor(white: 0, alpha: 0.0)
    let clearColor = UIColor(white: 0, alpha: 1.0)

    gradientLayer.colors = [blackColor.CGColor, clearColor.CGColor]

    gradientLayer.startPoint = CGPointMake(1.0, 0.5)
    gradientLayer.endPoint = CGPointMake(1.0, 1.0)
    gradientView.layer.mask = gradientLayer
}
```

If we run the app now, we can see that the data is more readable.

Building WeatherHourlyForecastView

This `WeatherHourlyForecastView` view is a horizontal `scrollView` object that contains seven cells:

```
class WeatherHourlyForecastView: UIView {
    private var didSetupConstraints = false
    private let scrollView = UIScrollView()
    private var forecastCells = Array<WeatherHourForecastView>()

    override init(frame: CGRect) {
        super.init(frame: frame)
        setup()
        style()
    }

    required init(coder aDecoder: NSCoder) {
        fatalError("init(coder:) has not been implemented")
    }
    override func updateConstraints() {
        if didSetupConstraints {
            super.updateConstraints()
            return
        }
        layoutView()
        super.updateConstraints()
```

```
            didSetupConstraints = true
        }
    }
```

The public part doesn't present anything new:

```
    // MARK: Setup
    private extension WeatherHourlyForecastView{
        func setup(){
            (0..<7).forEach { _ in
                let cell = WeatherHourForecastView(frame: CGRectZero)
                forecastCells.append(cell)
                scrollView.addSubview(cell)
            }
            scrollView.showsHorizontalScrollIndicator = false
            addSubview(scrollView)
        }
    }
```

The `setup()` function creates the cells and adds them to `scrollView`; we also use the `forEach()` internal iterator instead of using an external fast enumeration construct; technically, this doesn't change anything, but it is more *functional*.

We are saving the cells in an array in order to reference them later. I could have used `subviews` of `scrollView` instead of using another variable, but I don't like to mix presentation with business logic. It hides the intentions of the programmer:

```
    func layoutView(){
        constrain(self) {
            $0.height == 100
        }
        constrain(scrollView) {
            $0.edges == $0.superview!.edges
        }

        constrain(forecastCells.first!) {
            $0.left == $0.superview!.left
        }
        constrain(forecastCells.last!) {
            $0.right == $0.superview!.right
        }

        for idx in 0..<(forecastCells.count - 1) {
            let cell = forecastCells[idx]
            let nextCell = forecastCells[idx + 1]
            constrain(cell, nextCell) {
```

```
            $0.right == $1.left + 5
        }
    }
    forecastCells.forEach { cell in
        constrain(cell) {
            $0.width == $0.height
            $0.height == $0.superview!.height
            $0.top == $0.superview!.top
        }
    }
}
```

The `layout()` function stacks the cells horizontally:

```
// MARK: Render
extension WeatherHourlyForecastView{
    func render(){
        forecastCells.forEach {
            $0.render()
        }
    }
}
```

The `render()` function just calls the render of the cells. Before implementing the cell, we must not forget to remove the color set for the background:

```
func style(){
}
```

Then, add the render calls to `PrettyWeatherViewController`:

```
func renderSubviews() {
    currentWeatherView.render()
    hourlyForecastView.render()
}
```

Let's move on to `WeatherHourForecastView`:

```
import Cartography
import WeatherIconsKit

class WeatherHourForecastView: UIView {
    private var didSetupConstraints = false
    private let iconLabel = UILabel()
    private let hourLabel = UILabel()
    private let tempsLabel = UILabel()
```

```
override init(frame: CGRect) {
    super.init(frame: frame)
    setup()
    style()
}

required init(coder aDecoder: NSCoder) {
    fatalError("init(coder:) has not been implemented")
}
override func updateConstraints() {
    if didSetupConstraints {
        super.updateConstraints()
        return
    }
    layoutView()
    super.updateConstraints()
    didSetupConstraints = true
}
}
```

We create three labels:

```
// MARK: Setup
private extension WeatherHourForecastView{
    func setup(){
        addSubview(iconLabel)
        addSubview(hourLabel)
        addSubview(tempsLabel)
    }
}

// MARK: Layout
private extension WeatherHourForecastView{
    func layoutView() {
        constrain(iconLabel) {
            $0.center == $0.superview!.center
            $0.height == 50
        }
        constrain(hourLabel) {
            $0.centerX == $0.superview!.centerX
            $0.top == $0.superview!.top
        }
        constrain(tempsLabel) {
            $0.centerX == $0.superview!.centerX
            $0.bottom == $0.superview!.bottom
```

```
                }
            }
        }
```

After adding the three labels to the view, we set them like this: one at the top, the second in the center, and the last at the bottom:

```
// MARK: Style
private extension WeatherHourForecastView{
    func style(){
        iconLabel.textColor = UIColor.whiteColor()
        hourLabel.font = UIFont.latoFontOfSize(20)
        hourLabel.textColor = UIColor.whiteColor()
        tempsLabel.font = UIFont.latoFontOfSize(20)
        tempsLabel.textColor = UIColor.whiteColor()
    }
}


// MARK: Render
extension WeatherHourForecastView{
    func render(){
        var dateFormatter = NSDateFormatter()
        dateFormatter.dateFormat = "HH:mm"
        hourLabel.text = dateFormatter.stringFromDate(NSDate())
        iconLabel.attributedText = WIKFontIcon.
wiDaySunnyIconWithSize(30).attributedString()

        tempsLabel.text = "5° 8°"
    }
}
```

When run it at this stage, the app starts to look gorgeous!

Seeing the next day's forecast in WeatherDaysForecastView

The WeatherDaysForecastView view is pretty similar to WeatherHourForecastView; the only difference is that the cells are stacked vertically, not horizontally:

```
private var forecastCells = Array<WeatherDayForecastView>()
```

Again, we add an array to the cells:

```
func setup(){
    (0..<7).forEach { _ in
        let cell = WeatherDayForecastView(frame: CGRectZero)
        forecastCells.append(cell)
        addSubview(cell)
    }
}
```

We created the `setup()` function and added it to the `WeatherDaysForecastView` and the `internal` array:

```
// MARK: Layout
private extension WeatherDaysForecastView{
    func layoutView(){
        constrain(forecastCells.first!) {
            $0.top == $0.superview!.top
        }

        for idx in 0..<(forecastCells.count - 1) {
            let cell = forecastCells[idx]
            let nextCell = forecastCells[idx+1]
            constrain(cell, nextCell) {
                $0.bottom == $1.top
            }
        }

        forecastCells.forEach { cell in
            constrain(cell) {
                $0.left == $0.superview!.left
                $0.right == $0.superview!.right
            }
        }

        constrain(forecastCells.last!) {
            $0.bottom == $0.superview!.bottom
        }
    }
}
```

We lay them out, paying attention to disabling the translation from `autoresizingMask` to Auto Layout constraints for the view itself. Cartography disables it, but in this case we set constraints only on `subviews`, leaving the view without explicit constraints at this level:

```
// MARK: Render
extension WeatherDaysForecastView{
    func render(){
        forecastCells.forEach {
            view.render()
        }
    }
}
```

Again, the render only forwards functions. We remove the set of the background color:

```
// MARK: Style
private extension WeatherDaysForecastView{
    func style(){
    }
}
```

We add the render method to `PrettyWeatherViewController`:

```
func renderSubviews() {
    currentWeatherView.render()
    hourlyForecastView.render()
    daysForecastView.render()
}
```

The `WeatherDayForecast` class is similar to `WeatherHourForecastView`:

```
import Foundation
import Cartography
import WeatherIconsKit

class WeatherDayForecastView: UIView {
    private var didSetupConstraints = false
    private let iconLabel = UILabel()
    private let dayLabel = UILabel()
    private let tempsLabel = UILabel()

    override init(frame: CGRect) {
        super.init(frame: frame)
        setup()
```

```
            style()
    }

    required init(coder aDecoder: NSCoder) {
        fatalError("init(coder:) has not been implemented")
    }
    override func updateConstraints() {
        if didSetupConstraints {
            super.updateConstraints()
            return
        }
        layoutView()
        super.updateConstraints()
        didSetupConstraints = true
    }
}
```

We add the labels:

```
// MARK: Setup
private extension WeatherDayForecastView{
    func setup(){
        addSubview(dayLabel)
        addSubview(iconLabel)
        addSubview(tempsLabel)
    }
}


// MARK: Layout
private extension WeatherDayForecastView{
    func layoutView() {
        constrain(self) {
            $0.height == 50
        }

        constrain(iconLabel) {
            $0.centerY == $0.superview!.centerY
            $0.left == $0.superview!.left + 20
            $0.width == $0.height
            $0.height == 50
        }

        constrain(dayLabel, iconLabel) {
            $0.centerY == $0.superview!.centerY
            $0.left == $1.right + 20
```

```
        }

        constrain(tempsLabel) {
            $0.centerY == $0.superview!.centerY
            $0.right == $0.superview!.right - 20
        }
    }
}
```

As usual, the layout part is long but straightforward:

```
// MARK: Style
private extension WeatherDayForecastView{
    func style(){
        iconLabel.textColor = UIColor.whiteColor()
        dayLabel.font = UIFont.latoFontOfSize(20)
        dayLabel.textColor = UIColor.whiteColor()
        tempsLabel.font = UIFont.latoFontOfSize(20)
        tempsLabel.textColor = UIColor.whiteColor()
    }
}

// MARK: Render
extension WeatherDayForecastView{
    func render(){
        var dateFormatter = NSDateFormatter()
        dateFormatter.dateFormat = "EEEE"
        dayLabel.text = dateFormatter.stringFromDate(NSDate())
        iconLabel.attributedText = WIKFontIcon.
wiDaySunnyIconWithSize(30).attributedString()

        tempsLabel.text = "7°     11°"
    }
}
```

Now, run the app; it is really gorgeous! The only thing missing from a UI point of view is blurring the background when `scrollView` reaches the bottom.

Blurring the background

The first naïve idea would be to change the level of blurriness depending on the position of `scrollView`, but this will be really inefficient because the blur operation is CPU-intensive, and it won't be smooth on older devices.

So, the idea is to trick the user. Instead of blurring the image at every change of position of `scrollView`, we blur the image, only before setting it to `UIImageView`. Then, we set the alpha channel to 0 (which means transparent). Next, we change the alpha depending on the position, reaching opaque when the `scrollView` offset reaches half.

First of all, we need to import the framework to blur the image:

```
import FXBlurView
```

Then, we need to create the overlay view and set it as `subview`:

```
private let overlayView = UIImageView()
//...
func setup(){
    //...
    overlayView.contentMode = .ScaleAspectFill
    overlayView.clipsToBounds = true
    view.addSubview(overlayView)
    //...
    scrollView.delegate = self
    view.addSubview(scrollView)
}
func layoutView() {
    //...
    constrain(overlayView) {
        $0.edges ==  $0.superview!.edges
    }
}
```

Next, in the `render()` function, we set the blurred image:

```
func render(image: UIImage?){
    guard let image = image else {return}
    backgroundView.image = image
    overlayView.image = image.blurredImageWithRadius(10, iterations:
20, tintColor: UIColor.clearColor())
    overlayView.alpha = 0
}
```

Note that we set the image as transparent.

I believe you've noticed that we set **View Controller** as a delegate of `scrollView`. This allows us to detect the change in position during scrolling:

```
// MARK: UIScrollViewDelegate
extension PrettyWeatherViewController: UIScrollViewDelegate{
```

```
func scrollViewDidScroll(scrollView: UIScrollView) {
    let offset = scrollView.contentOffset.y
    let treshold: CGFloat = CGFloat(view.frame.height)/2
    overlayView.alpha = min (1.0, offset/treshold)


}
}
```

As you can see, the code is straightforward; we set the alpha channel to be proportional to the position. Now, by running the app, we can see how good it looks.

 You can find the code for this version at https://github.com/gscalzo/Swift2ByExample/tree/4_PrettyWeather_3_UI.

Downloading the background image

Before moving on to downloading the actual forecast, we'll introduce the topic of networking downloading a geo-localized background image.

Searching in Flickr

To get an image, we'll use the API of Flickr, a famous image-hosting website, using a convenient Pod. First of all, we override the `viewWillAppear` function in `PrettyWeatherApp` so that a new image will be downloaded every time **View Controller** appears:

```
override func viewWillAppear(animated: Bool) {
    super.viewWillAppear(animated)

    let lat:Double = 48.8567
    let lon:Double = 2.3508

    FlickrDatastore().retrieveImageAtLat(lat, lon: lon){ image in
        self.render(image)
    }
}
```

To implement the searching feature, we set a dummy value using the coordinates of Paris. Then, we create a new file named `FlickrDatastore`:

```
import FlickrKit

class FlickrDatastore {
    private let OBJECTIVE_FLICKR_API_KEY = "CREATE_API_KEY"
    private let OBJECTIVE_FLICKR_API_SHARED_SECRET = "CREATE_SHARED_
SECRET"
    private let GROUP_ID = "1463451@N25"

    func retrieveImageAtLat(lat: Double, lon: Double, closure: (image:
UIImage?) -> Void){
    }

    private func extractImageFk(fk: FlickrKit, response: AnyObject?,
        error: NSError?, closure: (image: UIImage?) -> Void) {
    }
}
```

To use the Flickr API, you need to request an API key and a secret key. These can be requested for free after logging in.

 The API key can be requested at `https://www.flickr.com/services/apps/create/`.

To get images that are suitable for our app, we select pictures from a group where users upload images related to the weather:

```
func retrieveImageAtLat(lat: Double, lon: Double, closure: (image:
UIImage?) -> Void){
    let fk = FlickrKit.sharedFlickrKit()
    fk.initializeWithAPIKey(OBJECTIVE_FLICKR_API_KEY, sharedSecret:
OBJECTIVE_FLICKR_API_SHARED_SECRET)

    fk.call("flickr.photos.search", args: ["group_id": GROUP_ID,
"lat": "\(lat)", "lon": "\(lon)", "radius": "10"],
maxCacheAge: FKDUMaxAgeOneHour) { (response, error) -> Void in
    self.extractImageFk(fk, response: response, error: error,
closure: closure)
    }
}
```

As you can see, using `FlickrKit` is really straightforward. However, the result is a JSON string, and parsing a JSON string in Swift is not as simple as it is in Objective-C.

The reasons for this lie in the heterogeneity of the result. This means that JSON can contain different types, whereas Swift pushes for the homogeneity of containers and the intrinsic optionality of the dictionary as a container, which means that we need to check the existence of every value we get from a dictionary.

The implementation of `extractImage()` will explain the problem better:

```
private func extractImageFk(fk: FlickrKit, response: AnyObject?,
    error: NSError?, closure: (image: UIImage?) -> Void) {
    if let response = response as? [String:AnyObject]{
        if let photos = response["photos"] as? [String:AnyObject]{
            if let listOfPhotos: AnyObject = photos["photo"] {
                if listOfPhotos.count > 0 {
                    let randomIndex = Int(arc4random_uniform(
                    UInt32(listOfPhotos.count)))
                    let photo = listOfPhotos[randomIndex] as!
                    [String:AnyObject]
```

```
                    let url = fk.photoURLForSize(
                    FKPhotoSizeMedium640, fromPhotoDictionary:
                    photo)
                    let image = UIImage(data: NSData(
                    contentsOfURL: url)!)
                    dispatch_async(dispatch_get_main_queue()){
                        closure(image: image!)
                    }
                }
            }
        }
    } else {
        println(error)
        println(response)
    }
}
```

The format of the JSON returned is as follows:

```
{photos: {
    page: 1,
    pages: 3,
    perpage: 250,
    photo: [
            {
             farm = 8,
             id = 16172607518,
             ...
            },
            {
             farm = 2,
             id = 16132447518,
             ...
            },
            ...
          ]
    }
}
```

We need the array of a photo. This can be reached by accessing two nested dictionaries, and because every access to a value using a key is optional, we need to verify that the values are not *nil* when creating this unpleasant cascade effect.

When we get the array, we extract a random element and download the image.

Because the response from the server runs in a background thread, it is safe to download the image synchronously without fear of freezing the UI.

As you can imagine, the nested conditions lead to poor readability of the code, but after Swift 1.2, released in Xcode 6.3, Apple made optional unwrapping it with more power. This allows you to unwrap more optional values in the same condition, and you can also add logical conditions to the `if` block using the `where` keyword.

Hence, the previous code can be written in more concise way, like this:

```
if let response = response as? [String:AnyObject],
    photos = response["photos"] as? [String:AnyObject],
    listOfPhotos: AnyObject = photos["photo"]
    where listOfPhotos.count > 0 {

} else {
    println(error)
    println(response)
}
```

By running the app, we get random images of Paris.

This code can be found at `https://github.com/gscalzo/ Swift2ByExample/tree/4_PrettyWeather_4_DownloadImage`.

Geolocalising the app

As a test, we have used dummy coordinates, but we have a powerful GPS on board, and it's time to use it.

Using Core Location

To use the Core Location framework service, we need to instruct iOS that our app is using it.

To do this, we must add the `NSLocationAlwaysUsageDescription` key with a string; for example, this application requires location services to get the weather of your current location in `Info.plist`.

Then, we add a new property to `PrettyWeatherViewController`:

```
private var locationDatastore: LocationDatastore?
```

Next, we change the `viewWillAppear` function:

```
override func viewWillAppear(animated: Bool) {
    super.viewWillAppear(animated)
    locationDatastore = LocationDatastore() { [weak self] location
in
        FlickrDatastore().retrieveImageAtLat(location.lat, lon:
location.lon){ image in
            self?.render(image)
        }
    }
}
```

Our simple wrapper around `LocationManager` basically calls the provided closure when the location changes. The implementation is straightforward:

```
import CoreLocation

struct Location {
    let lat: Double
    let lon: Double
}

class LocationDatastore: NSObject, CLLocationManagerDelegate {
    private let locationManager = CLLocationManager()

    typealias LocationClosure = (Location) -> Void
    private let onLocationFound: LocationClosure

    init(closure: LocationClosure){
        onLocationFound = closure
        super.init()
        locationManager.delegate = self
        locationManager.requestAlwaysAuthorization()
        startUpdating()
    }


    private func startUpdating() {
        locationManager.startUpdatingLocation()
    }

    private func stopUpdating() {
        locationManager.stopUpdatingLocation()
    }
```

```swift
    func locationManager(manager: CLLocationManager!, didFailWithError
error: NSError!) {
        locationManager.stopUpdatingLocation()
        NSLog("Error: \(error)")
        dispatch_async(dispatch_get_main_queue()){
            self.onLocationFound(Location(lat: 37.3175, lon:
122.0419))
        }
    }

    func locationManager(manager: CLLocationManager!,
didUpdateLocations locations: [AnyObject]) {
        var locationArray = locations as NSArray
        var locationObj = locationArray.lastObject as! CLLocation
        var coord = locationObj.coordinate

        dispatch_async(dispatch_get_main_queue()){
            self.onLocationFound(Location(lat: coord.latitude, lon:
coord.longitude))
        }

        stopUpdating()
    }

    func locationManager(manager: CLLocationManager!,
        didChangeAuthorizationStatus status: CLAuthorizationStatus) {
            switch status {
            case .Restricted:
                NSLog("Denied access: Restricted Access to location")
            case .Denied:
                NSLog("Denied access: User denied access to location")
            case .NotDetermined:
                NSLog("Denied access: Status not determined")
            default:
                NSLog("Allowed to location Access")
                startUpdating()
            }
        }
    }
}
```

If you run the app now, a pop-up asking for permission to use the location services appears, as shown in the following screenshot. If you deny the permission, in order to simplify the error handling, hardcoded coordinates are passed.

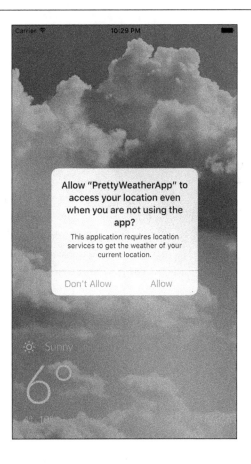

 You can find the code for this version at `https://github.com/gscalzo/Swift2ByExample/tree/4_PrettyWeather_5_GeoLocalisation`.

Retrieving the actual forecast

We have almost completed the app, but it is still missing the most important part: the weather forecast.

Getting the forecast from OpenWeatherMap

There are plenty of services that provide forecasts for free or for a small amount of money.

For our app, we'll use `http://openweathermap.org`, whose API is free for a small number of calls.

First of all, we create the `WeatherCondition` struct to handle the forecast:

```
import Foundation
struct WeatherCondition {
    let cityName: String?
    let weather: String
    let icon: IconType?
    let time: NSDate
    let tempKelvin: Double
    let maxTempKelvin: Double
    let minTempKelvin: Double

    var tempFahrenheit: Double {
        get {
            return tempCelsius * 9.0/5.0 + 32.0
        }
    }

    var maxTempFahrenheit: Double {
        get {
            return maxTempCelsius * 9.0/5.0 + 32.0
        }
    }
    var minTempFahrenheit: Double {
        get {
            return minTempCelsius * 9.0/5.0 + 32.0
        }
    }

    var tempCelsius: Double {
        get {
            return tempKelvin - 273.15
        }
    }
    var maxTempCelsius: Double {
        get {
            return maxTempKelvin - 273.15
        }
    }
    var minTempCelsius: Double {
        get {
            return minTempKelvin - 273.15
        }
    }
}
```

Because the service returns the temperature in Kelvin, we provide the computed properties to get the temperature in either degrees Celsius or degrees Fahrenheit.

The `IconType` enumeration is just an enumeration of the possible icons returned from the server:

```
enum IconType: String {
    case i01d = "01d"
    case i01n = "01n"
    case i02d = "02d"
    case i02n = "02n"
    case i03d = "03d"
    case i03n = "03n"
    case i04d = "04d"
    case i04n = "04n"
    case i09d = "09d"
    case i09n = "09n"
    case i10d = "10d"
    case i10n = "10n"
    case i11d = "11d"
    case i11n = "11n"
    case i13d = "13d"
    case i13n = "13n"
    case i50d = "50d"
    case i50n = "50n"
}
```

 The code for the forecast can be found at
http://openweathermap.org/weather-conditions.

Then, we change the `viewWillAppear` function in `PrettyWeatherViewController` again. We do this to raise three calls to get the current weather and forecast:

```
override func viewWillAppear(animated: Bool) {
    super.viewWillAppear(animated)
    locationDatastore = LocationDatastore() { [weak self] location
in
        FlickrDatastore().retrieveImageAtLat(location.lat, lon:
location.lon){ image in
            self?.render(image)
            return
        }
        let weatherDatastore = WeatherDatastore()
```

```
          weatherDatastore.retrieveCurrentWeatherAtLat(location.lat,
lon: location.lon) {
              currentWeatherConditions in
              self?.renderCurrent(currentWeatherConditions)
              return
          }
          weatherDatastore.retrieveHourlyForecastAtLat(location.lat,
lon: location.lon) {
              hourlyWeatherConditions in
              self?.renderHourly(hourlyWeatherConditions)
              return
          }
          weatherDatastore.retrieveDailyForecastAtLat(location.lat,
lon: location.lon, dayCnt: 7) {
              hourlyWeatherConditions in
              self?.renderDaily(hourlyWeatherConditions)
              return
          }
      }
  }
```

The renders are just functions used to forward the requests to `subviews`:

```
func renderCurrent(currentWeatherConditions: WeatherCondition){
    currentWeatherView.render(currentWeatherConditions)
}

func renderHourly(weatherConditions: Array<WeatherCondition>){
    hourlyForecastView.render(weatherConditions)
}

func renderDaily(weatherConditions: Array<WeatherCondition>){
    daysForecastView.render(weatherConditions)
}
```

Don't forget to remove the `renderSubviews()` function.

Rendering CurrentWeatherView

After removing the dummy `render()` function, we add this function:

```
func render(weatherCondition: WeatherCondition){
    iconLbl.attributedText = iconStringFromIcon(weatherCondition.
icon!, 20)
    weatherLbl.text = weatherCondition.weather
```

```
    var usesMetric = false
    if let localeSystem =
NSLocale.currentLocale().objectForKey(NSLocaleUsesMetricSystem) as?
Bool {
        usesMetric = localeSystem
    }

    if usesMetric {
        minTempLbl.text =
"\(weatherCondition.minTempCelsius.roundToInt())°"
        maxTempLbl.text =
"\(weatherCondition.maxTempCelsius.roundToInt())°"
        currentTempLbl.text =
"\(weatherCondition.tempCelsius.roundToInt())°"
    } else {
        minTempLbl.text =
"\(weatherCondition.minTempFahrenheit.roundToInt())°"
        maxTempLbl.text =
"\(weatherCondition.maxTempFahrenheit.roundToInt())°"
        currentTempLbl.text =
"\(weatherCondition.tempFahrenheit.roundToInt())°"
    }

    cityLbl.text = weatherCondition.cityName ?? ""
}
```

Because we want to represent the temperature as an integer and not as a double, we
have created a convenience category for `double`:

```
extension Double {
    func roundToInt() -> Int{
        return Int(round(self))
    }
}
```

Also, we have added a function to convert `IconType` into an icon in
`WeatherIconsKit`:

```
import WeatherIconsKit

func iconStringFromIcon(icon: IconType, size: CGFloat) ->
NSAttributedString {
    switch icon {
    case .i01d:
        return WIKFontIcon.wiDaySunnyIconWithSize(size).
attributedString()
    case .i01n:
```

```
            return WIKFontIcon.wiNightClearIconWithSize(size).
attributedString()
        case .i02d:
            return WIKFontIcon.wiDayCloudyIconWithSize(size).
attributedString()
        case .i02n:
            return WIKFontIcon.wiNightCloudyIconWithSize(size).
attributedString()
        case .i03d:
            return WIKFontIcon.wiDayCloudyIconWithSize(size).
attributedString()
        case .i03n:
            return WIKFontIcon.wiNightCloudyIconWithSize(size).
attributedString()
        case .i04d:
            return WIKFontIcon.wiCloudyIconWithSize(size).
attributedString()
        case .i04n:
            return WIKFontIcon.wiCloudyIconWithSize(size).
attributedString()
        case .i09d:
            return WIKFontIcon.wiDayShowersIconWithSize(size).
attributedString()
        case .i09n:
            return WIKFontIcon.wiNightShowersIconWithSize(size).
attributedString()
        case .i10d:
            return WIKFontIcon.wiDayRainIconWithSize(size).
attributedString()
        case .i10n:
            return WIKFontIcon.wiNightRainIconWithSize(size).
attributedString()
        case .i11d:
            return WIKFontIcon.wiDayThunderstormIconWithSize(size).
attributedString()
        case .i11n:
            return WIKFontIcon.wiNightThunderstormIconWithSize(size).
attributedString()
        case .i13d:
            return WIKFontIcon.wiSnowIconWithSize(size).attributedString()
        case .i13n:
            return WIKFontIcon.wiSnowIconWithSize(size).attributedString()
        case .i50d:
            return WIKFontIcon.wiFogIconWithSize(size).attributedString()
        case .i50n:
            return WIKFontIcon.wiFogIconWithSize(size).attributedString()
        }
    }
```

The code is verbose, but it is actually straightforward—just a way to the map icon to the `attributedString` that describe the image.

Rendering WeatherHourlyForecastView

The render function just iterates through all the `subviews` and calls the `render()` function:

```
// MARK: Render
func render(weatherConditions: Array<WeatherCondition>){
    zip(forecastCells, weatherConditions).forEach {
        $0.render($1)
    }
}
```

The `zip()` function is a function brought in from Haskell that *merges* two arrays in a single array containing tuples of each element for every row of the arrays; the following example will explain this better:

The arrays are as follows:

```
let a = [1,2,3,4]
let b = ["a","b","c","d"]
```

The function is as follows:

```
zip(a, b)
```

The previous function returns the following result:

```
[(1,"a"),(2,"b"),(3,"c"),(4,"d")]
```

To continue adding our code to the render, in `WeatherHourForecastView`, we use the same approach that we used for the current weather:

```
// MARK: Render
extension WeatherHourForecastView{
    func render(weatherCondition: WeatherCondition){
        var dateFormatter = NSDateFormatter()
        dateFormatter.dateFormat = "HH:mm"
        hourLabel.text = dateFormatter.
stringFromDate(weatherCondition.time)
        iconLabel.attributedText = iconStringFromIcon(weatherConditi
on.icon!, 30)

        var usesMetric = false
```

```
            if let localeSystem = NSLocale.currentLocale().objectForKey(NS
LocaleUsesMetricSystem) as? Bool {
                usesMetric = localeSystem
            }

            if usesMetric {
                tempsLabel.text = "\(weatherCondition.minTempCelsius.
roundToInt())° \(weatherCondition.maxTempCelsius.roundToInt())°"
            } else {
                tempsLabel.text = "\(weatherCondition.minTempFahrenheit.
roundToInt())° \(weatherCondition.maxTempFahrenheit.roundToInt())°"
            }
        }
    }
}
```

Again, there's nothing particularly complicated, and it permits us to see the data in the cells.

Rendering WeatherDaysForecastView

Even in this case, the flow is exactly the same. First, we iterate to forward the call to subviews:

```
extension WeatherDaysForecastView{
        func render(weatherConditions: Array<WeatherCondition>){
        zip(forecastCells, weatherConditions).forEach {
            $0.render($1)
        }
    }
}
```

Then, in `WeatherDayForecast`, we render the weather condition:

```
// MARK: Render
extension WeatherDayForecastView{
    func render(weatherCondition: WeatherCondition){
        var dateFormatter = NSDateFormatter()
        dateFormatter.dateFormat = "EEEE"
        dayLabel.text = dateFormatter.stringFromDate(weatherCondition.
time)
        iconLabel.attributedText = iconStringFromIcon(weatherConditi
on.icon!, 30)

        var usesMetric = false
        if let localeSystem = NSLocale.currentLocale().objectForKey(NS
LocaleUsesMetricSystem) as? Bool {
```

```
            usesMetric = localeSystem
        }

        if usesMetric {
            tempsLabel.text = "\(weatherCondition.minTempCelsius.
roundToInt())°    \(weatherCondition.maxTempCelsius.roundToInt())°"
        } else {
            tempsLabel.text = "\(weatherCondition.minTempFahrenheit.
roundToInt())°    \(weatherCondition.maxTempFahrenheit.
roundToInt())°"
        }
    }
}
```

Connecting to the server

Finally, we are ready to get the forecast data, and for that, we'll use a nice service called OpenWeatherMap, `http://openweathermap.org`, which offers a free tier as well.

To get access to the free tier, first of all we need to register to the site and then create a new API key, which will be passed as a parameter in every call to the server.

With this information, let's implement `WeatherDatastore`.

This class uses Alamofire, the Swift equivalent of AFNetworking, the most used third-party library to help handle network communications in iOS. It also uses SwiftyJson, which eliminates the problem of nested checks for optional values during the decoding of JSON (short for JavaScript Object Notation, a lightweight data interchange format) data:

```
import Foundation
import CoreLocation
import Alamofire
import SwiftyJSON

class WeatherDatastore {
    let APIKey = "CREATE_API_KEY"

    func retrieveCurrentWeatherAtLat(lat: CLLocationDegrees, lon:
CLLocationDegrees,
        block: (weatherCondition: WeatherCondition) -> Void) {
        }
    func retrieveDailyForecastAtLat(lat: Double,
        lon: Double,
```

```
        dayCnt: Int,
        block: (weatherConditions: Array<WeatherCondition>) -> Void) {
}
```

The first method asks for the current weather and parses the JSON response to convert it to our struct:

```
func retrieveCurrentWeatherAtLat(lat: CLLocationDegrees, lon:
CLLocationDegrees,
    block: (weatherCondition: WeatherCondition) -> Void) {
        let url = "http://api.openweathermap.org/data/2.5/weather
?APPID=\(APIKey)"
        let params = ["lat":lat, "lon":lon]

        Alamofire.request(.GET, url, parameters: params)
        .responseJSON { request, response, result in
            switch result {
                case .Success(let json):
                    let json = JSON(json)
                    block(weatherCondition:
self.createWeatherConditionFronJson(json))
                case .Failure(_, let error):
                    print("Error: \(error)")
            }
        }
}
```

The `createWeatherConditionFromJson()` function is responsible for the conversion:

```
private extension WeatherDatastore {
    func createWeatherConditionFronJson(json: JSON) ->
WeatherCondition{
        let name = json["name"].string
        let weather = json["weather"][0]["main"].stringValue
        let icon = json["weather"][0]["icon"].stringValue
        let dt = json["dt"].doubleValue
        let time = NSDate(timeIntervalSince1970: dt)
        let tempKelvin = json["main"]["temp"].doubleValue
        let maxTempKelvin = json["main"]["temp_max"].doubleValue
        let minTempKelvin = json["main"]["temp_min"].doubleValue

        return WeatherCondition(
            cityName: name,
            weather: weather,
            icon: IconType(rawValue: icon),
            time: time,
```

```
                tempKelvin: tempKelvin,
                maxTempKelvin: maxTempKelvin,
                minTempKelvin: minTempKelvin)
        }
    }
```

Here, as we can see, `SwiftyJson` permits us to write denser code because the `SwiftJson` dictionary handles the optional result in a clever way using internal optional chaining; the expression returns `nil` if any of its components returns nil.

The `retrieveHourlyForecast()` function is basically the same as the current weather; the only difference is that it returns an array of `WeatherCondition`:

```
func retrieveHourlyForecastAtLat(lat: CLLocationDegrees,
    lon: CLLocationDegrees,
    block: (weatherConditions: Array<WeatherCondition>) -> Void) {
        let url =
"http://api.openweathermap.org/data/2.5/forecast?APPID=\(APIKey)"
        let params = ["lat":lat, "lon":lon]
        Alamofire.request(.GET, url, parameters: params)
        .responseJSON { request, response, result in
            switch result {
                case .Success(let json):
                    let json = JSON(json)
                    let list: Array<JSON> =
                    json["list"].arrayValue

                    let weatherConditions: Array
                    <WeatherCondition> = list.map() {
                        return
self.createWeatherConditionFronJson($0)
                }
                block(weatherConditions: weatherConditions)
                    case .Failure(_, let error):
                        print("Error: \(error)")
                }
            }
    }
```

Finally, the `retrieveDailyForecast()` function returns an array for the forecast of the upcoming days. Note that OpenWeatherMap returns an array of days that contains the actual day as well; so, we need to get rid of the first element:

```
func retrieveDailyForecastAtLat(lat: Double,
    lon: Double,
    dayCnt: Int,
```

```
block: (weatherConditions: Array<WeatherCondition>) -> Void) {
    let url = "http://api.openweathermap.org/data/2.5/
forecast/daily?APPID=\(APIKey)"
    let params = ["lat":lat, "lon":lon,
"cnt":Double(dayCnt+1)]
    Alamofire.request(.GET, url, parameters: params)
        .responseJSON { request, response, result in
            switch result {
                case .Success(let json):
                    let json = JSON(json)
                    let list: Array<JSON> =
json["list"].arrayValue
                    let weatherConditions: Array<WeatherCondition>
= list.map(){
                    return self.createDayForecastFronJson($0)
                }
                let count = weatherConditions.count
                let daysWithoutToday =
Array(weatherConditions[1..<count])
                block(weatherConditions: daysWithoutToday)
                case .Failure(_, let error):
                    print("Error: \(error)")
            }
        }
}
```

Unfortunately, the format of the response is a little different from the responses to the former requests; hence, we need to build a new conversion function:

```
func createDayForecastFronJson(json: JSON) -> WeatherCondition{
    let name = ""
    let weather = json["weather"][0]["main"].stringValue
    let icon = json["weather"][0]["icon"].stringValue
    let dt = json["dt"].doubleValue
    let time = NSDate(timeIntervalSince1970: dt)
    let tempKelvin = json["temp"]["day"].doubleValue
    let maxTempKelvin = json["temp"]["max"].doubleValue
```

```
let minTempKelvin = json["temp"]["min"].doubleValue

return WeatherCondition(
    cityName: name,
    weather: weather,
    icon: IconType(rawValue: icon),
    time: time,
    tempKelvin: tempKelvin,
    maxTempKelvin: maxTempKelvin,
    minTempKelvin: minTempKelvin)
}
```

The last thing missing is the configuration of the **App Transport Security (ATS)**; to enhance the security, since iOS 9, the default transport protocol has been HTTPS unless exceptions are set in `Info.plist`, as you can find out by looking at the logs:

`2015-09-30 23:46:23.280 PrettyWeatherApp[8879:12527303] Allowed to location Access`

`2015-09-30 23:46:23.438 PrettyWeatherApp[8879:12527722] App Transport Security has blocked a cleartext HTTP (http://) resource load since it is insecure. Temporary exceptions can be configured via your app's Info. plist file.`

`Error: Error Domain=NSURLErrorDomain Code=-1022 "The resource could not be loaded because the App Transport Security policy requires the use of a secure connection`

Because the free tier of **openweathermap.org** is only HTTP, we must add the following keys to `Info.plist`:

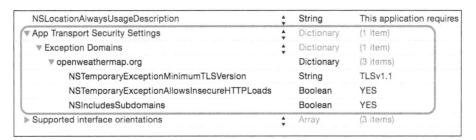

NSLocationAlwaysUsageDescription		String	This application requires
▼ App Transport Security Settings		Dictionary	(1 item)
▼ Exception Domains		Dictionary	(1 item)
▼ openweathermap.org		Dictionary	(3 items)
NSTemporaryExceptionMinimumTLSVersion		String	TLSv1.1
NSTemporaryExceptionAllowsInsecureHTTPLoads		Boolean	YES
NSIncludesSubdomains		Boolean	YES
▶ Supported interface orientations		Array	(3 items)

And, with this, our pretty weather app is done! The following screenshot shows how the app will look:

 You can find the code for this version at `https://github.com/gscalzo/Swift2ByExample/tree/4_PrettyWeather_6_Complete`.

Where do we go from here?

Although our app is almost complete, the possibilities for its expansion are endless.

Starting from this source, you can do the following:

- Make it more robust in handling error situations. Currently, if anything goes wrong, nothing happens on the user's side because the app just logs the error. A good strategy would be to present a warning somewhere and provide a chance to the user to retry the operation.

- The app works well if the user allows the use of GPS, but it will stop working if the user denies it. How about adding a functionality to view the weather for more cities than one, swiping horizontally to view a new city?

- In the app, the background is chosen using only coordinates, but because the images in that group are tagged with the weather, it would be nice to show an image that matches the weather and, maybe, with the correct time of the day or night.

- A straightforward but really useful feature would be to add the pull-to-refresh functionality to request the weather again.

- We presented a minimal amount of data. OpenWeatherMap offers more data, and it can be presented in a nice way:

To verify that the separation layers are solid, it would be interesting to add the chance to use a different weather provider (that is, Weather Underground or `http://forecast.io/`), and to ensure that we don't need to change anything outside the data store.

Summary

This was a long chapter, again—full of information and first-hand experience.

We consolidated our architecture of classes and the way in which we build the UI. You have finally learned how to connect to a server and how the option cascade chain can be solved.

After having implemented two utility apps, in the next couple of chapters we are going to implement a game again. It is one of the most iconic games in recent years, *Flappy Bird*.

6
Flappy Swift

After having explored how to build normal apps with the previous two apps, let's go back to games.

These apps will use two useful frameworks that iOS provides for casual game developers: SKSprite and SKScene. The former is a handy and powerful 2D game framework that provides a physics engine based on Box2D (http://box2d.org/). The latter allows indie game developers to implement three-dimensional games.

Let's start using the first framework by implementing a nice clone of *Flappy Bird*.

The app is...

Only someone who has been living under a rock for the past 2 years could have not heard of *Flappy Bird*, but to ensure that everybody understands the game, let's go through a brief introduction.

Flappy Bird is a simple but addictive game where the player controls a bird that must fly between a series of pipes. Gravity pulls the bird down but, by touching the screen, the player can make the bird flap and move toward the sky, driving the bird through a gap in a couple of pipes. The goal is to pass through as many pipes as possible.

Our implementation will be a high-fidelity tribute to the original game, with the same simplicity and difficulty level. The app will consist of only two screens: a clean menu screen and the game itself, as shown in the following screenshot:

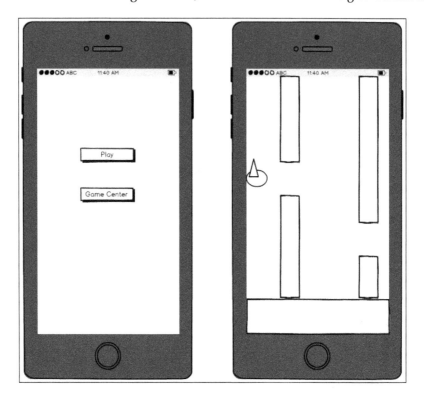

Building the skeleton of the app

Let's start by implementing the skeleton of our game using the SpriteKit game template.

Creating the project

To implement a SpriteKit game, Xcode provides a convenient template, which prepares a project with all the useful settings:

1. Go to **New** | **Project** and select the **Game** template, as shown in the following screenshot. Click Next:

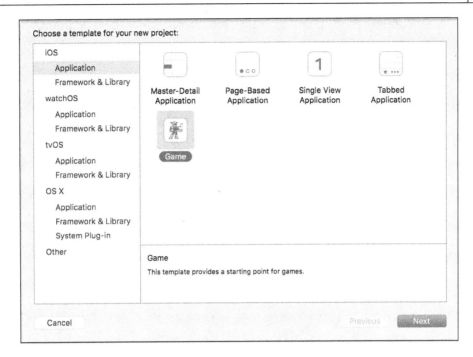

2. In the following screen, after filling in all the fields, pay attention and select **SpriteKit** under **Game Technology**, like this:

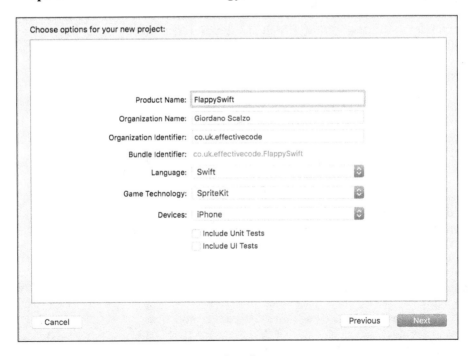

3. After running the app and touching the screen, you will be delighted by the cute, rotating airplanes.

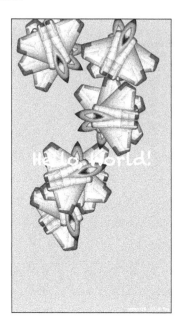

Implementing the menu

First of all, let's add `CocoaPods`, which is a dependency manager for Objective-C projects; write the following code in `Podfile`:

```
use_frameworks!
inhibit_all_warnings!

target 'FlappySwift' do
    pod 'Cartography', :git =>
"https://github.com/robb/Cartography.git", :tag => '0.6.0'
    pod 'HTPressableButton', '~> 1.3.2'
end
```

Then, install `CocoaPods` by running the `pod install` command. As usual, we are going to implement the UI without using Interface Builder and Storyboards. Go to **App Delegate** and add these lines to create the main view controller:

```
func application(application: UIApplication,
didFinishLaunchingWithOptions launchOptions: [NSObject: AnyObject]?)
-> Bool {
    let viewController = MenuViewController()
```

```
let mainWindow = UIWindow(frame: UIScreen.mainScreen().bounds)
mainWindow.backgroundColor = UIColor.whiteColor()
mainWindow.rootViewController = viewController
mainWindow.makeKeyAndVisible()
window = mainWindow

return true
}
```

MenuViewController, as the name suggests, implements a nice menu to choose between the game and the Game Center, which we'll see in the next chapter:

```
import UIKit
import HTPressableButton
import Cartography

class MenuViewController: UIViewController {
    private let playButton = HTPressableButton(frame: CGRectMake(0, 0,
260, 50), buttonStyle: .Rect)
    private let gameCenterButton = HTPressableButton(frame:
CGRectMake(0, 0, 260, 50), buttonStyle: .Rect)

    override func viewDidLoad() {
        super.viewDidLoad()
        setup()
        layoutView()
        style()
        render()
    }
}
```

As you can see, we are using the usual structure. Just for the sake of making the UI pretty, we are using HTPressableButtons instead of the default buttons.

Despite the fact that we are using Auto Layout, the implementation of this custom button requires that we instantiate it by passing a frame to it:

```
// MARK: Setup
private extension MenuViewController{
    func setup(){
        playButton.addTarget(self, action: "onPlayPressed:",
forControlEvents: .TouchUpInside)
        view.addSubview(playButton)
        gameCenterButton.addTarget(self, action:
"onGameCenterPressed:", forControlEvents: .TouchUpInside)
```

```
            view.addSubview(gameCenterButton)
        }

    @objc func onPlayPressed(sender: UIButton) {
        let vc = GameViewController()
        vc.modalTransitionStyle = .CrossDissolve
        presentViewController(vc, animated: true, completion: nil)
    }

    @objc func onGameCenterPressed(sender: UIButton) {
        print("onGameCenterPressed")
    }
}
```

The only thing to note is that, because we are setting the function to be called when the button is pressed using the addTarget() function, we must prefix the designed methods using @objc. Otherwise, it will be impossible for the Objective-C runtime to find the correct method when the button is pressed. This is because they are implemented in a private extension; of course, you can set the extension as internal or public and you won't need to prepend @objc to the functions:

```
// MARK: Layout
extension MenuViewController{
    func layoutView() {
        constrain(playButton) { view in
            view.bottom == view.superview!.centerY - 60
            view.centerX == view.superview!.centerX
            view.height == 80
            view.width == view.superview!.width - 40
        }
        constrain (gameCenterButton) { view in
            view.bottom == view.superview!.centerY + 60
            view.centerX == view.superview!.centerX
            view.height == 80
            view.width == view.superview!.width - 40
        }
    }
}
```

The layout functions simply put the two buttons in the correct places on the screen:

```
// MARK: Style
private extension MenuViewController{
    func style(){
        playButton.buttonColor = UIColor.ht_grapeFruitColor()
```

```
            playButton.shadowColor = UIColor.ht_grapeFruitDarkColor()
            gameCenterButton.buttonColor = UIColor.ht_aquaColor()
            gameCenterButton.shadowColor = UIColor.ht_aquaDarkColor()
        }
    }


    // MARK: Render
    private extension MenuViewController{
        func render(){
            playButton.setTitle("Play", forState: .Normal)
            gameCenterButton.setTitle("Game Center", forState: .Normal)
        }
    }
```

Finally, we set the colors and text for the titles of the buttons. The following screenshot shows the complete menu:

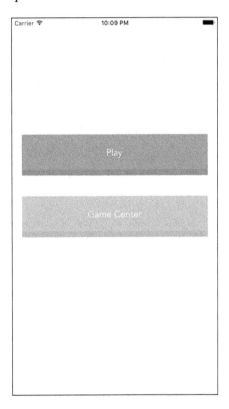

You will notice, when you click on **Play** button, the app crashes. This is because the template is using the view defined in the storyboard, and we are directly using the controllers.

Let's change the code in `GameViewController`:

```
class GameViewController: UIViewController {
    private let skView = SKView()

    override func viewDidLoad() {
        super.viewDidLoad()
        skView.frame = view.bounds
        view.addSubview(skView)
        if let scene = GameScene.unarchiveFromFile("GameScene") as?
GameScene {
            scene.size = skView.frame.size
            skView.showsFPS = true
            skView.showsNodeCount = true
            skView.ignoresSiblingOrder = true
            scene.scaleMode = .AspectFill
            skView.presentScene(scene)
        }
    }
}
```

We are basically creating `SKView` programmatically and setting its size just as we did for the main view's size.

To read the scene from a file, we added a class convenience method to `SKNode`:

```
extension SKNode {
    class func unarchiveFromFile(file : NSString) -> SKNode? {
        if let path = NSBundle.mainBundle().pathForResource(file as
String, ofType: "sks") {
            let sceneData = try! NSData(contentsOfFile: path, options:
.DataReadingMappedIfSafe)
            let archiver = NSKeyedUnarchiver(forReadingWithData:
sceneData)

            archiver.setClass(self.classForKeyedUnarchiver(),
forClassName: "SKScene")
            let scene = archiver.decodeObjectForKey(NSKeyedArchiveRoot
ObjectKey) as! GameScene
            archiver.finishDecoding()
            return scene
        } else {
            return nil
        }
    }
}
```

Note that NSData throws an error during init but, because we are expecting the file to be in the right place, we can skip the check using the try block.

We can run the app now in order to check whether everything is working fine.

 You can find the code for this version at https://github.com/gscalzo/Swift2ByExample/tree/5_FlappySwift_1_Menu.

A stage for a bird

Let's kick-start the game by implementing the background, which is not as straightforward as it might sound.

SpriteKit in a nutshell

SpriteKit is a powerful but easy-to-use game framework introduced in iOS 7.

Basically, it provides the infrastructure to move images onto the screen and interact with them.

It also provides a physics engine (based on Box2D), a particles engine, and basic sound playback support, making it particularly suitable for casual games.

The content of the game is drawn inside SKView, which is a particular kind of UIView, so it can be placed inside a normal hierarchy of UIViews.

The content of the game is organized into scenes, represented by subclasses of SKScene. Different parts of the game, such as the menu, levels, and so on, must be implemented in different SKScene classes. You can consider an SK in SpriteKit as an equivalent of UIViewController.

Inside SKScene, the elements of the game are grouped in the SKNode's tree, which tells SKScene how to render the components.

SKNode can be either a drawable node, such as SKSpriteNode or SKShapeNode, or it can be something to be applied to the subtree of its descendants, such as SKEffectNode or SKCropNode.

 SKScene is SKNode itself.

Nodes are animated using SKAction.

SKAction is a change that must be applied to a node, such as a move to a particular position, a change of scaling, or a change in the way the node appears. Actions can be grouped together so they run in parallel or wait for the end of a previous action.

Finally, we can define physics-based relations between objects, defining the mass, gravity, and how the nodes interact with each other.

That said, the best way to understand and learn SpriteKit is by starting to play with it. So, without further ado, let's move on to the implementation of our tiny game. In this way, you'll get a complete understanding of the most important features of SpriteKit.

Explaining the code

In the previous section, we implemented the menu view, leaving the code in a state similar to what was created by the template. With a basic knowledge of SpriteKit, you can now start understanding the code:

```
class GameViewController: UIViewController {
    private let skView = SKView()

    override func viewDidLoad() {
        super.viewDidLoad()
        skView.frame = view.bounds
        view.addSubview(skView)
        if let scene = GameScene.unarchiveFromFile("GameScene") as?
GameScene {
            scene.size = skView.frame.size
            skView.showsFPS = true
            skView.showsNodeCount = true
            skView.ignoresSiblingOrder = true
            scene.scaleMode = .AspectFill
            skView.presentScene(scene)
        }
    }
}
```

This is UIViewController, which starts the game; it creates SKView to present the complete screen. Then, it instantiates the scene from GameScene.sks, which can be considered the equivalent of a storyboard. Next, it enables some debug information before presenting the scene.

Now it's clear that we must implement the game inside the GameScene class.

Simulating a three-dimensional world using parallax

To simulate depth in the in-game world, we are going to use the technique of parallax scrolling, a really popular method wherein distant images on the game screen move more slowly than close ones.

In our case, we have three different levels, and we'll use three different speeds. The following screenshot shows the use of parallax scrolling:

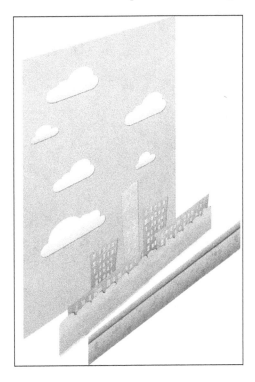

Before implementing the scrolling background, we must import the images into our project, remembering to set each image as 2x in the assets.

 You can find the code for this version at `https://github.com/gscalzo/Swift2ByExample/raw/5_FlappySwift_2_ParallaxLevels/FlappySwift/assets/assets.zip`.

The `GameScene` class basically sets up the background levels:

```
import SpriteKit

class GameScene: SKScene {
    private var screenNode: SKSpriteNode!
    private var actors: [Startable]!

    override func didMoveToView(view: SKView) {
        screenNode = SKSpriteNode(color: UIColor.clearColor(), size:
self.size)
        screenNode.anchorPoint = CGPoint(x: 0, y: 0)
        addChild(screenNode)
        let sky = Background(textureNamed: "sky", duration:60.0).
addTo(screenNode, zPosition: 0)
        let city = Background(textureNamed: "city", duration:20.0).
addTo(screenNode, zPosition: 1)
        let ground = Background(textureNamed: "ground", duration:5.0).
addTo(screenNode, zPosition: 2)
        actors = [sky, city, ground]

        for actor in actors {
            actor.start()
        }
    }
}
```

The only implemented function is `didMoveToView()`, which can be considered the equivalent of `viewDidAppear` for `UIVIewController`.

We define an array of `Startable` objects, where `Startable` is a protocol for creating the life cycle of the scene, `uniform` scene:

```
import SpriteKit

protocol Startable {
    func start()
    func stop()
}
```

This will give us an easy and handy way to stop the game later, when we either reach the final goal or our character dies. The `Background` class holds the behavior for a scrollable level:

```
import SpriteKit

class Background {
```

```
private let parallaxNode: ParallaxNode
private let duration: Double

init(textureNamed textureName: String, duration: Double) {
    parallaxNode = ParallaxNode(textureNamed: textureName)
    self.duration = duration
}

func addTo(parentNode: SKSpriteNode, zPosition: CGFloat) -> Self {
    parallaxNode.addTo(parentNode, zPosition: zPosition)
    return self
}
}
```

As you can see, the class saves the requested duration of a cycle, and then it forwards the calls to a class called `ParallaxNode`. The `addTo()` function connects the node to the parent, the scene itself, passing `zPosition` as well. It defines the order in which each node will be rendered on top of the parent node: the larger the node, the sooner it gets rendered; this is useful to cut down on the rendering. If a node is covered by another node with higher `zPosition`, the covered part is not rendered:

```
// Startable
extension Background : Startable {
    func start() {
        parallaxNode.start(duration: duration)
    }

    func stop() {
        parallaxNode.stop()
    }
}
```

The `Startable` protocol is implemented by forwarding the methods to `ParallaxNode`.

How to implement scrolling

The idea of implementing scrolling is really straightforward: we implement a node where we put two copies of the same image in a tiled format. We then place the node such that we have the left half fully visible. Then, we move the entire node to the left until we fully present the left node. Finally, we reset the position to the original one and restart the cycle.

The following figure explains this algorithm:

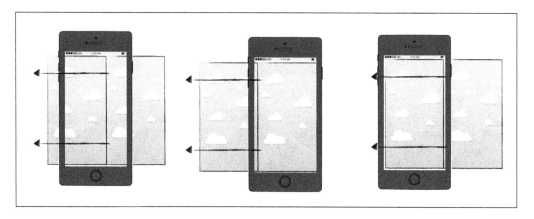

The code for this is as follows:

```
import SpriteKit

class ParallaxNode {
    private let node: SKSpriteNode!

    init(textureNamed: String) {
        let leftHalf = createHalfNodeTexture(textureNamed, offsetX: 0)
        let rightHalf = createHalfNodeTexture(textureNamed, offsetX:
leftHalf.size.width)

        let size = CGSize(width: leftHalf.size.width + rightHalf.size.
width,
            height: leftHalf.size.height)

        node = SKSpriteNode(color: UIColor.clearColor(), size: size)
        node.anchorPoint = CGPointZero
        node.position = CGPointZero
        node.addChild(leftHalf)
        node.addChild(rightHalf)
    }

    func zPosition(zPosition: CGFloat) -> ParallaxNode {
        node.zPosition = zPosition
        return self
    }
```

```
        func addTo(parentNode: SKSpriteNode, zPosition: CGFloat) ->
ParallaxNode {
            parentNode.addChild(node)
            node.zPosition = zPosition
            return self
        }
}
```

The `init()` method simply creates the two halves, puts them side by side, and sets the position of the node:

```
// Mark: Private
private func createHalfNodeTexture(textureNamed: String, offsetX:
CGFloat) -> SKSpriteNode {
    let node = SKSpriteNode(imageNamed: textureNamed, normalMapped:
true)
    node.anchorPoint = CGPointZero
    node.position = CGPoint(x: offsetX, y: 0)
    return node
}
```

The half node is just a node with the correct offset for the *x* coordinate:

```
// Mark: Startable
extension ParallaxNode {
    func start(duration duration: NSTimeInterval) {
        node.runAction(SKAction.repeatActionForever(SKAction.sequence(
            [
                SKAction.moveToX(-node.size.width/2.0, duration:
duration),
                SKAction.moveToX(0, duration: 0)
            ]
        )))
    }

    func stop() {
        node.removeAllActions()
    }
}
```

Finally, the `Startable` protocol is implemented using two actions in a sequence. First, we move half the size—which means an image width—to the left, and then we move the node to the original position to start the cycle again.

This is what the final result looks like:

 You can find the code for this version at `https://github.com/gscalzo/Swift2ByExample/raw/5_FlappySwift_2_ParallaxLevels`.

A flying bird

Now, it's time to implement our hero.

Adding the Bird node

First of all, we must add a new character to the `GameScene` class:

```
class GameScene: SKScene {
    private var bird: Bird!
    //...
    override func didMoveToView(view: SKView) {
        //...
```

```
        bird = Bird(textureNames: ["bird1.png", "bird2.png"]).
addTo(screenNode)
        bird.position = CGPointMake(30.0, 400.0)

        actors = [sky, city, ground, bird]
        //...
    }
}
```

We can see that this new class behaves like the other, which we have already implemented:

```
import SpriteKit

class Bird : Startable {
    private var node: SKSpriteNode!
    private let textureNames: [String]

    var position : CGPoint {
        set { node.position = newValue }
        get { return node.position }
    }

    init(textureNames: [String]) {
        self.textureNames = textureNames
        node = createNode()
    }

    func addTo(scene: SKSpriteNode) -> Bird{
        scene.addChild(node)
        return self
    }
}
```

In the public part, we build the node and add it to the parent. Note that the `position` property is implemented as a `computed` property, which forwards `set` and `get` to SKNode:

```
// Creators
private extension Bird {
    func createNode() -> SKSpriteNode {
        let birdNode = SKSpriteNode(imageNamed: textureNames.first!)
        birdNode.zPosition = 2.0
        return birdNode
    }
}
```

The node is built using the first frame of the passed textures. Also, zposition is set to be on top of all the background images:

```
// Startable
extension Bird : Startable {
    func start() {
        animate()
    }

    func stop() {
        node.physicsBody!.dynamic = false
        node.removeAllActions()
    }
}
// Private
extension Bird {
    private func animate(){
        let animationFrames = textureNames.map { texName in
            SKTexture(imageNamed: texName)
        }

        node.runAction(
            SKAction.repeatActionForever(
                SKAction.animateWithTextures(animationFrames,
timePerFrame: 0.5)
            ))
    }
}
```

The start() function animates the bird by alternating between the provided textures. The stop() function stops the animation and the physics engine. You'll understand better what this means in the next section:

```
// Actions
extension Bird {
    func update() {
        switch node.physicsBody!.velocity.dy {
        case let dy where dy > 30.0:
            node.zRotation = (3.14/6.0)
        case let dy where dy < -100.0:
            node.zRotation = -1*(3.14/4.0)
        default:
            node.zRotation = 0.0
        }
    }
}
```

Finally, the `update` method changes the rotation as per the vertical speed. Because the framework calls the update method of the current scene for every frame refresh, we need to forward it to the bird:

```
class GameScene: SKScene {
//...
    override func update(currentTime: CFTimeInterval) {
        bird.update()
    }
//..
}
```

If we run the app now, we will see a cute bird flying, but it is stuck in the middle of the screen!

Making the bird flap

To implement the flight of the bird, we'll leverage the physics engine provided by SpriteKit. To use a physics engine, we must define a gravity force and then define the mass for each element we want to animate by following the laws of physics. This might sound complex, but in reality it's relatively straightforward.

First of all, we must define the gravity in the scene:

```
class GameScene: SKScene {
    override func didMoveToView(view: SKView) {
        physicsWorld.gravity = CGVector(dx: 0, dy: -3)
        //..
    }
}
```

Next, we add touch handling:

```
class GameScene: SKScene {
//...
    override func touchesBegan(touches: Set<UITouch>, withEvent event:
UIEvent?) {
        bird.flap()
    }
}
```

This is a low-level touching interception, and the proper Apple way is to use a gesture recognizer: a gesture recognizer is a component that can be attached to `UIView` and that recognizes a particular touch action, (a single tap, or a slide, for example), and then calls an appropriate function when the gesture happens. In this way, we can define the different code to be executed for different gestures.

Then, we add a physics body to the bird:

```
private extension Bird {
    func createNode() -> SKSpriteNode {
        let birdNode = SKSpriteNode(imageNamed: textureNames.first!)
        birdNode.zPosition = 2.0
        birdNode.physicsBody = SKPhysicsBody.rectSize(birdNode.size) {
$0.dynamic = true
  }
        return birdNode
    }
}
```

The usual way to set up SKPhysicsBody is to create a body first and then mutate it by changing the values of its properties. As we prefer immutability, we extend SKPhysicsBody to handle the builder pattern, and this allows us to build and set SKPhysics in only one place and return an immutable object:

```
extension SKPhysicsBody {
    typealias BodyBuilderClosure = (SKPhysicsBody) -> ()

    class func rectSize(size: CGSize,
        builderClosure: BodyBuilderClosure) -> SKPhysicsBody {
            let body = SKPhysicsBody(rectangleOfSize: size)
            builderClosure(body)
            return body
    }
}
```

To simulate a flap, we apply an impulse to the bird in the opposite direction to gravity:

```
// Actions
extension Bird {
    func flap() {
        node.physicsBody!.velocity = CGVector(dx: 0, dy: 0)
        node.physicsBody!.applyImpulse(CGVector(dx: 0, dy: 8))
    }
    //...
}
```

By running the app now, we can make our bird fly:

 You can find the code for this version at `https://github.com/gscalzo/Swift2ByExample/tree/5_FlappySwift_3_Bird`.

Pipes!

Now the bird is flapping but there are no enemies, so the game is pretty boring. It's time to add some obstacles: pipes!

Implementing the pipes node

To implement the pipes as they were in the original game, we need two classes: `PipesNode`, which contains the top and bottom pipes, and `Pipes`, which creates and handles `PipesNode`.

Let's begin with `Pipes` and add it as an actor to `GameScene`:

```
//...
let pipes = Pipes(topPipeTexture: "topPipe.png", bottomPipeTexture:
"bottomPipe").addTo(screenNode)

actors = [sky, city, ground, bird, pipes]
//...
```

The `Pipes` class holds the texture name, and it is added to the node tree:

```
import SpriteKit

class Pipes {
    private class var createActionKey : String { get {return
"createActionKey"} }
    private var parentNode: SKSpriteNode!
    private let topPipeTexture: String
    private let bottomPipeTexture: String

    init(topPipeTexture: String, bottomPipeTexture: String) {
        self.topPipeTexture = topPipeTexture
        self.bottomPipeTexture = bottomPipeTexture
    }

    func addTo(parentNode: SKSpriteNode) -> Pipes {
        self.parentNode = parentNode
        return self
    }
}
```

You can see here that the `Pipes` `public` interface is similar to that of the other nodes we have implemented so far:

```
//MARK: Startable
extension Pipes : Startable {
    func start() {
        let createAction = SKAction.repeatActionForever(
            SKAction.sequence(
                [
                    SKAction.runBlock {
                        self.createNewPipesNode()
                    },
                    SKAction.waitForDuration(3)
                ]
            ) )
```

```
        parentNode.runAction(createAction, withKey: Pipes.
createActionKey)
    }

    func stop() {
        parentNode.removeActionForKey(Pipes.createActionKey)

        let pipeNodes = parentNode.children.filter {
            $0.name == PipesNode.kind
        }
        for pipe in pipeNodes {
            pipe.removeAllActions()
        }
    }
}
```

The `start` function basically creates a new `PipesNode` objects after every 3 seconds, and the `stop` function removes the current action and the actions of the working `PipesNode` objects

```
//MARK: Private
private extension Pipes {
    func createNewPipesNode() {
        PipesNode(topPipeTexture: topPipeTexture, bottomPipeTexture:bo
ttomPipeTexture, centerY: centerPipes()).addTo(parentNode).start()
    }

    func centerPipes() -> CGFloat {
        return parentNode.size.height/2 - 100 + 20 *
CGFloat(arc4random_uniform(10))
    }
}
```

The `createNewPipesNode()` function creates a new `Pipes` pair. Add it to `parentNode` and start it. To create a pair of differently placed pipes every time, we use a function that calculates a random place for the center:

```
import SpriteKit

class PipesNode{
    class var kind : String { get {return "PIPES"} }
    private let gapSize: CGFloat = 50

    private let pipesNode: SKNode
    private let finalOffset: CGFloat!
```

```
        private let startingOffset: CGFloat!

        init(topPipeTexture: String, bottomPipeTexture: String, centerY:
    CGFloat){
            pipesNode = SKNode()
            pipesNode.name = PipesNode.kind

            let pipeTop = createPipe(imageNamed: topPipeTexture)
            let pipeTopPosition = CGPoint(x: 0, y: centerY + pipeTop.size.
    height/2 + gapSize)
            pipeTop.position = pipeTopPosition
            pipesNode.addChild(pipeTop)

            let pipeBottom = createPipe(imageNamed: bottomPipeTexture)
            let pipeBottomPosition = CGPoint(x: 0, y: centerY -
    pipeBottom.size.height/2 - gapSize)
            pipeBottom.position = pipeBottomPosition
            pipesNode.addChild(pipeBottom)

            finalOffset = -pipeBottom.size.width
            startingOffset = -finalOffset
        }
```

PipesNode is a node on top of which we place the two pipes' sprites. Note that, in the
constructor, we also calculate the starting and ending points of the pipes:

```
        func addTo(parentNode: SKSpriteNode) -> PipesNode {
            let pipePosition = CGPoint(x: parentNode.size.width +
    startingOffset, y: 0)
            pipesNode.position = pipePosition
            pipesNode.zPosition = 4

            parentNode.addChild(pipesNode)
            return self
        }

        func start() {
            pipesNode.runAction(SKAction.sequence(
                [
                    SKAction.moveToX(finalOffset, duration: 6.0),
                    SKAction.removeFromParent()
                ]
                ))
        }
```

These values are used in the `addTo()` function in order to set the starting point and in the `start()` function, where the first action commands the node to move toward the left, outside the screen, before removing the node from the parent:

```
// Creators
func createPipe(#imageNamed: String) -> SKSpriteNode {
    let pipeNode = SKSpriteNode(imageNamed: imageNamed)
    return pipeNode
}
```

With the implementation of this `constructor` function, we are ready to run the app and see how it looks.

And it looks really pretty! But the pipes are in front of the ground, not behind it as expected. This issue can be solved easily by changing the `zPosition` of the ground, making it greater than that of the pipes.

Let's change the value of `zPosition` when instantiating the ground to be bigger than one of the pipes:

```
let ground = Background(textureNamed: "ground", duration:5.0).
addTo(screenNode, zPosition: 5)
```

Run the app now; everything works as expected, as shown in this screenshot:

You can find the code for this version at `https://github.com/gscalzo/Swift2ByExample/tree/5_FlappySwift_4_Pipes`.

Making the components interact

Although the app is colorful and seeing the bird fly is fun, we need to create a real-world scene, where collision with an obstacle typically brings you to a halt.

Setting up the collision-detection engine

The SpriteKit physics engine provides us with a really simple mechanism to detect collisions between objects. Basically, we need to set a bitmask for each component and then a collision-detection delegate. Let start defining the bitmask; for it, we define an enumeration in `GameScene`:

```
enum BodyType : UInt32 {
    case bird = 0b0001
    case ground = 0b0010
    case pipe = 0b0100
    case gap = 0b1000
}
```

Pay attention to two things. First, we must define the bitmask as a power of 2 so that we can detect what touches what using a bitwise `or` operation. Second, we've added a gap identifier, a component we haven't defined yet.

A gap is the hole between two pipes, and we need to detect the moment when the bird passes through this hole in order to increase the score.

Let's start setting up the pipes:

```
private func createPipe(imageNamed imageNamed: String) -> SKSpriteNode
{
    let pipeNode = SKSpriteNode(imageNamed: imageNamed)
    let size = CGSize(width: pipeNode.size.width, height: pipeNode.
size.height)
    pipeNode.physicsBody = SKPhysicsBody.rectSize(size) {
        body in
        body.dynamic = false
        body.affectedByGravity = false
        body.categoryBitMask = BodyType.pipe.rawValue
        body.collisionBitMask = BodyType.pipe.rawValue
```

```
        }

        return pipeNode
    }
```

Basically, we have defined the physics for the pipes. Also, we took advantage of being here already in order to add the `gap` component:

```
        private func createGap(size size: CGSize) -> SKSpriteNode {
        let gapNode = SKSpriteNode(color: UIColor.clearColor(),
            size: size)
        gapNode.zPosition = 6
        gapNode.physicsBody = SKPhysicsBody.rectSize(size) {
            body in
            body.dynamic = false
            body.affectedByGravity = false
            body.categoryBitMask = BodyType.gap.rawValue
            body.collisionBitMask = BodyType.gap.rawValue
        }
        return gapNode
    }
```

The definition is pretty similar to that of the `Pipes` class:

```
        init(topPipeTexture: String, bottomPipeTexture: String, centerY:
    CGFloat){
    //...
        pipesNode.addChild(pipeBottom)

        let gapNode = createGap(size: CGSize(
            width: pipeBottom.size.width,
            height: gapSize*2))
        gapNode.position = CGPoint(x: 0, y: centerY)
        pipesNode.addChild(gapNode)
        //...
    }
```

The `gap` node is simply set as a node and put in the node tree. Let's move on to the bird now:

```
    // Creators
    private extension Bird {
        func createNode() -> SKSpriteNode {
            let birdNode = SKSpriteNode(imageNamed: textureNames.first!)
            birdNode.zPosition = 2.0
```

```
            birdNode.physicsBody = SKPhysicsBody.rectSize(birdNode.size.
    scale(0.8)){
                body in
                body.dynamic = true
                body.categoryBitMask = BodyType.bird.rawValue
                body.collisionBitMask = BodyType.bird.rawValue
                body.contactTestBitMask = BodyType.ground.rawValue |
                    BodyType.pipe.rawValue |
                    BodyType.gap.rawValue
            }

            return birdNode
        }
    }
```

We are concentrating the detection logic inside the `bird` class, saying that the bird touches the ground, the pipe, or the gap.

 We are reducing the actual size of the related body of the bird. This is because the bird's frames have a transparent border in order to contain the wing animation, and using the entire frame would have made the detection area larger than required.

Pay attention to this code; `scale()` is an extension we add to `CGSize`:

```
// CGSize Private
extension CGSize {
    func scale(factor: CGFloat) -> CGSize {
        return CGSize(width: self.width * factor, height: self.height
* factor)
    }
}
```

We set the delegate in `GameScene`:

```
        override func didMoveToView(view: SKView) {
            physicsWorld.contactDelegate = self
            //...
        }
```

After setting it, we implement the protocol:

```
// Contacts
extension GameScene: SKPhysicsContactDelegate {
    func didBeginContact(contact: SKPhysicsContact) {
```

```
        let contactMask = contact.bodyA.categoryBitMask | contact.
bodyB.categoryBitMask

            switch (contactMask) {
            case BodyType.pipe.rawValue | BodyType.bird.rawValue:
                println("Contact with a pipe")
            case BodyType.ground.rawValue | BodyType.bird.rawValue:
                println("Contact with ground")
                for actor in actors {
                    actor.stop()
                }
            default:
                return
            }

        }


    func didEndContact(contact: SKPhysicsContact) {
        let contactMask = contact.bodyA.categoryBitMask | contact.
bodyB.categoryBitMask

            switch (contactMask) {
            case BodyType.gap.rawValue | BodyType.bird.rawValue:
                println("Contact with gap")
            default:
                return
            }
        }
    }
```

From the code, you can see that using the bitmask helps us know which two objects are colliding without requiring knowledge of which object is in bodyA and which is in bodyB.

By running the app now, you can see that everything works fine when the bird collides with either the pipes or the gap, but nothing happens in the case of the ground. This is because the ground is currently SKSpriteNode, and it has nothing associated with it.

Let's solve this issue by adding a function to GameScene. This function creates a body for the ground:

```
override func didMoveToView(view: SKView) {
//...
ground.zPosition(5)
screenNode.addChild(bodyTextureName("ground"))
//...
}
```

The function to create the body is really straightforward:

```
private extension GameScene{
    func bodyTextureName(textureName: String) -> SKNode{
        let image = UIImage(named: textureName)
        let width = image!.size.width
        let height = image!.size.height
        let groundBody = SKNode()
        groundBody.position = CGPoint(x: width/2, y: height/2)

        groundBody.physicsBody = SKPhysicsBody.rectSize(CGSize(width:
width, height: height)){ body in
            body.dynamic = false
            body.affectedByGravity = false
            body.categoryBitMask = BodyType.ground.rawValue
            body.collisionBitMask = BodyType.ground.rawValue
        }

        return groundBody
    }
}
```

Before trying the app, we set up the debug settings to show the shape of every physics body in the game:

```
class GameViewController: UIViewController {
override func viewDidLoad() {
    //...
    if let scene = GameScene.unarchiveFromFile("GameScene") as?
GameScene {
        //...
        skView.showsPhysics = true
        //...
        }
    }
}
```

By running the app now, we can see from the log that we are interacting with all the required components, as shown in the following screenshot:

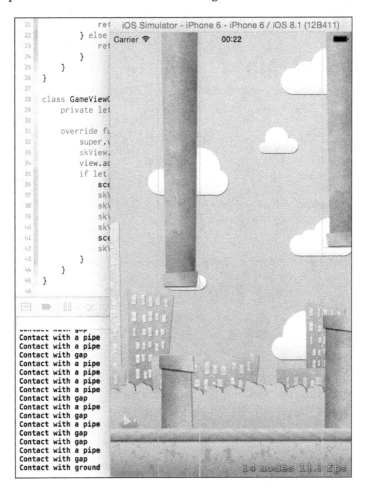

 You can find the code for this version at https://github.com/gscalzo/Swift2ByExample/tree/5_FlappySwift_5_Collisions.

Completing the game

Almost everything is done now, and in this final section, we are going to add the correct interaction between all the elements of the game.

Colliding with pipes

When the bird touches a pipe, we need to push it down so that it touches the ground and dies:

```
extension GameScene: SKPhysicsContactDelegate {
    func didBeginContact(contact: SKPhysicsContact!) {
    //...
    case BodyType.pipe.rawValue | BodyType.bird.rawValue:
    println("Contact with a pipe")
    bird.pushDown()
    //...
}
```

To push it, we can use the same technique that we used for the flapping — applying an impulse:

```
func pushDown() {
    dying = true
    node.physicsBody!.applyImpulse(CGVector(dx: 0, dy: -10))
}
```

Although the impulse has been applied correctly, you might notice that you can continue flapping after touching a pipe, and sometimes the bird starts flying again.

To solve this issue, we add a `status` variable to the bird. This variable indicates whether the bird is dying or is alive:

```
class Bird : Startable {
    //...
private var dying = false
    //...
}
extension Bird {
    func flap() {
        if !dying {
            node.physicsBody!.velocity = CGVector(dx: 0, dy: 0)
            node.physicsBody!.applyImpulse(CGVector(dx: 0, dy: 6))
        }
    }
    //...
}
```

Now the bird has no way to save itself after hitting a pipe!

Adding the score

The last feature that is missing is the score.

First of all, we implement a Score class. It holds the current score and the label used to present it:

```
import SpriteKit

class Score {
    private let score = SKLabelNode(text: "0")
    var currentScore = 0

func addTo(parentNode: SKSpriteNode) -> Score {
        score.fontName = "MarkerFelt-Wide"
        score.fontSize = 30
        score.position = CGPoint(x: parentNode.size.width/2, y:
parentNode.size.height - 40)
        parentNode.addChild(score)
        return self
    }

    func increase() {
        currentScore += 1
        score.text = "\(currentScore)"
    }
}
```

Then, we need to add it to the main screen:

```
class GameScene: SKScene {
    //...
    private var score = Score()

    override func didMoveToView(view: SKView) {
        //...
        score.addTo(screenNode)
        //...
    }
}
```

Next, we increase the score after the bird leaves a gap:

```
func didEndContact(contact: SKPhysicsContact!) {
    //...
    switch (contactMask) {
        case BodyType.gap.rawValue | BodyType.bird.rawValue:
        println("Contact with gap")
        score.increase()
        //...
    }
}
```

Then, we can play and see our score increase.

Adding a restart pop-up

You must surely noticed that, after the bird dies, the only way to play again is by restarting the app. Pretty annoying, isn't it?

Let's add a pop-up to present the final score and allow the player to play again. To get a nicer alert view, we use the `SIAlertView` pod by adding the pod `SIAlertView', '~> 1.3'` line to our `Podfile`.

Then we add a handler to manage the end of the game:

```
case BodyType.ground.rawValue | BodyType.bird.rawValue:
    println("Contact with ground")
    for actor in actors {
        actor.stop()
    }
    askToPlayAgain()
```

The `askToPlayAgain()` function basically builds the pop-up:

```
// Private
private extension GameScene {
    func askToPlayAgain() {
        let alertView = SIAlertView(title: "Ouch!!", andMessage:
"Congratulations! Your score is \(score.currentScore). Play again?")

        alertView.addButtonWithTitle("OK", type: .Default) { _ in
self.onPlayAgainPressed() }
        alertView.addButtonWithTitle("Cancel", type: .Default) { _ in
self.onCancelPressed() }
        alertView.show()
    }
}
```

Don't forget to import the correct framework and add two public properties to hold the callbacks associated with the two buttons:

```
import SpriteKit
import SIAlertView
class GameScene: SKScene {
//...
var onPlayAgainPressed:(()->Void)!
var onCancelPressed:(()->Void)!
```

Next, we need to refactor the `GameViewController` class to extract the creation of the scene in an independent function to permit calling inside the callback:

```
class GameViewController: UIViewController {
    private let skView = SKView()

    override func viewDidLoad() {
        super.viewDidLoad()
        skView.frame = view.bounds
        view.addSubview(skView)

        createTheScene()
    }

    private func createTheScene() {
        do {
            let scene = try GameScene.unarchiveFromFile("GameScene")
            if let scene = scene as? GameScene {
                scene.size = skView.frame.size
                skView.showsFPS = true
                skView.showsNodeCount = true
                skView.ignoresSiblingOrder = true
                scene.scaleMode = .AspectFill

                scene.onPlayAgainPressed = { [weak self] in
                    self?.createTheScene()
                }

                scene.onCancelPressed = { [weak self] in
                    self?.dismissViewControllerAnimated(true,
completion: nil)
                }
                skView.presentScene(scene)
            }
        }catch (let error) {
            fatalError("Error \(error) while unarchiving 'GameScene'")
        }
    }
}
```

Finally, the game has all the required features, and they make it fun.

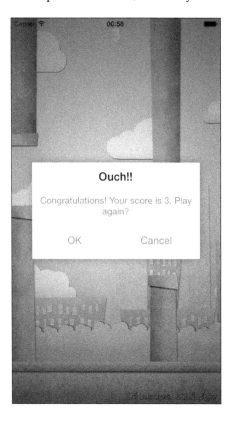

 You can find the code for this version at `https://github.com/gscalzo/FlappySwift/tree/full_plain_game`.

Summary

In this chapter, we shifted gears and introduced a new framework. You learned about the most common and useful features when it comes to building a video game.

You also learned how to implement scrolling using different speeds to simulate depth. Then, we added a character, animated it, and made it move.

Finally, we introduced a physics engine. It is useful for many purposes, including collision detection. Although the game is functionally complete, in the next chapter we'll continue to polish it by adding music, video, sound effects, and a connection to the Game Center.

7
Polishing Flappy Swift

We ended the previous chapter with a complete clone of Flappy Bird.

Although the game is fun and you can play exactly as you do in the original, you might have noticed that the game is lacking something that makes professional games more interesting to play.

The goal of this chapter is to fill this lacuna by adding some juiciness and integrating the game with the Game Center to create a leaderboard and increase the engagement of your players.

Adding juiciness

Juiciness in a game or an app can be defined as all the effects such as sounds, zooming, or shaking elements. Although they are not indispensable to the game, they make the experience of gaming more pleasant.

Let there be sounds!

The first thing we add is sound effects in order to give feedback to the user when something, either good or bad, happens in the game. For example, we could notify that the bird is flapping, or has hit the pipes, using a sound.

Basically, there are two ways for an indie game developer, which means a developer without any video game publisher's financial support, to add sounds to the game: creating them or searching for them from sound collections, such as https://www.freesound.org or http://www.freesfx.co.uk.

Because the aim of this book is to teach you how to create apps using Swift, we'll use some resources found in a free collection.

In the master branch, you can find `.zip` files with all the required sounds.

 You can find the sounds at `https://github.com/gscalzo/`
`Swift2ByExample/raw/5_FlappySwift_7_Juicy/`
`FlappySwift/assets/sounds.zip`.

Let's start adding sound files to the project by creating a new `sounds` folder in it, like this:

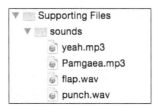

SpriteKit provides us with a convenient action to play a sound, and we don't have to worry about the format of the sound.

However, you must pay attention to the fact that uncompressed files, such as `.wav`, can have a large size, and the resulting app can become larger than expected. So, I advise that you always convert sound files into `.mp3` files.

That said, let's add the sound of flapping to be played when the player touches the screen. Add this code to the `GameScene` file:

```
override func touchesBegan(touches: NSSet, withEvent event: UIEvent) {
    runAction(SKAction.playSoundFileNamed("flap.wav",
waitForCompletion: false))
    bird.flap()
}
```

By starting the app now, we can hear a sound effect when the bird flaps its wings.

As you can imagine, adding a *bump* sound when the bird hits a pipe or the ground is just a matter of writing a similar function call in the correct place:

```
func didBeginContact(contact: SKPhysicsContact!) {
    //...
    switch (contactMask) {
        case BodyType.pipe.rawValue | BodyType.bird.rawValue:
            println("Contact with a pipe")
            runAction(SKAction.playSoundFileNamed("punch.wav",
waitForCompletion: false))
            bird.pushDown()
```

```
        case BodyType.ground.rawValue | BodyType.bird.rawValue:
            println("Contact with ground")
            runAction(SKAction.playSoundFileNamed("punch.wav",
waitForCompletion: false))
            for actor in actors {
                actor.stop()
            }
            //...
    }
```

Finally, we add a cheerful sound when the player gets a point:

```
func didEndContact(contact: SKPhysicsContact!) {
    //...
    switch (contactMask) {
        case BodyType.gap.rawValue |  BodyType.bird.rawValue:
            println("Contact with gap")
            runAction(SKAction.playSoundFileNamed("yeah.mp3",
waitForCompletion: false))
            score.increase()
            //...
    }
```

When you play the app, you will notice that it's already very pleasant to play.

Playing the soundtrack

Kevin MacLeod's site, `http://incompetech.com`, is a virtually infinite source of amazing free video game and movie soundtracks. Here, you can find tons of amazing `.mp3` files under the Creative Commons Attribution License. We are going to use one of Kevin's files, `Pamgaea`, which can be found at `http://incompetech.com/wordpress/2013/09/pamgaea/`.

Although we can use the SpriteKit action to play the soundtrack, it is better to use `AVFoundation`. This can give us more flexibility in playing a long sound file.

Let's start implementing a proper class, which is `MusicPlayer`, to handle the player:

```
import Foundation
import AVFoundation

enum MusicPlayerError: ErrorType {
    case ResourceNotFound
}
```

```
class MusicPlayer {
    private var player: AVAudioPlayer? = nil

    init(filename: String, type: String) throws {
        if let resource =
        NSBundle.mainBundle().pathForResource(filename, ofType:
        type) {
            let url = NSURL(fileURLWithPath: resource)
            player = try AVAudioPlayer(contentsOfURL: url)
            player?.numberOfLoops = -1
            player?.prepareToPlay()
        } else {
            throw MusicPlayerError.ResourceNotFound
        }
    }
}
```

This class basically wraps `AVPlayer` to configure it to play infinite loops (this is the meaning of the `player?.numberOfLoops = -1` statement). It also preloads part of the song in its internal cache before it receives the `play()` call.

Because the `AVAudioPlayer` function throws an error if the URL doesn't contain a valid file, we throw that error again; also, we declare a custom error to handle when the resource is not found.

The only two functions we need are `play()` and `stop()`, which are basically forwards to the actual `AVPlayer` function:

```
class MusicPlayer {
    //...
    func play() {
        player?.play()
    }
    func stop() {
        player?.stop()
    }
}
```

We want to start playing when the app starts, so we add the player to the `MenuViewController` class:

```
class MenuViewController: UIViewController {
    //...
    private var player: MusicPlayer?

    override func viewDidLoad() {
```

```
        super.viewDidLoad()
        do {
            player = try MusicPlayer(filename: "Pamgaea", type:
            "mp3")
            player!.play()
        } catch {
            print("Error playing soundtrack")
        }
        //...
    }
}
```

Start the app. A funny tune will follow, playing during the gameplay.

Shaking the screen!

If you have ever played the original game, you might remember that the screen shook whenever the bird hit the ground. Although an action to make a node shake doesn't exist, we can add a new action, which is basically a sequence of moving around the center:

```
import SpriteKit

extension SKAction {
    // Thanks to Benzi: http://stackoverflow.com/a/24769521/288379
    class func shake(duration:CGFloat, amplitudeX:Int = 3,
amplitudeY:Int = 3) -> SKAction {
        let numberOfShakes = duration / 0.015 / 2.0
        var actionsArray:[SKAction] = []
        for _ in 1 Int(numberOfShakes) {
            let dx =
            CGFloat(arc4random_uniform(UInt32(amplitudeX))) -
            CGFloat(amplitudeX / 2)
            let dy =
            CGFloat(arc4random_uniform(UInt32(amplitudeY))) -
            CGFloat(amplitudeY / 2)
            let forward = SKAction.moveByX(dx, y:dy, duration: 0.015)
            let reverse = forward.reversedAction()
            actionsArray.append(forward)
            actionsArray.append(reverse)
        }
        return SKAction.sequence(actionsArray)
    }
}
```

In this code, we create a number of shake actions, each of them with a random amplitude; each action is added to the collection of the actions, with the opposite of the same shake as well, so that the screen is in the original position and is ready for the next shake.

We use this action when the bird hits the ground. It is applied to the `screen` node:

```
extension GameScene: SKPhysicsContactDelegate {
    func didBeginContact(contact: SKPhysicsContact!) {
        //...
        case BodyType.ground.rawValue | BodyType.bird.rawValue:
        //...
            let shakeAction = SKAction.shake(0.1, amplitudeX: 20,
            amplitudeY: 20)
            screenNode.runAction(shakeAction)
            self.askToPlayAgain()
        //...
    }
```

By playing the app, you will notice that the screen shakes, but the effect is reduced by the appearance of the popup asking for a restart. The fastest way to fix this issue is to add a small delay before the popup appears.

Because the function for the executing of a delayed block could be handy for other apps, we wrap the actual **Grand Central Dispatch (GCD)** function in a function:

```
import Foundation
func execAfter(delay:Double, closure:()->()) {
    dispatch_after(
        dispatch_time(
            DISPATCH_TIME_NOW,
            Int64(delay * Double(NSEC_PER_SEC))
        ),
    dispatch_get_main_queue(), closure)
}
```

So, we can delay the popup in this way:

```
let shakeAction = SKAction.shake(0.1, amplitudeX: 20,
                                      amplitudeY: 20)
screenNode.runAction(shakeAction)
execAfter(1) {
    self.askToPlayAgain()
}
```

The app is now complete from the features point of view, and we can move on to adding Game Center support.

 You can find the code for this version at https://github.com/ gscalzo/Swift2ByExample/tree/5_FlappySwift_7_Juicy.

Integrating with Game Center

Game Center can be defined as a social gaming network that offers multiplayer features. It was made available in iOS 4.1, and it has been updated with new gaming options ever since.

What Game Center provides

The features provided by Game Center are as follows:

- **Leaderboards**: This is a shared database containing the scores of the players of the game. It allows them to add their personal results and compare them with the scores of other players.

- **Achievements**: These are the goals defined inside the game that cause players to maintain interest in the game. Some examples of achievements can be *Destroyed 50 Enemies*, *Run during the Night*, and so on.

- **Multiplayer**: This feature allows the developer to implement a networked game where players can compete with each other, either in real time or in a turn-based manner.

Incorporating Game Center in an app is a two-step project. First of all, we need to set up the app in iTunes Connect, enabling Game Center support and setting up the leaderboards. Then, we need to add the code to send the score to Game Center.

Setting up Game Center

We'll use Xcode to automate the tasks to be done in order to set up Game Center:

1. The first thing we need to do is to add **Apple ID** to **Xcode**. Go to **Xcode Menu | Preferences** and select the **Accounts** icon, as shown in this screenshot:

2. Then, we add **Apple ID**, as shown in the following screenshot:

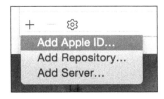

3. Now, in **Project Navigator**, select the project and the correct name of the **Team**, which should be the name of the developer, like this:

4. Finally, click on **Capabilities** at the top of the window and turn the switch **ON** for Game Center, as shown in this screenshot:

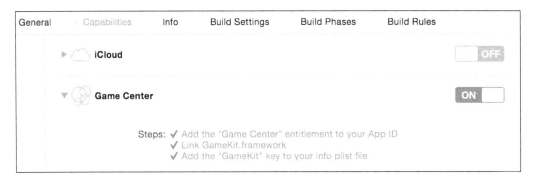

Before implementing the code, we need to set up the app on iTunes Connect.

Creating an app record on iTunes Connect

Creating a record on iTunes Connect is not mandatory for integration with Game Center, but it is required in order to create any leaderboard. If you feel comfortable with this process, you can skip this section and go to the next section:

1. First of all, log in to iTunes Connect (`http://itunesconnect.apple.com`) using your credentials. Then, add a new app by selecting the following icon:

2. By pressing the **+** sign at the top, we can add the app, as shown in this screenshot:

3. To complete the creation of the app, we fill in all of the required data, as shown in the following screenshot:

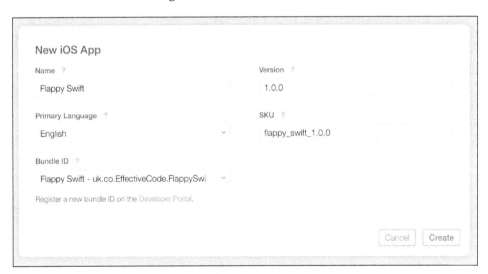

As you can see, the app ID we created in Xcode is presented in the **Bundle ID** drop-down window so that we can add it as **Bundle ID**.

4. Here is a screenshot that shows the expected properties of the **Flappy Swift** app:

Enabling Game Center

We have already enabled Game Center for the app in Xcode. We need to do this for the app in iTunes Connect.

To do this, we must select Game Center from the menu of the app, as shown in the preceding screenshot.

Because we don't have a suite of games to share leaderboards. Follow these steps to enable Game Center in your app:

1. Click on the **Enable for Single Game** button, as shown in the following screenshot:

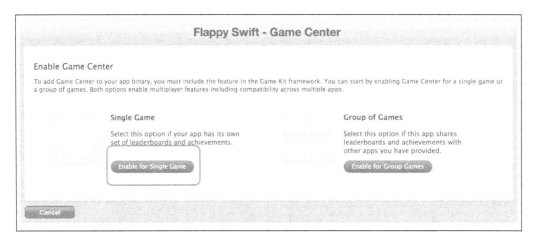

2. The following screenshot shows the enabled **Game Center** dashboard in our app:

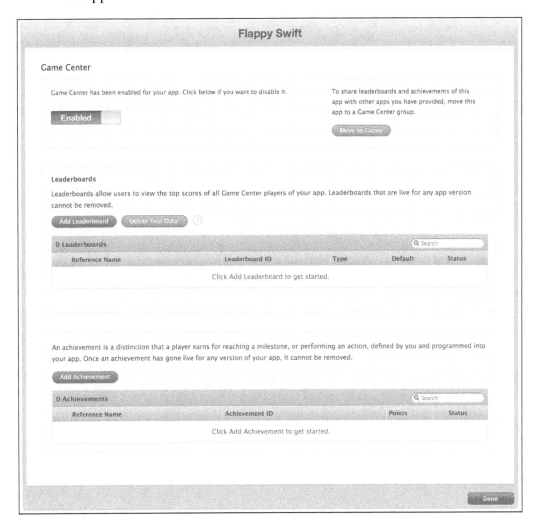

3. As you can see, we have the ability to add, change, and configure several leaderboards and achievements, but for the sake of simplicity, we will create only one leaderboard. We do this by clicking on the **Add Leaderboard** button and filling in the form, as shown in this screenshot:

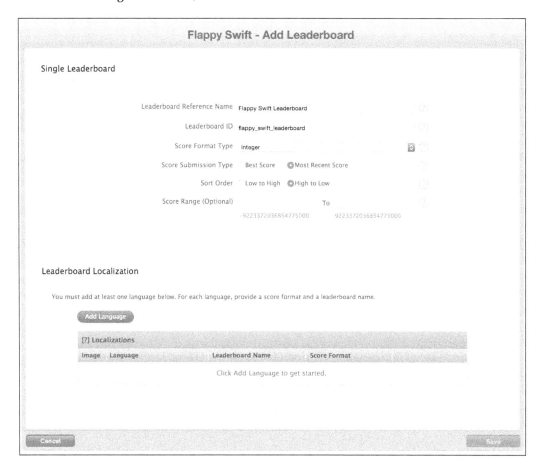

Finally, we have set up the leaderboard for our game.

Creating fake user accounts to test Game Center

Although not mandatory, it is definitely a good practice to have fake test accounts for use during the development of a game that supports Game Center. Otherwise, you might risk having a not-yet-published app featured in Game Center. The following are the steps to create a fake user account to test your game:

1. To create new users, go back to the home page of iTunes Connect and then select the **Users and Roles** icon, which looks like this:

2. Then, select **Sandbox Testers**, as shown in the following screenshot:

3. Finally, create a **Tester** by filling in the form, like this:

Pay attention; the e-mail must be real and it will be used as a login to test the Game Center feature in the app.

Although this process could seem awkward and long, after you learn to do it for an app, you'll notice that it will be always the same for all other apps you'll create supporting Game Center.

We are finally ready to add the code to enable the sharing of the code on Game Center.

Authenticating a player

The first thing that we must handle with the integration of Game Center is to authenticate the player. Once the player is connected to Game Center, then all the features implemented in the app are available for them; otherwise, they are simply not available.

Apple recommends that you implement the authentication in `AppDelegate`, but we prefer to implement it as the first action in the `MenuViewController` class. To do this, we create a `GameCenter` wrapper class and use it in the `viewDidLoad()` function of `MenuViewController`:

```
class MenuViewController: UIViewController {
    //...
    private let gameCenter = GameCenter()
    override func viewDidLoad() {
        super.viewDidLoad()
        gameCenter.authenticateLocalPlayer()
    //...
```

Let's start implementing the `GameCenter` class:

```
import GameKit
import SIAlertView

class GameCenter: NSObject {
    private var gameCenterEnabled = false
    private var leaderboardIdentifier = ""

    func authenticateLocalPlayer() {
        let localPlayer = GKLocalPlayer.localPlayer()
        localPlayer.authenticateHandler = { (viewController,
        error) in
            if let vc = viewController {
                let topViewController =
                UIApplication.sharedApplication().delegate!
                .window!!.rootViewController
                topViewController?.presentViewController(vc,
                animated: true, completion: nil)
            } else if localPlayer.authenticated {
                self.gameCenterEnabled = true
                localPlayer.
loadDefaultLeaderboardIdentifierWithCompletionHandler({
(leaderboardIdentifier, error) -> Void in
                    self.leaderboardIdentifier =
                    leaderboardIdentifier!
                })
            }
        }
    }
}
```

This class has two properties: a Boolean indicating whether Game Center is enabled or not and the identifier for the leaderboard. Although we have set the name of the leaderboard and it is a constant, it's safer to retrieve it from the server in order to give us the flexibility to change it after the app has been published.

The code is really straightforward because it relies on the API of Game Center. Everything is handled by the `authenticateHandler()` closure, which is called by passing two optional values: `UIViewController` and an error.

The former is the login view controller that we must present when the user is not logged in. To find the topmost view controller, we ask the root view controller of the main window. If the user is connected, we retrieve the identifier of the leaderboard.

When the app is run, either the login screen or a banner with the name of the logged-in player should be presented, like this:

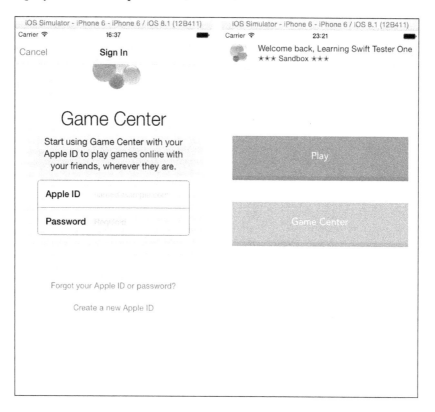

The rest of the class is just a function meant to report the scores, which basically transforms the score into an integer for the proper class:

```
class GameCenter: NSObject {
    //...
    func reportScore(score: Int){
        if !gameCenterEnabled {
            return
        }
        let gkScore = GKScore(leaderboardIdentifier:
leaderboardIdentifier)
        gkScore.value = Int64(score)
GKScore.reportScores([gkScore], withCompletionHandler: nil)
    }
}
```

The last of the required functions is a way of presenting the leaderboard:

```
class GameCenter: NSObject {
    //...
func showLeaderboard() {
        if !gameCenterEnabled {
            let alertView = SIAlertView(title: "Game Center
Unavailable", andMessage: "Player is not signed in")

            alertView.addButtonWithTitle("OK", type: .Default)
            { _ in}
            alertView.show()
            return
        }
        let gcViewController = GKGameCenterViewController()

        gcViewController.gameCenterDelegate = self
        gcViewController.viewState = .Leaderboards
        gcViewController.leaderboardIdentifier =
        leaderboardIdentifier

        let topViewController = UIApplication.sharedApplication().
delegate!.window!!.rootViewController
        topViewController?.presentViewController(gcViewController,
animated: true, completion: nil)
    }
}
```

The GKGameCenterControllerDelegate protocol implementation simply dismisses the leaderboard view controller:

```
extension GameCenter: GKGameCenterControllerDelegate {
    func gameCenterViewControllerDidFinish(gameCenterViewController:
GKGameCenterViewController) {
        gameCenterViewController.dismissViewControllerAnimated(true,
completion: nil)
    }
}
```

After implementing these functions, we need to add them to the MenuViewController class:

```
    @objc func onPlayPressed(sender: UIButton) {
        let vc = GameViewController()
        vc.gameCenter = gameCenter
        //...
    }

    @objc func onGameCenterPressed(sender: UIButton) {
        gameCenter.showLeaderboard()
    }
```

GameViewController forwards the class to GameScene:

```
class GameViewController: UIViewController {
    var gameCenter: GameCenter?
    //...
private func createTheScene() {
        if let scene = GameScene.unarchiveFromFile("GameScene") as?
GameScene {
            scene.gameCenter = gameCenter
```

In the GameScene class, we report the score when the bird hits the ground:

```
class GameScene: SKScene {
  var gameCenter: GameCenter?
    //...
}
extension GameScene: SKPhysicsContactDelegate {
    func didBeginContact(contact: SKPhysicsContact!) {
        //...
        case BodyType.ground.rawValue | BodyType.bird.rawValue:
        //...
gameCenter?.reportScore(score.currentScore)
```

With this code in place, after pressing the proper button, we can finally see the leaderboard, as shown in this screenshot:

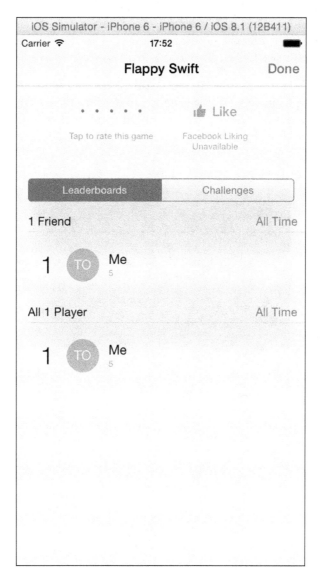

 You can find the code for this version at https://github.com/ gscalzo/Swift2ByExample/tree/5_FlappySwift_8_ GameCenter.

Summary

This chapter was a bit different from the others because for the first time, we probably spent more time configuring iTunes Connect than performing actual coding. However, this is a necessary step in order to include Game Center support, so it's worth gaining solid knowledge of how to do it.

With this chapter done by adding juiciness and Game Center support *Flappy Swift* is ready to be published. So, it's time to move on to the next chapter, where we'll explore the other game development frameworks brought in by iOS 8 by implementing a clone of an endless three-dimensional runner game called *Cube Runner*.

8
Cube Runner

In the last two chapters, we saw how easy it is to implement a 2D game using SpriteKit.

Most of you probably think that implementing a 3D game is something that only professional game developers can do because it requires a knowledge of 3D graphics, math, rendering, lights, and so on, as well as external tools such as Unity.

This may have been true until Apple released SceneKit, a really simple 3D rendering framework created mainly for hobbyists and casual game developers. First introduced in OS X Mountain Lion, it became even more powerful in 2014 with the addition of particle effects, physics simulations, and multipass rendering. It was added to iOS 8, allowing the community of iOS developers to implement 3D applications using a model similar to Sprite Kit and UIKit in general.

In this chapter, after a brief introduction to SceneKit using Playground, we'll implement an iOS clone of a fun Flash game.

The app is…

The world of Flash games is a never-ending source of inspiration; however, because Flash is not available in iOS, the most entertaining Flash games must be remade in a native way.

Cube Runner is a rare case in which simplicity and fun come together to create a really addictive game. Implemented in 2006 by Max Abernethy, it is a predecessor of the infinite runner game where the player, who is driving a triangular spaceship, must survive in an alien landscape by avoiding cubes he encounters during the run.

The view is from a cam following the hero, and as he turns the jet, the tridimensional world changes accordingly, as shown in the following screenshot:

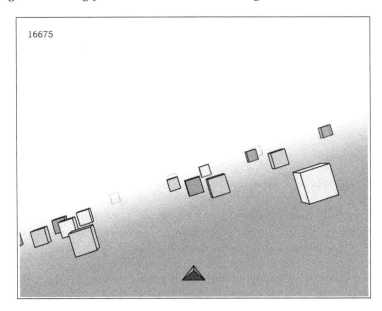

As is usual in endless runner games, the score increments in a time-based fashion; the longer the player survives, the bigger the score.

Introduction to SceneKit

Before diving into the development of the game, let's introduce SceneKit briefly.

What is SceneKit?

SceneKit is a rendering engine that's based on a hierarchy of nodes, a similar way to SpriteKit. The most important kinds of nodes are lights, the camera, geometry objects, boxes, spheres, and so on. Actually, all of these are attributes of a node, but for the sake of simplicity in the way we look at them, let's consider these as different entities.

To these nodes, we can apply several actions, such as moving, rotating, and so on. We can also add a physical body to a node and put it into a physical world, which is again really similar to SpriteKit.

Building an empty scene

To get our feet wet, we'll use the playground again as we did in the *Chapter 1, Welcome to the World of Swift*.

Let's start by creating a new iOS playground called `SceneKitPlayground`, and import the frameworks needed to perform our experiment:

```
import UIKit
import SceneKit
import XCPlayground
```

The latter is the framework that allows us to display the scene on the Playground console, so don't forget to open the console by going to **View | Assistant Editor | Show Assistant Editor**.

We start by creating `SCNView`, which is `UIView` that displays the SceneKit scene. Then, we add the scene, which is the stage where everything happens, and finally, we show the view in the console:

```
var sceneView = SCNView(frame:
    CGRect(x: 0, y: 0,
    width: 400, height: 400))
var scene = SCNScene()
sceneView.scene = scene
XCPlaygroundPage.currentPage.liveView = sceneView
```

This is what the playground presents:

```
  <   >   ⬚ SceneKitPlayground
1 import UIKit
2 import SceneKit
3 import XCPlayground
4
5 var sceneView = SCNView(frame:            SCNView
6     CGRect(x: 0, y: 0,
7         width: 400, height: 400))
8 var scene = SCNScene()                    <SCNScene: 0x7ffaebd28c70>
9 sceneView.scene = scene                   SCNView
10 XCPlaygroundPage.currentPage.liveView =
       sceneView
```

To enable rendering, we need to open the console. Go to **View** | **Assistant Editor** | **Show Assistant Editor**, as shown in this screenshot:

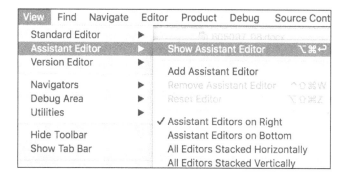

Now, let's start adding the nodes to the scene, starting with the camera:

```
var cameraNode = SCNNode()
cameraNode.camera = SCNCamera()
cameraNode.position = SCNVector3(x: 0, y: 0, z: 4)
scene.rootNode.addChildNode(cameraNode)
```

As mentioned earlier, the camera is an attribute of a node that can be positioned and rotated in the space of the scene. As you can see, `SCNScene` has a predefined `rootNode` to which we add children to create the object hierarchy.

Let's utilize this snippet of code to introduce the coordinate system of SceneKit, as follows:

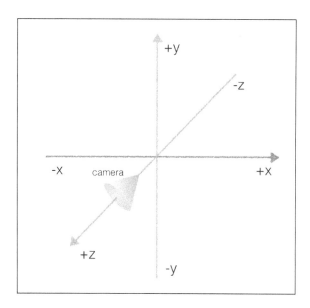

As you can see, the x and y axes are placed on the plane in front of the user, with the y axis being positive from the bottom to the top, which is the opposite of UIKit. The z axis runs from the user to the screen, with positive values toward the user. The camera aims at $-z$. It's really important to be clear in your mind how these axes are orientated. Otherwise, it may become really difficult to place objects in the scene and debug them if the scene is not rendered as expected.

Adding a green torus

Now, let's add an object to the scene:

```
var torus = SCNTorus(ringRadius: 1, pipeRadius: 0.35)
var torusNode = SCNNode(geometry: torus)
torusNode.position = SCNVector3(x: 0.0, y: 0.0, z: 0.0)
scene.rootNode.addChildNode(torusNode)
```

Despite us having added a camera and an object, nothing is shown in the scene.

This is because we haven't defined the material of the object yet. By material, we mean a collection of attributes associated with a surface that define its appearance when rendered. Using the material's properties, we can define it as opaque or transparent, how much light it can reflect or diffuse, and so on.

Let's define the torus as a green object that reflects white light:

```
torus.firstMaterial?.diffuse.contents = UIColor.greenColor()
torus.firstMaterial?.specular.contents = UIColor.whiteColor()
```

Finally, a torus is rendered onto the scene.

However, it's not really appealing. Because of the position of the camera, what we are seeing is basically the side of the torus. Also, instead of looking like it's 3D, it appears really flat, like this:

Let's solve the first issue by rotating the torus by $\pi/4$ around the x axis:

```
torusNode.rotation = SCNVector4(x: 1.0, y: 0.0, z: 0.0, w: Float(M_
PI/4.0))
```

To rotate a node, we first need to define the vector around which the node will rotate and then the angle of the rotation. Now, the torus is nicely visible, as shown here:

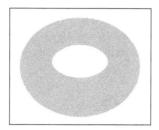

Let there be light!

The flatness is because the scene is lacking light, so let's add light:

```
var light = SCNLight()
light.type = SCNLightTypeSpot
var lightNode = SCNNode()
lightNode.light = light
lightNode.position = SCNVector3(x: 0, y: 0, z: 6)
scene.rootNode.addChildNode(lightNode)
```

After running the code, the torus will look like the following:

Now the torus definitely looks better.

Let's make it move!

As mentioned earlier, we can apply actions to nodes in the same way as we do in SpriteKit; for example, we can forever move the light to the left and right:

```
let moveAction = SCNAction.sequence([
    SCNAction.moveByX(-2, y: 0, z: 0, duration: 1),
    SCNAction.moveByX(2, y: 0, z: 0, duration: 1),
```

```
    SCNAction.moveByX(2, y: 0, z: 0, duration: 1),
    SCNAction.moveByX(-2, y: 0, z: 0, duration: 1)
])
lightNode.runAction(SCNAction.repeatActionForever(moveAction))
```

We can also make the torus rotate:

```
let rotateAction = SCNAction.rotateByAngle(CGFloat(M_PI),
    aroundAxis: SCNVector3(x: 1.0, y: 0.0, z: 0.0),
    duration: 4.0)

torusNode.runAction(SCNAction.repeatActionForever(rotateAction))
```

It's amazing what we can build with just a few lines of code in such an interactive way:

In this brief introduction, we have just scratched the surface of what we can do with SceneKit. Nevertheless, we have introduced its key concepts, which will help us implement our game without any problems.

Implementing Cube Runner

After experimenting a bit with SceneKit, let's start implementing our game.

The game skeleton

As usual, let's start by selecting the correct Xcode project template—the **Game** template in this case, which looks like this:

In the next screen, we add the requested data and select **SceneKit** as the technology, as shown here:

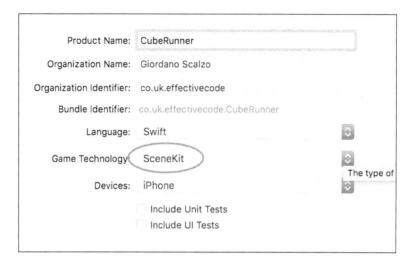

After selecting only **Portrait** as the **Device Orientation**, as shown in the following screenshot, we can run the example project:

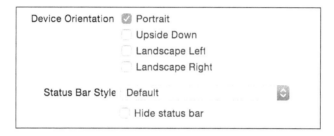

The demo app shows a gorgeous rotating 3D airplane, thus showing us what we can achieve using this framework. Here is a screenshot of the plane:

Implementing the menu

As the first task in building the app, we prepare `Podfile`, which contains a few pods that we'll use to build the **Menu** view:

```
inhibit_all_warnings!
use_frameworks!

target 'CubeRunner' do
    pod 'Cartography', :git => "https://github.com/robb/Cartography.
git", :tag => '0.6.0'
    pod 'HTPressableButton', '~> 1.3.2'
    pod 'BitwiseFont', '~> 0.1.0'
end
```

The first is the usual Auto Layout helper library, the second is for the buttons of the menu, and the latter is the custom font that reminds us of the font used in old arcade video games.

After running the usual `pod install` command, we are ready to implement the `MenuViewController` class.

The code of this class is basically the same as we used from the previous game, so it shouldn't need any further explanation. First, we need to add the builder to `AppDelegate`:

```
    func application(application: UIApplication,
  didFinishLaunchingWithOptions launchOptions: [NSObject: AnyObject]?)
  -> Bool {
        let viewController = MenuViewController()
        let mainWindow = UIWindow(frame: UIScreen.mainScreen().bounds)
        mainWindow.backgroundColor = UIColor.whiteColor()
        mainWindow.rootViewController = viewController
        mainWindow.makeKeyAndVisible()
        window = mainWindow
        return true
    }
```

Then, we implement the view controller, which presents us with the menu from which we can select game sections, and a label with the name of the game using a cool font:

```
import UIKit
import HTPressableButton
import Cartography
import BitwiseFont

class MenuViewController: UIViewController {
    private let playButton = HTPressableButton(frame: CGRectMake(0, 0,
260, 50), buttonStyle: .Rect)
    private let gameCenterButton = HTPressableButton(frame:
CGRectMake(0, 0, 260, 50), buttonStyle: .Rect)
    private let titleLbl = UILabel()

    override func viewDidLoad() {
        super.viewDidLoad()
        setup()
        layoutView()
        style()
        render()
    }
}
```

The setup prepares the components and transitions for other view controllers:

```
// MARK: Setup
private extension MenuViewController{
    func setup(){
        playButton.addTarget(self, action: "onPlayPressed:",
forControlEvents: .TouchUpInside)
        view.addSubview(playButton)
        gameCenterButton.addTarget(self, action:
"onGameCenterPressed:", forControlEvents: .TouchUpInside)
        view.addSubview(gameCenterButton)
        view.addSubview(titleLbl)
    }

    @objc func onPlayPressed(sender: UIButton) {
        let vc = GameViewController()
        vc.modalTransitionStyle = .CrossDissolve
        presentViewController(vc, animated: true, completion: nil)
    }

    @objc func onGameCenterPressed(sender: UIButton) {
        print("onGameCenterPressed")
    }
}
```

The components are centered horizontally and placed on the screen to fill it in a uniform way:

```
// MARK: Layout
extension MenuViewController{
    func layoutView() {
        constrain(titleLbl) { view in
            view.top == view.superview!.top + 60
            view.centerX == view.superview!.centerX
        }
        constrain (playButton) { view in
            view.bottom == view.superview!.centerY - 60
            view.centerX == view.superview!.centerX
            view.height == 80
            view.width == view.superview!.width - 40
        }
        constrain (gameCenterButton) { view in
            view.bottom == view.superview!.centerY + 60
            view.centerX == view.superview!.centerX
```

```
            view.height == 80
            view.width == view.superview!.width - 40
        }
    }
}
```

The `style()` function uses the flat UI colors that `HTPressableButtons` brought with it:

```swift
// MARK: Style
private extension MenuViewController{
    func style(){
        playButton.buttonColor = UIColor.ht_grapeFruitColor()
        playButton.shadowColor = UIColor.ht_grapeFruitDarkColor()
        playButton.titleLabel?.font = UIFont.bitwiseFontOfSize(30)
        gameCenterButton.buttonColor = UIColor.ht_aquaColor()
        gameCenterButton.shadowColor = UIColor.ht_aquaDarkColor()
        gameCenterButton.titleLabel?.font = UIFont.
bitwiseFontOfSize(30)
        titleLbl.textColor = UIColor.ht_midnightBlueColor()
        titleLbl.font = UIFont.bitwiseFontOfSize(50)
    }
}
```

Finally, the render inserts text as the caption of the components:

```swift
// MARK: Render
private extension MenuViewController{
    func render(){
        playButton.setTitle("Play", forState: .Normal)
        gameCenterButton.setTitle("Game Center", forState: .Normal)
        titleLbl.text = "Cube Runner"
    }
}
```

Run the app. The menu has a fancy retro taste, as shown in this screenshot:

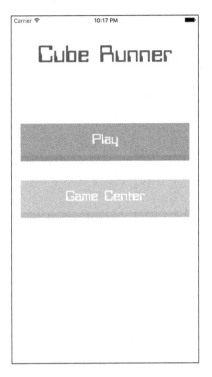

 You can find the code for this version at `https://github.com/gscalzo/Swift2ByExample/tree/6_CubeRunner_1_Menu`.

Flying in a 3D world

Let's now build a scene where we can fly by skipping colorful cubes.

Setting up a scene

By running the app built so far, you might have noticed that, when you select the **Play** button, the app crashes. This is because `GameViewController` expects to be set up by the Storyboard where the view is actually `SCNView`; because the view is a plain `UIView`, it crashes.

To fix this issue, we need to build a slim `GameViewController` from scratch:

```
import UIKit
import QuartzCore
import SceneKit

class GameViewController: UIViewController {
    private let scnView = SCNView()
    private var scene: SCNScene!

    override func viewDidLoad() {
        super.viewDidLoad()
        scnView.frame = view.bounds
        view.addSubview(scnView)

        createContents()
    }
    override func prefersStatusBarHidden() -> Bool {
        return true
    }
}
```

The `createContents()` function creates all the elements of the game, and it'll be handy to have it as a separate function when we need to implement the restart feature:

```
// MARK: content builder
private extension GameViewController {
    func createContents() {
        scene = SCNScene()
  scnView.showsStatistics = true
        scnView.scene = scene
    }
}
```

Now the game no longer crashes, but the game controller presents a plain white view.

The first node we create is the `camera` node. We need it to observe the scene. Because we'll need to apply an action to the camera, let's save it as an instance variable:

```
class GameViewController: UIViewController {
  //...
    private var cameraNode: SCNNode!
    //...
```

Then, in `createContents()`, we create and add it to the scene:

```
func createContents() {
    //...
    cameraNode = createCamera()
    scene.rootNode.addChildNode(cameraNode)
    scnView.scene = scene
}
```

The function that creates the node is really straightforward. It just enters the expected position and the correct rotation pointing it to the center:

```
func createCamera() -> SCNNode{
    let cameraNode = SCNNode()
    cameraNode.camera = SCNCamera()
    cameraNode.position = SCNVector3Make(0, 7, 20)
    cameraNode.rotation = SCNVector4Make(1, 0, 0, -atan2f(7,
20.0))
    return cameraNode
}
```

The code presented in `createCamera()` is basic trigonometry. The only unusual notation is the one for the rotation, where we first define the axis around which we want to rotate the object, x in this case. Then, we define the angle of rotation; a `tan2(y, x)` is the angle in radians between the positive x axis of a plane and the point given by the (x, y) coordinates on it. The value of this angle is positive for counterclockwise angles (the upper-half plane — that is, $y > 0$), and negative for clockwise angles (the lower-half plane — that is, $y < 0$).

If you recall the diagram of the coordinates you saw earlier, it should not be difficult to imagine where the camera is, but the following diagram should also help you visualize it:

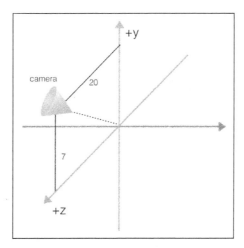

Adding a fighter

A powerful feature of SceneKit is that it can import a 3D scene model exported to COLLADA (`https://www.khronos.org/collada/`), which is a royalty-free XML format for interchange of 3D models.

This means that a graphic artist can create a scene using their usual tools, such as Maya or Blender. Then, a developer imports the file into the iOS app without any need for further processing phases.

Moreover, this format enables the use of models that can be bought or downloaded for free from a marketplace, such as `http://www.turbosquid.com`. Indeed, from this marketplace, we'll use a royalty-free jet fighter model that fits the mood of our game perfectly.

Looking at the project window, we notice that there is a folder called `art.scnassets`, where we must put the 3D assets. This folder is mapped to the filesystem of the project. This means that there is a directory with the same name in the filesystem of the project; by adding a file to that directory, the file is automatically added to the project:

Let's download the model and add it to the project.

 The model can be downloaded from `https://github.com/gscalzo/Swift2ByExample/blob/6_CubeRunner_2_PlainScene/CubeRunner/assets/model/eurofighter.dae.zip`.

By selecting **jetfighter**, as shown in the following screenshot, we can see what constitutes the scene:

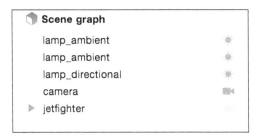

The scene components are different types of lights, a camera, and the jet fighter.

We can play with each of them, changing position, materials, and so on. The result will be rendered in the right-hand panel of the screen, like this:

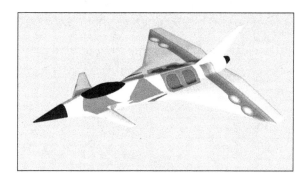

Now that we have added the model of the scene to the project, let's add it to the game.

First of all, instead of creating an empty SCNScene, we need to load the scene from the model:

```
func createContents() {
    scene = SCNScene(named: "art.scnassets/eurofighter.dae")
    scnView.showsStatistics = true
    //...
```

Then, we search for the jetfighter object, change its size to fit into our scene, and place it between the camera and the center:

```
    let jetfighterNode = createJetfighter()
    scnView.scene = scene
}

func createJetfighter() -> SCNNode{
    let jetfighterNode = scene!.rootNode.
childNodeWithName("jetfighter", recursively: true)!

    jetfighterNode.scale = SCNVector3(x: 0.03, y: 0.03, z: 0.03)
    jetfighterNode.position = SCNVector3(x: 0, y: 1.0, z: 13)
    jetfighterNode.rotation = SCNVector4(x: 0, y: 1, z: 0, w:
Float(M_PI))
    return jetfighterNode
}
```

Note that we must search for the node within the whole tree; this means we must use recursively equal to true. Otherwise, the node will be searched for only in the immediate children of the node.

We also need to rotate it to make it point in the same direction as the camera; to do this, we must rotate the jet fighter by 180 degrees about the *y* axis.

Upon running the app, we can finally see something like this:

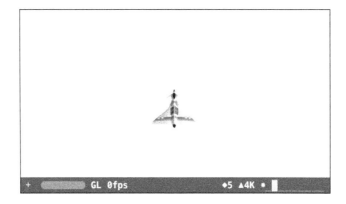

Texturing the world

A texture is an image that can be added to the surface of a 3D model, making it more realistic. We have already used a texture to add a skin to the jet fighter.

Now, we'll add textures to the sky and floor.

> The images for this purpose can be downloaded from
> https://github.com/gscalzo/Swift2ByExample/
> blob/6_CubeRunner_2_PlainScene/CubeRunner/
> assets/images/images.zip.

Add the icon and two images, ensuring you to set them as 2x in their respective panels.

First of all, we set the sky as the texture for the background of the scene:

```
func createContents() {
    scene = SCNScene(named: "art.scnassets/eurofighter.dae")
    scene.background.contents = UIImage(named: "sky")
    scnView.showsStatistics = true
    //...
```

Then, we add a special node, `SCNFloor`. It acts as the base of the scene:

```
func createContents() {
//...
let jetfighterNode = createJetfighter()
    scene.rootNode.addChildNode(createFloor())
    //...
```

The `createFloor()` function basically creates a floor and applies a texture on top of it:

```
func createFloor() -> SCNNode {
    let floor = SCNFloor()
    floor.firstMaterial!.diffuse.contents = UIImage(named: "moon")
    floor.firstMaterial!.diffuse.contentsTransform =
SCNMatrix4MakeScale(2, 2, 1)
    floor.reflectivity = 0
    return SCNNode(geometry: floor)
}
```

To apply the texture in the correct place and with the correct scale, we move it using a transformation of its coordinates:

```
floor.firstMaterial!.diffuse.contentsTransform.
```

Now the app has started looking like a real game:

Make it move

As we saw in the introduction, applying actions to nodes is really straightforward. So, making the jet fighter fly on the moon is just a matter of adding an action to make the camera, and the fighter itself, move toward the horizon:

```
func createContents() {
    //...
  let moveForwardAction = SCNAction.repeatActionForever(
        SCNAction.moveByX(0, y: 0, z: -100, duration: 7))
      cameraNode.runAction(moveForwardAction)
      jetfighterNode.runAction(moveForwardAction)
      //...
      scnView.scene = scene
```

Obviously, the speed can be tweaked and also selected, depending on the level of difficulty.

To pilot the jet, we'll use a motion detector so that the plane responds to the rotation of the iPhone by the player. The first thing we need to do is to import `CoreMotion`:

```
import SceneKit
import CoreMotion
```

We need to save the `motionManager` variable that we'll create in a property:

```
class GameViewController: UIViewController {
    //...
    private var motionManager : CMMotionManager?
```

In `createContents()`, we create the `coreManager` object, and set the closure that will be called at every change in position of the iPhone:

```
func createContents() {
    //...
    motionManager = CMMotionManager()
    motionManager?.deviceMotionUpdateInterval = 1.0 / 60.0
    motionManager?.
    startDeviceMotionUpdatesUsingReferenceFrame(
        CMAttitudeReferenceFrame.XArbitraryZVertical,
        toQueue: NSOperationQueue.mainQueue(),
        withHandler: { (motion: CMDeviceMotion?, error:
        NSError?) -> Void in
guard let motion = motion else {return}
            let roll = CGFloat(motion.attitude.roll)
```

```
let rotateCamera =
SCNAction.rotateByAngle(roll/20.0,
aroundAxis: SCNVector3(x: 0, y: 0, z: 1),
                          duration: 0.1)
self.cameraNode.runAction(rotateCamera)

let rotateJetfighter =
SCNAction.rotateByAngle(roll/10.0,
aroundAxis: SCNVector3(x: 0, y: 0, z: 1),
                          duration: 0.1)
jetfighterNode.runAction(rotateJetfighter)

let actionMove =
SCNAction.moveByX(roll, y: 0, z: 0, duration: 0.1)
self.cameraNode.runAction(actionMove)
jetfighterNode.runAction(actionMove)
})
//...
```

We are getting the value of a roll, which is the rotation around the vertical axis of the physical iPhone when it is in portrait mode. We use the retrieved value to move and rotate the camera and jet fighter accordingly.

Because we want to add more visual feedback to the game, we must have the jet rotating more than the camera, so we need to create two different actions for the rotation. One of them will have a greater angle of rotation than the other.

All of these values are calculated using trial and error and by running the app to take a look at how they change the animation. You can change these values to experiment and better understand how these things work.

 You can find the code for this version at https://github. com/gscalzo/Swift2ByExample/tree/6_CubeRunner_2_ PlainScene.

Adding cubes

In the original game, sections of random cubes are interleaved with sections of an elaborated path.

For simplicity, our version will present a smooth, curved path that repeats itself in a section of 200 steps.

To create the path, we need to calculate a cubic spline, which is a curve that connects several points smoothly.

To do this, we'll use the `SwiftCubicSpline` pod, which creates a curve like this one:

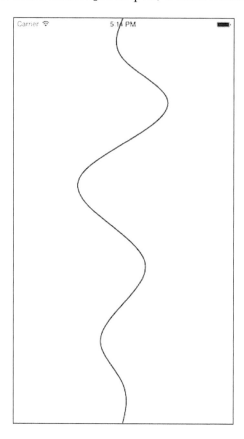

Because it's a pod, it is straightforward to use; just add this to the `Podfile`:

pod 'SwiftCubicSpline', '~> 0.1.0'

After running the `pod install` command, we are ready to use the cubic spline interpolation to create a path. Let's import the framework and create a constant spline:

```
import SwiftCubicSpline
class GameViewController: UIViewController {
    //...
    private let spline = CubicSpline(points: [
        CGPoint(x: 0.0, y: 0.5),
        CGPoint(x: 0.1, y: 0.5),
        CGPoint(x: 0.2, y: 0.8),
        CGPoint(x: 0.4, y: 0.2),
        CGPoint(x: 0.6, y: 0.6),
```

```
            CGPoint(x: 0.8, y: 0.4),
            CGPoint(x: 0.9, y: 0.5),
            CGPoint(x: 1.0, y: 0.5)
            ])
    //...
```

In `createContents()`, after creating `motionManager` object, we call the function to create the first section of the lane:

```
func createContents() {
//...
motionManager?.startDeviceMotionUpdatesUsingReferenceFrame(
            //...
    })
        buildTheLane()
        //...
```

This function just iterates for each step of the section and calls another function to create the actual piece of the lane:

```
func buildTheLane() {
    for var zPos = 0; zPos < 200; zPos += 3 {
        let z = cameraNode.position.z - Float(zPos)
        buildCubesAtPosition(z)
    }
}
```

The `buildCubesAtPosition()` function is a little more complicated:

```
func buildCubesAtPosition(zPos: Float){
    let laneWidth: CGFloat = 40

    let zPosInSection = zPos%200
    let normalizedZ = CGFloat(fabs(zPosInSection/200))
    let normalizedX = Float((spline.interpolate(normalizedZ) -
0.5)*laneWidth)

    let cubeAtLeft = cube()
    cubeAtLeft.position = SCNVector3(x: normalizedX - 6, y: 1.0,
z: zPos)
    scene.rootNode.addChildNode(cubeAtLeft)
    let cubeAtRight = cube()
    cubeAtRight.position = SCNVector3(x: normalizedX + 6, y: 1.0,
z: zPos)
    scene.rootNode.addChildNode(cubeAtRight)
}
```

First, we get the position inside the current section. Then, because the spline is in the 0 to 1 range, we normalize the position to be in the same range.

Given the normalized value, which means between 0 and 1, we calculate the *x* position in the spline and denormalize it again, which means adding a value to the center of the lane, to create a position that is within the coordinates of the screen.

The position we just calculated is central with respect to the screen, but we need two values for each of the cubes that creates the lane. Given the width of the lane of 12 steps, we set the cubes at each side:

```
func cube(size: CGFloat = 2.0) -> SCNNode {
    let cube = SCNBox(width: size, height: size, length: size,
chamferRadius: 0)
    let cubeNode = SCNNode(geometry: cube)

    cube.firstMaterial!.diffuse.contents = {
        switch arc4random_uniform(4) {
        case 0:
            return UIColor.ht_belizeHoleColor()
        case 1:
            return UIColor.ht_wisteriaColor()
        case 2:
            return UIColor.ht_midnightBlueColor()
        default:
            return UIColor.ht_pomegranateColor()
        }
    }()

    return cubeNode
}
```

The `cube()` function uses a primitive function of SceneKit to create a cube and set a random color for its face. Notice how we created an anonymous function and then called it in place in order to wrap the logic of selecting a random color.

The game is now pretty cool:

However, we have just created the first section; we need to create an infinite lane. To do this, we set a timer that creates a piece of lane every 1/5th of a second.

As we might need to invalidate the timer, we create a property for it:

```
class GameViewController: UIViewController {
  //...
    private var laneTimer: NSTimer!
```

Then, we set up the timer in the createContents() function:

```
    func createContents() {
//...
buildTheLane()
        laneTimer = NSTimer.scheduledTimerWithTimeInterval(0.2,
target: self,
        selector: "laneTimerFired", userInfo: nil, repeats: true)
```

Since the section is 200 steps long, we need to build a piece of lane that's 200 steps in front of the camera in the callback that's called when the timer fires:

```
@objc func laneTimerFired(){
    buildCubesAtPosition(cameraNode.position.z-200)
}
```

If you run the app now, you will find that the lane is endless, and it allows the player to race for a longer run.

However, there's still a small glitch that detracts from our game's credibility: we can see the cubes of the lane being built, popping up on the horizon. To fix this issue, we use a nice feature of SceneKit: long-distance fog. In our case, it will be black in order to simulate the night:

```
    func createContents() {
//...
laneTimer = NSTimer.scheduledTimerWithTimeInterval(0.2, target: self,
        selector: "laneTimerFired", userInfo: nil, repeats: true)
    scene!.fogStartDistance = 30
    scene!.fogEndDistance = 90
    scene!.fogColor = UIColor.blackColor()
```

By running the app now, we can see a nice night-like effect on the horizon, which seems as if the cubes appear from the darker side of the moon, like this:

Adding more obstacles

Although we haven't completed the game yet notably, collision detection is missing, we can already see that the game is too easy to play. One way to increase the difficulty of the path is to add a few cubes inside the path:

```
func buildCubesAtPosition(zPos: Float){
    //...
    if arc4random_uniform(5) < 1 {
        let centralCube = cube(size: 1.0)
        scene.rootNode.addChildNode(centralCube)
        let xOffset = arc4random_uniform(10)
        centralCube.position = SCNVector3(x: normalizedX +
Float(xOffset) - 5.0, y: 1.0, z: zPos)
    }
}
```

This code is added to the function that is responsible for building the lane when a certain z position is given. Using `arc4random_uniform(5)`, there is a one out of five probability of placing a small cube in every piece of the lane. In this way, the game can never be exactly the same as it was earlier.

The position of the cube inside the lane is random, as well. Although collision detection is still missing, the game is already fun to play:

You can find the code for this version at `https://github.com/gscalzo/Swift2ByExample/tree/6_CubeRunner_3_Cubes`.

Now that the way to add obstacles has been implemented, a good challenge for you would be to add more and different obstacles, for example, spheres of different radii or adding collected objects that would add points to the score. The sky is the limit.

Adding a few touches

Although a few things are still missing, either some parts of them are straightforward or we already implemented them in the previous chapters when we were building *Flappy Swift*.

The score

The score falls under the *straightforward* category, and it is worth implement it right now so that we can finish adding all the visual elements to the screen.

The goal of the game is for the player to keep going as long as they can without colliding with a cube. So, to implement the score, we just need to schedule a timer that fires every second, increasing the score. First of all, we need to add elements as properties:

```
class GameViewController: UIViewController {
    //...
    private var laneTimer: NSTimer!
    private let scoreLbl = UILabel()
    private var scoreTimer: NSTimer!
    private var score = 0
```

Then, we set up the score, calling `setupScore()` in `createContents()`:

```
    func createContents() {
//...
        scene!.fogColor = UIColor.blackColor()
        setupScore()
        //...
    }
```

The `setupScore()` function adds the label to the view hierarchy and sets the correct style:

```
func setupScore(){
    scnView.addSubview(scoreLbl)
    scoreLbl.frame.origin.x = 0
    scoreLbl.frame.origin.y = 0
    scoreLbl.frame.size.height = 50
    scoreLbl.frame.size.width = 200
    scoreLbl.font = UIFont.bitwiseFontOfSize(30)
    scoreLbl.textColor = UIColor.whiteColor()
    score = 0
    scoreLbl.text = "\(score)"
    scoreTimer = NSTimer.scheduledTimerWithTimeInterval(1, target:
self, selector: "scoreTimerFired", userInfo: nil, repeats: true)
}
```

Finally, the closure bound to `scoreTimer` increases the score and sets the value in the label:

```
@objc func scoreTimerFired(){
    score++
    scoreLbl.text = "\(score)"
}
```

The game now presents a fancy score in the top-left corner, with a juicy retro font:

Let's add music

We've already implemented music and we can reuse the `MusicPlayer` class we created for *Flappy Swift*:

```
import Foundation
import AVFoundation

enum MusicPlayerError: ErrorType {
    case ResourceNotFound
}

class MusicPlayer {
    private var player: AVAudioPlayer? = nil

    init(filename: String, type: String) throws {
        if let resource = NSBundle.mainBundle().
pathForResource(filename, ofType: type) {
            let url = NSURL(fileURLWithPath: resource)
            player = try AVAudioPlayer(contentsOfURL: url)
            player?.numberOfLoops = -1
            player?.prepareToPlay()
        } else {
            throw MusicPlayerError.ResourceNotFound
        }
    }

    func play() {
        player?.play()
    }
    func stop() {
        player?.stop()
    }
}
```

For the soundtrack, we again rely on Kevin MacLeod and his website at `http://incompetech.com`. We use a calm space song called Space 1990-B.

 The soundtrack file can be downloaded from `https://github.com/gscalzo/Swift2ByExample/blob/6_CubeRunner_3_Cubes/CubeRunner/assets/music/Space%201990-B.mp3`.

Let's add the `musicPlayer` class as a property:

```
class GameViewController: UIViewController {
    //...
    private var musicPlayer: MusicPlayer?
    //...
```

As usual, the player is instantiated during the loading of the view:

```
    //...
    override func viewDidLoad() {
        super.viewDidLoad()
        do {
            musicPlayer = try MusicPlayer(filename: "Space 1990-B",
type: "mp3")
            musicPlayer!.play()
        } catch {
            print("Error playing soundtrack")
        }
        //...
    }
```

Then, implement `viewWillAppear()` and `viewDidDisappear()` to start and stop the music respectively:

```
    override func viewWillAppear(animated: Bool) {
        super.viewWillAppear(animated)
        musicPlayer?.play()
    }
    override func viewDidDisappear(animated: Bool) {
        super.viewDidDisappear(animated)
        musicPlayer?.stop()
    }
```

That's it! As already mentioned, although it's unfinished, the game still looks complete and fun.

 You can find the code for this version at https://github. com/gscalzo/Swift2ByExample/tree/6_CubeRunner_4_ MusicScore.

Summary

The aim of this chapter was to introduce SceneKit, demystifying the idea that 3D game development is something that only professional game developers can do. We showed you how Playground can help you learn about a new library, for example, SceneKit. This allows you to build and modify nodes when they are shown in the Playground console.

Then, we began implementing a complete 3D game. Although it is not complete yet, we have almost created a prototype—a game that, in real life, can be played and also shared with other players in order to gather feedback and steer its development in the correct direction.

In the following chapter, we'll carry on with the development of this game by adding missing features, notably one feature that could make the game look gorgeous, that is, explosions!

9
Completing Cube Runner

In the previous chapter, we implemented most of the features of Cube Runner. In this chapter, we will finish implementing the game.

The most notable feature that is missing is collision detection, so we'll start with that in this chapter. As we have already said, when we built Flappy Swift, Game Center support made the game more interesting; thus, we'll add that to Cube Runner as well.

Let's get started with all of this, and much more, in this chapter.

Creating a real game

The first thing we must implement to make this a real game is collision detection. Then, we'll add an end to the game; otherwise, it will be really boring. Finally, a few extra touches will make the game more appealing.

Detecting collisions

Collision detection in SceneKit is implemented as it is in SpriteKit. For every node that can collide, we must create a physics body and attach it to the node, setting a unique identifier for that body. Finally, a `contact` delegate will receive a call when a collision is detected.

First of all, we define an enumeration to list all the possible types of bodies, of which there are only two in our case:

```
enum BodyType : Int {
    case jetfighter = 1
    case cube = 2
}
```

In `createJetfighter()`, we create a parallelepiped to act as a physics body for the jet fighter because employing the actual model we used for rendering is a waste of calculation resources. For the purpose of detecting a collision, a rough shape is enough:

```
func createJetfighter() -> SCNNode{
    //...
    let jetfighterBodyNode = SCNNode(geometry:
    SCNBox(width: 0.3, height: 0.2, length: 1, chamferRadius: 0))
    jetfighterNode.physicsBody = SCNPhysicsBody(type: .Kinematic,
    shape:
    SCNPhysicsShape(node: jetfighterBodyNode, options: nil))
    jetfighterNode.physicsBody!.categoryBitMask =
    BodyType.jetfighter.rawValue
    jetfighterNode.physicsBody!.contactTestBitMask =
    BodyType.cube.rawValue

    return jetfighterNode
}
```

The size of the box was calculated, making the box visible and trying different values until it doesn't have the same size as the jet.

We create the aforementioned parallelepiped, which is of the jetfighter type, as by the category bitmask, and it collides with a cube, as by the contact bitmask.

We can do something similar for cubes:

```
func cube(size: CGFloat = 2.0) -> SCNNode {
    //...
    let cubeNode = SCNNode(geometry: cube)
    cubeNode.physicsBody = SCNPhysicsBody(type: .Static, shape:
    SCNPhysicsShape(node: cubeNode, options: nil))
    cubeNode.physicsBody!.categoryBitMask = BodyType.cube.rawValue
    cubeNode.physicsBody!.contactTestBitMask =
    BodyType.jetfighter.rawValue
    //...
}
```

Although the code is the same, the category and contact bitmasks are the other way round. Finally, we must assign the `GameViewController` class as `contactDelegate`:

```
func createContents() {
    scene = SCNScene(named: "art.scnassets/eurofighter.dae")
    scene.physicsWorld.contactDelegate = self
    //...
```

Obviously, we must implement that protocol. The way we do this is similar to the method we used for Flappy Swift:

```
extension GameViewController: SCNPhysicsContactDelegate{
    func physicsWorld(world: SCNPhysicsWorld,
        didBeginContact contact: SCNPhysicsContact){
            let contactMask = contact.nodeA.physicsBody!.
categoryBitMask | contact.nodeB.physicsBody!.categoryBitMask
            switch (contactMask) {
            case BodyType.jetfighter.rawValue |
            BodyType.cube.rawValue:
                println("Contact!")
            default:
                return
            }

        }
}
```

Run the app to verify that everything works as expected, as shown here:

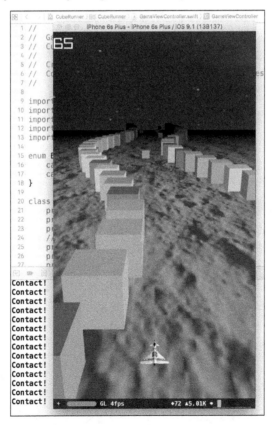

You can view the code of this version here: `https://github.com/` `gscalzo/Swift2ByExample/tree/6_CubeRunner_5_Collisions`.

Game over!

When the jet fighter touches a cube, we must do a few things to stop everything from moving; these include invalidating the timers, removing all node disabling `CoreMotion` manager, and so on.

This means that all of these objects must be accessible through the `delegate` method. To do this, we will put `jetfighterNode` as an instance variable, but to reduce the quantity of the code, we must change this. We create a property to hold the function that will be called in the `delegate` method. This function wraps the value of `jetfighterNode` so that we don't need to transform it into an `instance` variable.

First of all, we define the property:

```
class GameViewController: UIViewController {
    //...
    private var gameOver: () -> Void = {}
```

The function will be a function without any arguments and return values. Then, in `createContents()`, we assign the function's body:

```
func createContents() {
    //...
    setupScore()
    gameOver = { [unowned self] in
        self.laneTimer.invalidate()
        self.scoreTimer.invalidate()
        self.scene.physicsWorld.contactDelegate = nil
        self.cameraNode.removeAllActions()
        jetfighterNode.removeAllActions()
        self.motionManager?.stopDeviceMotionUpdates()
    }
```

As you can see, the body of the function is nothing more than the statements meant to stop everything.

Finally, we call the function after the `contact` delegate:

```
func physicsWorld(world: SCNPhysicsWorld,
    didBeginContact contact: SCNPhysicsContact){
        //..
        case BodyType.jetfighter.rawValue |
        BodyType.cube.rawValue:
        println("Contact!")
        gameOver()
```

By running the app, we see that the game stops when the jet fighter touches a cube — precisely what we were expecting. However, the only way to play again is by killing and restarting the app, which is not exactly convenient.

We need to implement a better way of restarting the game. To do that, we'll use the `SIAlertView` pod to ask the player whether they want to play again or whether they want to go back to the **Menu** view.

Of course, using a pod for **Alert Box** could be viewed as over-engineering, on the grounds that the iOS has great native alert boxes. However, `SIAlertView` is really good looking and its style suits the game; again, a good exercise for you could be replacing the `SIAlertView` pod with the native one.

First, we update the `Podfile` by adding this pod:

pod 'SIAlertView', '~> 1.3'

After installing the pods with `pod install`, we import the framework:

```
//...
import SwiftCubicSpline
import SIAlertView
```

We can now create a function to present the alert dialog:

```
func askToPlayAgain(#onPlayAgainPressed: () -> Void,
    onCancelPressed: () -> Void) {
        let alertView = SIAlertView(title: "Ouch!!", andMessage:
"Congratulations! Your score is \(score). Play again?")

        alertView.addButtonWithTitle("OK", type: .Default) { _ in
onPlayAgainPressed() }
        alertView.addButtonWithTitle("Cancel", type: .Default) { _ in
onCancelPressed() }
        alertView.show()
}
```

As you can see, depending on which button is pressed one of the functions passed as parameters is called. The functions are defined in the gameOver() function:

```
gameOver = { [unowned self] in
    //...
    self.motionManager?.stopDeviceMotionUpdates()
    self.askToPlayAgain(onPlayAgainPressed: {
        self.createContents()
        return
    },
    onCancelPressed: {
        self.dismissViewControllerAnimated(true, completion: nil)
        return
    })
}
```

The first function calls the createContents() function to restart the game, and now it is clear that grouping together the creation statements in a new function.

The second function dismisses the view controller to go back to the MenuViewController class. If we run the app now, it seems as if everything works as expected, but the pop-up is slightly delayed.

By putting a breakpoint in the body of the gameOver() function and running the debugger, we notice that the function is not called in the main thread but in the rendering thread rather than in the main thread, as shown in this screenshot:

The problem is that every change to the UI must be done in the main thread; otherwise, unexpected things — even crashes — can happen. What a rookie mistake!

This issue is easy to fix; create an execInMainThread convenience function to run a closure in the main thread:

```
func execInMainThread(closure:()->()) {
    dispatch_async(dispatch_get_main_queue(),closure)
}
```

In the `gameOver()` function, we wrap the call to `SIAlertView` using the previous function:

```
gameOver = { [unowned self] in
    //...
    self.motionManager?.stopDeviceMotionUpdates()
    execInMainThread(){
        self.askToPlayAgain(onPlayAgainPressed: {
            self.createContents()
        },
        onCancelPressed: {
            self.dismissViewControllerAnimated(true, completion:
            nil)
        })
    }
}
```

Finally, everything works as expected.

Adding the juice

As mentioned in the previous chapters, adding a few touches can make a game much more appealing.

Because the game is controlled using the motion of an iPhone, it is always in the hands of the player, so it will be nice to receive tactile feedback when the jet fighter crashes into a cube.

This can be easily implemented using vibrations, which can be triggered programmatically using an `AudioToolbox` service. Let's import the framework:

```
//...
import SIAlertView
import AudioToolbox.AudioServices
```

Then, add a function call to `gameOver()`:

```
gameOver = { [unowned self] in
    //...
    self.motionManager?.stopDeviceMotionUpdates()
    AudioServicesPlayAlertSound
    (SystemSoundID(kSystemSoundID_Vibrate))
```

A nice feature provided by `SceneKit` is a particle engine, which allows us to use a large number of small sprites to simulate certain fuzzy phenomena, such as fire, smoke, explosions, and so on.

First of all, let's add the `FireParticles.scnp` particle file and the `spark.png` sprite image to the project. To create or change the particle file, the particle console in Xcode is everything you need.

 You can find the resources at `https://github.com/gscalzo/Swift2ByExample/tree/6_CubeRunner_6_PlayableGame/CubeRunner/assets/explosion`.

Upon selecting the particle file and opening it with Xcode, you will notice that you can tweak its value, and Xcode presents the result in a nice console view, like this:

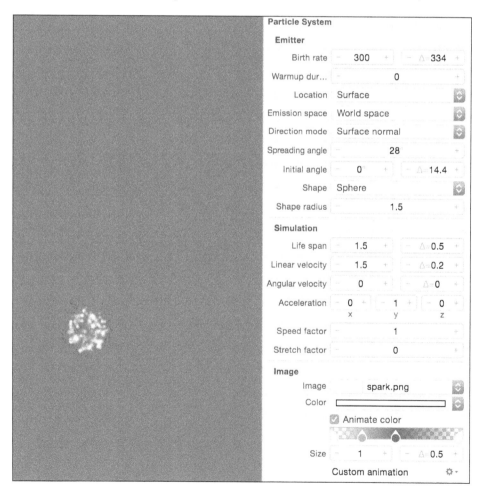

The idea is to make both the jet fighter and the cube explode when the former hits the latter. Let's create a function to add a particle system to a node:

```
func explodeNode(node: SCNNode){
    let fire = SCNParticleSystem(named: "FireParticles",
    inDirectory: nil)
    fire.emitterShape = node.geometry
    node.addParticleSystem(fire)
}
```

As you can see, adding a particle system is really straightforward. However, we need to change the gameOver() signature to pass the two nodes:

```
class GameViewController: UIViewController {
    //...
    private var gameOver: (SCNNode, SCNNode) -> Void = {_,_ in}
```

Then, we change the body of gameOver():

```
gameOver = { [unowned self] nodeA, nodeB in
    //...
    self.cameraNode.removeAllActions()
    jetfighterNode.removeAllActions()
    self.explodeNode(nodeA)
    self.explodeNode(nodeB)
    //...
}
```

Finally, we change the call of the gameOver() function:

```
func physicsWorld(world: SCNPhysicsWorld,
didBeginContact contact: SCNPhysicsContact){
    //..
    case BodyType.jetfighter.rawValue |
    BodyType.cube.rawValue:
    gameOver(contact.nodeA, contact.nodeB)
```

To give the player a chance to see the jet fighter and the cube burning before being covered by the pop-up, we delay the appearance of the pop-up. From previous apps, we copy execAfter():

```
func execAfter(delay:Double, closure:()->()) {
    dispatch_after(
    dispatch_time(
    DISPATCH_TIME_NOW,
    Int64(delay * Double(NSEC_PER_SEC))),
    dispatch_get_main_queue(), closure)
}
```

Then, we replace the execInMainThreat() call in gameOver() to execAfter()
using 1 second as the delay:

```
gameOver = { [unowned self] nodeA, nodeB in
        self.laneTimer.invalidate()
        //...
        AudioServicesPlayAlertSound(
        SystemSoundID(kSystemSoundID_Vibrate))
        execAfter(1){
            self.askToPlayAgain(onPlayAgainPressed: {
```

Nice, isn't it?

 You can find the code for this version at https://github.
com/gscalzo/Swift2ByExample/tree/6_CubeRunner_6_
PlayableGame.

Game Center

The last thing that is missing is integration with Game Center. We'll use the code we wrote for *Flappy Swift* for this purpose.

You might remember that there is a tedious series of operations to be done on the Apple backend servers. To avoid wasting pages by duplicating information, the procedure described in *Chapter 6, Flappy Swift*, can be referred to.

After setting up the leaderboard and the test user, we can copy the `GameCenter` class we created for *Flappy Swift*:

```
import GameKit
import SIAlertView

class GameCenter: NSObject {
    private var gameCenterEnabled = false
    private var leaderboardIdentifier = ""

    func authenticateLocalPlayer() {
        let localPlayer = GKLocalPlayer.localPlayer()
        localPlayer.authenticateHandler = { (viewController, error) in
            if let vc = viewController {
                let topViewController = UIApplication.
sharedApplication().delegate!.window!!.rootViewController
                topViewController?.presentViewController(vc, animated:
true, completion: nil)
            } else if localPlayer.authenticated {
                self.gameCenterEnabled = true
                localPlayer.
loadDefaultLeaderboardIdentifierWithCompletionHandler({
(leaderboardIdentifier, error) -> Void in
                    self.leaderboardIdentifier =
leaderboardIdentifier!
                })
            }
        }
    }

    func reportScore(score: Int){
        if !gameCenterEnabled {
            return
        }
```

```
        let gkScore = GKScore(leaderboardIdentifier:
leaderboardIdentifier)
        gkScore.value = Int64(score)

        GKScore.reportScores([gkScore], withCompletionHandler: nil)
    }


    func showLeaderboard() {
        if !gameCenterEnabled {
            let alertView = SIAlertView(title: "Game Center
Unavailable", andMessage: "Player is not signed in")

            alertView.addButtonWithTitle("OK", type: .Default)
            { _ in}
            alertView.show()
            return
        }


        let gcViewController = GKGameCenterViewController()

        gcViewController.gameCenterDelegate = self
        gcViewController.viewState = .Leaderboards
        gcViewController.leaderboardIdentifier = leaderboardIdentifier

        let topViewController = UIApplication.sharedApplication().
delegate!.window!!.rootViewController
        topViewController?.presentViewController(gcViewController,
animated: true, completion: nil)
    }
}

extension GameCenter: GKGameCenterControllerDelegate {
    func gameCenterViewControllerDidFinish(gameCenterViewController:
GKGameCenterViewController){
        gameCenterViewController.dismissViewControllerAnimated(true,
completion: nil)
    }
}
```

Just a reminder of what this class is for: `GameCenter` is a wrapper class around the Game Center functionalities. It provides three features:

- **Authentication**: Through the `authenticateLocalPlayer()` function, the class permits automatic logon or shows a form with a username and a password
- **Reporting score**: The `reportScore()` function wraps the call to the Game Center server to send the current score
- **Showing the leaderboard**: The `showLeaderboard()` function opens a new view with the leaderboard or fails with an alert dialog if the player is not logged in

Once again, we set up the `GameCenter` class in the `MenuViewController` class:

```
class MenuViewController: UIViewController {
    //...
    private let gameCenter = GameCenter()
    override func viewDidLoad() {
        super.viewDidLoad()
        gameCenter.authenticateLocalPlayer()
        //...
```

Then, we call `showLeaderboard()` in the callback of the Game Center button:

```
@objc func onGameCenterPressed(sender: UIButton) {
    println("onGameCenterPressed")
    gameCenter.showLeaderboard()
}
```

Finally, we need to pass the instance of GameCenter to the GameViewController class:

```
@objc func onPlayPressed(sender: UIButton) {
    let vc = GameViewController()
    vc.gameCenter = gameCenter
    //...
}
```

In this class, we add a property to hold the instance of the `GameCenter` class:

```
class GameViewController: UIViewController {
    //...
    private var gameOver: (SCNNode, SCNNode) -> Void = {_,_ in}
    var gameCenter: GameCenter?
```

The score, which is in the body of gameOver(), is sent to the server when the game ends:

```
gameOver = { [unowned self] nodeA, nodeB in
    //...
    self.motionManager?.stopDeviceMotionUpdates()
    if let gameCenter = self.gameCenter{
        gameCenter.reportScore(self.score)
    }
    //...
```

Finally, we have completed the game and are ready to challenge our friends to see who can make the longest run between the cubes.

You can find the code for this version at https://github.com/gscalzo/Swift2ByExample/tree/6_CubeRunner_7_GameCenter.

Summary

This chapter was shorter than most of the other chapters in this book. Nevertheless, we finished building the *Cube Runner* game by adding a proper game-over features, explosions, and a vibration in the case of a crash with a cube. We set up Game Center to collect the scores.

Although the game is pretty entertaining, there's always room for improvement; for example, different lanes could easily be added, or you could use different building functions for every section. You might even want to change the texture and shape of the cube to create planets. A bullet shooting from the jet could be added to wipe out small cubes inside the lanes.

However, adding these enhancements could be challenging. Nevertheless, by now you must have a good amount of knowledge of Swift and its frameworks well enough to start developing iOS apps in Swift on your own.

10

ASAP – an E-commerce App in Swift

In this book, I've presented different kinds of apps such as utilities, games, and so on, trying to showcase how to program real applications for iOS.

However, I admit that almost 80 percent of the apps are basically applications that receive JSON data from a server, present them in a tabular or grid, get events from a user, and send back JSON to the server. If you learn how to build a skeleton of an app of this kind, in a flexible and modular way, you will be ready to be a professional iOS developer.

In the two final chapters of this book, we'll implement an app of this kind, and thanks to the fact that Swift is now open source, we'll implement a server that we'll feed this app into as well.

The app is...

Mobile e-commerce is a sector that's greatly expanding, and you will want to become the new Amazon of shoes and clothing delivery. By doing this, you will be ready to start a new company called *ASAP*.

In this frenzied age, we know that a customer doesn't have time to spend in several different screens, so our app aims to simplify things by having only three screens: a login and registration, which will appear only the first time, a grid to show the products, and a table to present the cart that's ready for checkout.

The first requirement: login and registration

Other e-commerce apps probably need a lot of data from their customers, such as their e-mail ID, address, phone number, and so on, but in *ASAP*, we strive for simplicity and an e-mail address is more than enough.

Therefore, the first screen should only present a text field with a **Sign Up** button, which is enabled only when a valid e-mail ID is inserted into the text field:

Also, because registration is needed only when we run the app for the first time, this screen must be presented only if the customer hasn't logged into the app.

The second requirement: the products grid

This is the most important screen of the app where all the products are presented.

The view is a simple two-column grid, where each cell shows an image, a description, name, and the price of the product:

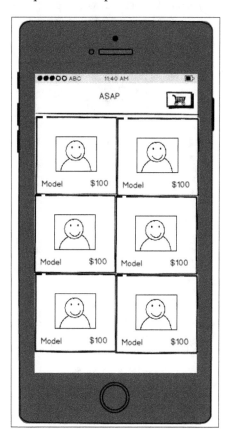

When the user taps on a cell, a specific product is added to the cart and a badge number is added along with a button and cart in the top-right corner of the screen.

If you tap on the same cell again, the product is removed from the cart and the badge decreases.

The cart button drives the app to the open cart.

The third requirement: the open cart

This screen allows the customer to see the content of the cart and buy the products.

The title of the screen shows the number of products.

When you slide a cell to the left, a **Delete** button appears, and if it's tapped, the product is removed from the cart. Therefore, the total amount and the grid status must change also accordingly.

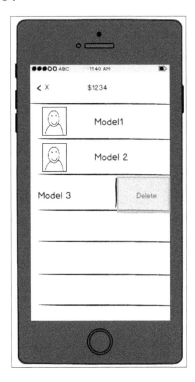

The skeleton app and register screen

Let's start the implementation of the app and let's begin with the **Register** screen.

The skeleton app

As usual, we create a new **Single View** application app, called *ASAP*, which, for the sake of simplicity, will be a portrait-only app:

1. Let's create a **Register** group where we'll add a `RegisterViewController` class and a Storyboard called `Register.storyboard`.

2. Add a `UIViewController` class to the scene, and define it as the `RegisterViewController` class:

3. To keep the instantiation simple, set it as the initial **View Controller** in the Storyboard:

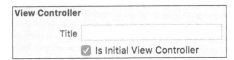

4. Moving to the class, we define a `factory` method to instantiate `RegisterViewController`:

```
import UIKit

class RegisterViewController: UIViewController {

    static func instantiate() -> RegisterViewController {
        return UIStoryboard(name: "Register",
        bundle: nil).instantiateInitialViewController()
        as! RegisterViewController
    }
}
```

This is a convenient way to set all the required information in order to create **View Controller** in the controller itself.

In `Appdelegate`, we instantiate the **View Controller** and set it as `rootViewController`:

```
import UIKit

@UIApplicationMain
class AppDelegate: UIResponder, UIApplicationDelegate {
    var window: UIWindow?
```

```
func application(application: UIApplication,
didFinishLaunchingWithOptions launchOptions:
[NSObject: AnyObject]?) -> Bool {
    self.window = UIWindow(frame:
    UIScreen.mainScreen().bounds)

    let initialViewController: UIViewController =
    RegisterViewController.instantiate()

    self.window?.rootViewController = initialViewController
    self.window?.makeKeyAndVisible()

    return true
}
}
```

Before moving on, let's add `Podfile` with some required libraries:

```
use_frameworks!
inhibit_all_warnings!

target 'ASAP' do
    pod 'SwiftyJSON', '~> 2.3.0'
    pod 'SDWebImage', '~> 3.7.3'
    pod 'FontAwesomeKit', :git =>
    'https://github.com/gscalzo/FontAwesomeKit'
    pod 'BBBadgeBarButtonItem', '~> 1.2'
    pod 'LatoFont', :git =>
    "https://github.com/gscalzo/LatoFont.git"
end
```

After using the `pod install` command, we'll add components to the Storyboard.

We'll use a really useful feature that Apple has added to iOS 9 called `UIStackView`.

`UIStackView` is a container of views, which can be stacked horizontally or vertically, defining their distribution, proportions, spacing and so on, without the need to add Auto Layout constraints to define how to position those views in the parent view.

Since `UIStackView` is lighter than the constraints, the performance is better; also, it's simpler to define the layout.

So, we add three components, a label, text field, and a button, as shown in the following screenshot:

Then, we select all the components:

After this, we click on the first new button in the Storyboard action bar:

This creates `UIStackView` with the following selected components:

It's clear that we need to set the missing constraints in order to make it pretty.

Let's begin defining the properties of **Stack View**.

Basically, we just set the spacing between the views, and we set the distribution as **Fill Equally**, which means that all the components will be of the same height:

Then, we set the size of the button:

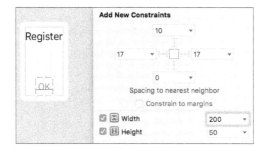

The text field must as the same size as the container so that we can set the leading and trailing:

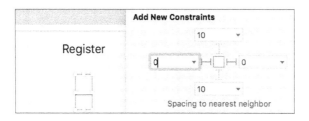

Finally, we set **Stack View** to be centered horizontally and at one quarter from the top of the screen:

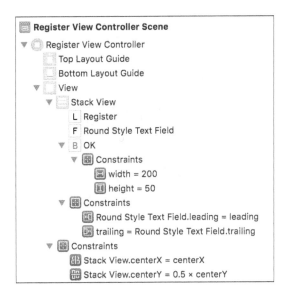

We customize the appearance a bit, making sure that the text field has a border and is without rounded corners, and then we set the e-mail **Keyboard Type**:

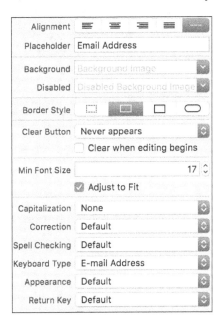

The previous screenshot presents the value to be changed in order to create a form similar to what is shown in this screenshot:

Let's now create outlets to connect the components:

```
import UIKit
import LatoFont

class RegisterViewController: UIViewController {
    @IBOutlet var okButton: UIButton! {
        didSet {
            okButton.enabled = false
            okButton.titleLabel?.font = UIFont.latoFontOfSize(18)
        }
    }

    @IBOutlet var emailTextField: UITextField! {
        didSet {
            emailTextField.becomeFirstResponder()
            emailTextField.font = UIFont.latoFontOfSize(18)
        }
    }
}
```

We use this nice pattern to set the properties of the outlets once they are set. In this way, the customization code is similar to the actual component.

Let's add the actions for the text field changes and button tap:

```
@IBAction func emailTextFieldChanged(sender: UITextField) {
    guard let text = sender.text else {
        return
    }
    okButton.enabled = text.isValidEmail()
}
```

```
@IBAction func signinTapped(sender: UIButton) {
    guard let text = emailTextField.text else {
        return
    }

}
```

Don't forget to connect them in the Storyboard, as shown in the following screenshots:

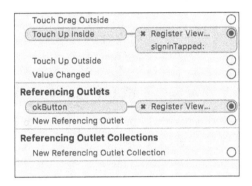

As you can see, we enable the **OK** button only if the text inside the text field is a valid e-mail address.

If you try implementing this code, you'll find that it is not a valid function of a string, so we need to create an extension:

```
extension String {
    func isValidEmail() -> Bool {
        let emailRegEx = "^[a-zA-Z0-9.!#$%&'*+/=?^_`{|}~-]+@
        [a-zA-Z0-9](?:[a-zA-Z0-9-]{0,61}[a-zA-Z0-9])?(?:\\.
        [a-zA-Z0-9](?:[a-zA-Z0-9-]{0,61}[a-zA-Z0-9])?)*$"

        let emailTest = NSPredicate(format:"SELF MATCHES %@",
        emailRegEx)
        return emailTest.evaluateWithObject(self)
    }
}
```

Now, we'll create a store to save the e-mail that's been inserted.

Although the correct destination should be the keychain, for simplicity's sake, we save the information in NSUserDefaults:

```
import Foundation

typealias Email = String

class UserStore {
    private struct Constants {
        static let emailKey = "emailKey"
    }

    func setUserEmail(email: Email) {
        NSUserDefaults.standardUserDefaults().setObject(email,
        forKey: Constants.emailKey)
    }

    func userEmail() -> Email? {
        return NSUserDefaults
            .standardUserDefaults()
            .objectForKey(Constants.emailKey) as? Email
    }

    func isUserSignedIn() -> Bool {
        return userEmail() != nil
    }
}
```

This store will be unique; hence, we create its instance in `AppDelegate` so that it can be easily accessed anywhere:

```
class AppDelegate: UIResponder, UIApplicationDelegate {

    var window: UIWindow?
    class func appdelegate() -> AppDelegate {
        return UIApplication.sharedApplication().delegate as!
        AppDelegate
    }

    var userStore = UserStore()
```

Now, in the `action` method of the **OK** button, we save the e-mail address:

```
@IBAction func signinTapped(sender: UIButton) {
    guard let text = emailTextField.text else {
        return
    }

    AppDelegate.appdelegate().userStore.setUserEmail(text)

    performSegueWithIdentifier("ShowEcommerceScene", sender:
    self)
}
```

As you can see, after saving the e-mail, we'll go to another view controller that has not been built yet. Let's implement the `EcommerceView` controller as usual by creating an `Ecommerce` group containing a `EcommerceViewController` class and `Ecommerce.storyboard`:

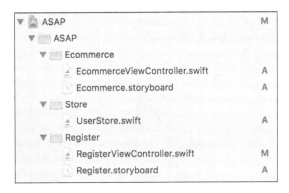

To move from one Storyboard to another, we use a nice feature by Xcode 7: the Storyboard reference. In the previous versions of Xcode, all the view controllers that are connected together using segues were in the same Storyboard, making a mess of the entire thing and really difficult to handle when working in a team. Using a Storyboard reference is now possible because it splits the view controllers into different Storyboards by preserving the possibility of connecting them using segues through the Storyboard references.

It's a kind of *label* that refers to a view controller in another storyboard:

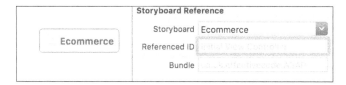

Next, we'll create a segue from the view controller to this reference, setting the identifier as ShowEcommerceScene:

The last feature that's missing is to go straight to the e-commerce screen if the user is already logged in when we launch the app.

For this, we can use UserStore in AppDelegate to check the user state and decide where to go on the first screen:

```
    func application(application: UIApplication,
didFinishLaunchingWithOptions launchOptions: [NSObject: AnyObject]?)
-> Bool {
        self.window = UIWindow(frame: UIScreen.mainScreen().bounds)

        UINavigationBar.appearance().titleTextAttributes =
[NSFontAttributeName : UIFont.latoBoldFontOfSize(18)]
```

```
let initialViewController: UIViewController

if !AppDelegate.appdelegate().userStore.isUserSignedIn() {
    initialViewController = RegisterViewController.
instantiate()
} else {
    initialViewController = EcommerceViewController.
instantiate()
}
```

To do this, we must define the `instantiate()` function in the controller:

```
class EcommerceViewController: UIViewController {

    static func instantiate() -> UIViewController {
        return UIStoryboard(name: "Ecommerce", bundle: nil).
instantiateInitialViewController()!
    }
}
```

Remember that to clean the saved e-mail, the quickest way is to reset the simulator:

This is what the app will then look like:

Now, we've completed our work on the first screen, and we are ready to implement the making of the actual e-commerce store.

You can find this code at `https://github.com/gscalzo/Swift2ByExample/tree/7_ASAP_1_Register`.

The ASAP e-commerce store

In this section, we'll implement the product, wrapping the connection with the server with a protocol so that we can implement the app using a fake local storage for this information.

The e-commerce product list

The list of the products stating the requirements for the app is simple: a grid with two columns is required, which we can implement using UICollectionView.

First of all, let's change the controller in the Storyboard from a simple UIViewController to UICollectionviewController, embed it into UINavigationController, add a UICollectionViewCell prototype, and change the parent class accordingly in the Swift file.

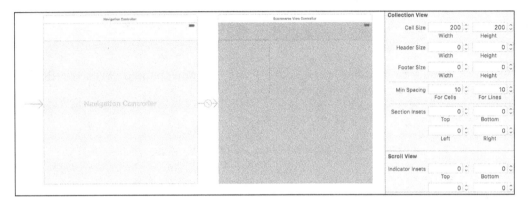

Although we are going to set up the collection using a custom flow, we'll set the size of the cell to be a little bigger in order to help us lay out the components:

```swift
import UIKit

class EcommerceViewController: UICollectionViewController {

    static func instantiate() -> UIViewController {
        return UIStoryboard(name: "Ecommerce", bundle: nil).
instantiateInitialViewController()!
    }

    override func viewDidLoad() {
        super.viewDidLoad()
        title = "ASAP"
    }
}
```

Next, we'll create an empty `ProductCollectionViewCell`, which also contains the product components:

```
import UIKit

class ProductCollectionViewCell: UICollectionViewCell {
}
```

Set this class as the custom class for `Cell`, and add the `Cell` identifier to enable the usage of the cells again.

While we are changing the Storyboard, let's set the background of `CollectionView` to white.

Let's now write some code to create fake cells in the controller and verify whether everything has been connected correctly:

```
extension EcommerceViewController {
    override func collectionView(collectionView:
    UICollectionView, numberOfItemsInSection section: Int) ->
    Int {
        return 40
    }

    override func collectionView(collectionView:
    UICollectionView, cellForItemAtIndexPath indexPath:
    NSIndexPath) -> UICollectionViewCell {
        let cell = collectionView.
        dequeueReusableCellWithReuseIdentifier("Cell",
        forIndexPath: indexPath) as! ProductCollectionViewCell

        switch arc4random_uniform(4) {
        case 0:
            cell.backgroundColor = UIColor.redColor()
        case 1:
            cell.backgroundColor = UIColor.greenColor()
        case 2:
            cell.backgroundColor = UIColor.blueColor()
        default:
            cell.backgroundColor = UIColor.orangeColor()
        }

        return cell
    }
}
```

When we run the app, we'll see the cells but they aren't perfectly laid out:

The problem here is that we haven't set a two-column layout yet.

Let's write the code for this two-column layout:

```
import UIKit

class TwoColumnFlowLayout: UICollectionViewFlowLayout {
    private struct Constants {
        static let NumberColumns = CGFloat(2.0)
        static let InteritemSpacing = CGFloat(1.0)
    }

    override func prepareLayout() {
        super.prepareLayout()
```

```
            configureItemSpacing()
            configureItemSize()
        }
    }

    private extension TwoColumnFlowLayout {
        func configureItemSpacing() {
            minimumInteritemSpacing = Constants.InteritemSpacing
            minimumLineSpacing = Constants.InteritemSpacing
        }

        func configureItemSize() {
            let itemSide = (collectionViewContentSize()
            .width / Constants.NumberColumns) -
            (Constants.InteritemSpacing * 0.5)
            itemSize = CGSizeMake(itemSide, itemSide)
        }
    }
```

In the Storyboard, we'll set the two-column layout as the flow layout; finally, CollectionView looks the way it's supposed to:

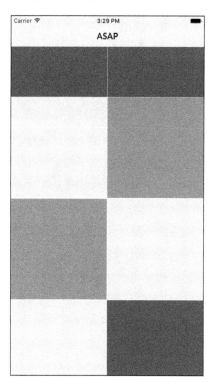

The product cell

The implementation of the product cell is just a way to encapsulate the components in `stackviews`, add the correct spacing, and present them in an appropriate way.

Recalling the requirement, we can implement the cell using this layout:

The model label and price label are contained in a horizontal **Stack View**, which is vertically stacked with the image and description.

The first **Stack View** has **Top Alignment** with **Equal Spacing Distribution**:

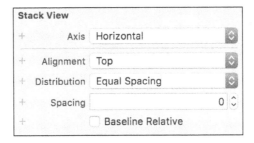

We also set a height of 21 to the **Model** label to define the height of **Stack View** as well.

Then we add the image, which has an aspect ratio constraint of 1:1, and the **Description Label**, with a height constraint that's equal to 21. We embed them in a **Vertical Stack View** with **Center Alignment** and **Fill Distribution**.

To define the width of the first **Stack View**, we add two constraints, leading and trailing, with a two point distance from the parent.

Finally, we set the space of the external **Stack View** with regard to its parent, setting it to two points everywhere, except at the top, where we set it to five.

To conclude, this is the cell:

The following is the components' tree where we'll take a look at the constraints:

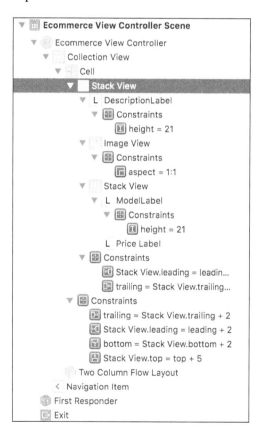

Although using **Interface Builder** is the method that's been indicated by Apple, as you can see, explaining it isn't the easiest thing to do. So, if you have any doubts or the code you've implemented doesn't work as expected, I suggest that you take a look at a project that's already been made on GitHub.

Now that we have the layout in place, let's add the outlets:

```
class ProductCollectionViewCell: UICollectionViewCell {
    @IBOutlet var nameLabel: UILabel! {
        didSet {
            nameLabel.font = UIFont.latoFontOfSize(18)
        }
    }
    @IBOutlet var imageView: UIImageView!
    @IBOutlet var descriptionLabel: UILabel! {
        didSet {
            descriptionLabel.font = UIFont.latoFontOfSize(18)
        }
    }
    @IBOutlet var priceLabel: UILabel! {
        didSet {
            priceLabel.font = UIFont.latoBoldFontOfSize(18)
        }
    }
}
```

Don't forget to connect the outlets in **Interface Builder**!

Now, verify whether everything works; let's add a configuration in the view controller:

```
override func collectionView(collectionView:
UICollectionView, cellForItemAtIndexPath indexPath:
NSIndexPath) -> UICollectionViewCell {
    let cell = collectionView.
    dequeueReusableCellWithReuseIdentifier("Cell",
    forIndexPath: indexPath) as! ProductCollectionViewCell

    cell.modelLabel.text = "Ex Model"
    cell.descriptionLabel.text = "Ex Description"
    cell.imageView.sd_setImageWithURL(NSURL(string:
    "http://lorempixel.com/400/400/food/")!)
    cell.priceLabel.text = "$123"

    cell.backgroundColor = UIColor.clearColor()

    return cell
}
```

An important thing to remember when handling the image in the table view or CollectionViews is to not synchronously download images, otherwise scrolling will be affected at the time of downloading images; instead, download the images in an asynchronous way, either implementing the code using NSURLSession or using a library, such as SDWebImage, as we are currently doing.

Ensure that you don't forget to import the framework:

```
import SDWebImage
```

Because the image has been downloaded from a non-secure host, we need to allow it in plist:

| ▼ App Transport Security Settings | ‡ | Dictionary | (1 item) |
| Allow Arbitrary Loads | ‡ | Boolean | YES |

Here is the app with the implemented cells:

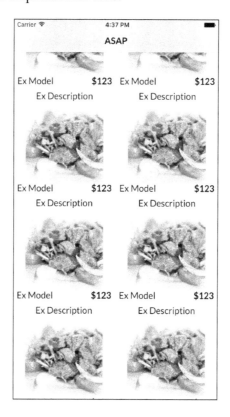

You can find the code for this version at `https://github.com/`
`gscalzo/Swift2ByExample/tree/7_ASAP_2_ProductList.`

Parsing and storing products

It's now time to add realistic products to our app.

Since this is the first local implementation and we aim to download products for a server, we'll wrap all the supposed calls to a server in a protocol, which will be implemented with the help of a local storage in this chapter and a server in the next one.

Let's start implementing the `Product` entity:

```
import Foundation

struct Product {
    let id: String
    let name: String
    let price: Double
    let description: String
    let imageURL: NSURL
}
```

Now, define a protocol to retrieve raw products in the form of a single JSON string from the storage, and let's call it `ProductGateway`:

```
protocol ProductGateway {
    func getProducts(completion: (String) -> Void)
}
```

This is the seam that can be used to change the implementation, and thus the kind of storage, without affecting the code using it.

As done earlier for the `User` class, we define a `store` object to hold the `Product` entities, and, in this case, call the `gateway` and `translate` functions from JSON to `Product` entities:

```
import Foundation
import SwiftyJSON

class ProductStore {
    private struct ProductKeys {
        static let products = "products"
```

```
        static let ID = "id"
        static let name = "name"
        static let price = "price"
        static let description = "description"
        static let imageURL = "imageURL"
    }

    private let gateway: ProductGateway

    init(gateway: ProductGateway) {
        self.gateway = gateway
    }

    func retrieve(completion: ([Product] -> Void)) {

        gateway.getProducts() { productsJSON in
            if let dataFromString = productsJSON.
            dataUsingEncoding(NSUTF8StringEncoding,
            allowLossyConversion: false) {
                let json = JSON(data: dataFromString)

                let productsJSON = json[ProductKeys.products]

                let products = productsJSON.map {
                (index, product) in
                    Product(
                        id: product[ProductKeys.ID].stringValue,
                        name: product[ProductKeys.name].
                        stringValue,
                        price: product[ProductKeys.price].
                        doubleValue,
                        description: product
                        [ProductKeys.description].stringValue,
                        imageURL: NSURL(string: product
                        [ProductKeys.imageURL].stringValue)!
                    )
                }
                completion(products)
            }
        }
    }
}
```

Since parsing JSON is not too convenient in Swift, we exploit again in the SwiftyJSON library.

We now add the store into `CollectionViewController`:

```
class EcommerceViewController: UICollectionViewController {
    let productStore = ProductStore(gateway: LocalProductGateway())
    private var products: [Product] = []
```

As you can see, we inject a particular implementation of the gateway during the creation of the store. `LocalProductGateway` isn't implemented yet but it will be soon enough.

We also add a `Product` array, which is the model of `CollectionView`.

We then call a method to get the products in `viewDidLoad`:

```
override func viewDidLoad() {
    super.viewDidLoad()
    title = "ASAP"

    productStore.retrieve { [weak self] products in
        self?.products = products
        self?.collectionView?.reloadData()
    }
}
```

If you remember, we faked the `CollectionViewDatasource` methods to create cells, but we now have the model and can implement the actual cells:

```
extension EcommerceViewController {
    override func collectionView(collectionView: UICollectionView,
    numberOfItemsInSection section: Int) -> Int {
        return products.count
    }

    override func collectionView(collectionView: UICollectionView,
    cellForItemAtIndexPath indexPath: NSIndexPath) ->
    UICollectionViewCell {
        let cell = collectionView.
        dequeueReusableCellWithReuseIdentifier("Cell",
        forIndexPath: indexPath) as! ProductCollectionViewCell

        let product = products[indexPath.row]
        cell.nameLabel.text = product.name
        cell.descriptionLabel.text = product.description
        cell.imageView.sd_setImageWithURL(product.imageURL)
        cell.priceLabel.text = "$\(product.price)"
```

```
        cell.backgroundColor = UIColor.clearColor()

        return cell
    }
}
```

The code does nothing more than bind the product entity fields with the appropriate components in `Cell`.

The last missing class is `LocalProductGateway`, which simply reads a string from a file:

```swift
import Foundation

class LocalProductGateway: ProductGateway {
    func getProducts(completion: (String) -> Void) {

        let path = NSBundle.mainBundle().pathForResource
        ("products", ofType: "json")

        do {
            completion(try String(contentsOfFile: path!,
            encoding: NSUTF8StringEncoding))
        } catch {
            completion("[:]")
        }
    }
}
```

The `products.json` example file contains example products that can be used to simulate the server.

> The example file can be downloaded from `https://raw.githubusercontent.com/gscalzo/Swift2ByExample/7_ASAP_3_Products/ASAP/ASAP/products.json`.

One last note: when you check open source or tutorial code, you'll notice that authors uses the same technique, but call the protocol using the Protocol suffix, or `ProductGatewayProtocol` in our case, and call the concrete class without the `ProductGateway` or `ProtocolGatewayConcrete` suffix, personally, I don't like this style because it leaks technical details (the client doesn't need to know that they're using a protocol instead of a class, for example), so I prefer calling the protocol in the most generic way and calling the class in a specific way to implement that protocol, for example, `LocalProductGateway` or `ServerProductGateway`.

That said, our app correctly shows the products now:

 You can find the code for this version at `https://github.com/gscalzo/Swift2ByExample/tree/7_ASAP_3_Products`.

The ASAP cart

An e-commerce app is not complete as it only shows the products without giving the possibility of buying them.

In this section, we'll implement the cart using the same technique presented in the previous section to wrap the call to a server.

Adding a product to the cart

Let's start by defining what a cart should do, as follows:

- Adding a product
- Removing a product
- Buying the cart

Given these commands, we define the gateway in this way:

```
import Foundation

protocol CartGateway {
    func addProductID(productID: String)
    func removeProductID(productID: String)
    func buy()
}
```

The local implementation is basically an empty implementation of the protocol:

```
class LocalCartGateway: CartGateway {
    func addProductID(productID: String){
    }

    func removeProductID(productID: String){
    }

    func buy() {
    }
}
```

The CartStore class is nothing more than a wrapper around a dictionary that sends the command to the gateway:

```
class CartStore {
    private var products = [String:Product]()
    private let gateway: CartGateway

    init(gateway: CartGateway) {
        self.gateway = gateway
    }

    func containsProductID(productID: String) -> Bool {
        return products[productID] != nil
    }
}
```

```
func addProduct(product: Product) {
    products[product.id] = product
    gateway.addProductID(product.id)
}

func removeProduct(product: Product) {
    products.removeValueForKey(product.id)
    gateway.removeProductID(product.id)
}

func buy() {
    products = [:]
    gateway.buy()
}

func count() -> Int {
    return products.count
}
}
```

The cart must be instantiated as a property in the `EcommerceViewController` class:

```
class EcommerceViewController: UICollectionViewController {
    let productStore = ProductStore(gateway: LocalProductGateway())
    private var products: [Product] = []
    let cartStore = CartStore(gateway: LocalCartGateway())
```

The product cell's background must change its background color depending on the state of the product and if it is in the cart or not:

```
override func collectionView(collectionView: UICollectionView,
cellForItemAtIndexPath indexPath: NSIndexPath) ->
UICollectionViewCell {
    let cell = collectionView.
    dequeueReusableCellWithReuseIdentifier("Cell",
    forIndexPath: indexPath) as! ProductCollectionViewCell
    //...
    if cartStore.containsProductID(product.id) {
        cell.backgroundColor = UIColor.lightGrayColor()
    } else {
        cell.backgroundColor = UIColor.clearColor()
    }

    return cell
}
```

Finally, we add or remove the product by tapping on a product's cell:

```
override func collectionView(collectionView:
UICollectionView, didSelectItemAtIndexPath indexPath:
NSIndexPath) {
    let product = products[indexPath.row]

    if cartStore.containsProductID(product.id) {
        cartStore.removeProduct(product)
    } else {
        cartStore.addProduct(product)
    }
    collectionView.reloadData()
}
```

To show the customer the number of the products inside the cart, we use a badge in the navigation bar, which will eventually show us the open cart.

To implement the button, we use a pod called BBBadgeBarButtonItem and FontAwesomeKit to use the cart icon:

```
import BBBadgeBarButtonItem
import FontAwesomeKit
```

The code basically creates a button in the navigation bar and through a convenience function, it changes the number inside the badges:

```
extension EcommerceViewController {
    func setupCart() {
        let button = UIButton(type: .Custom)
        let icon = FAKFontAwesome.shoppingCartIconWithSize(20)
        button.setAttributedTitle(icon.attributedString(),
        forState: .Normal)
        button.addTarget(self, action: "cartButtonTapped:",
        forControlEvents: .TouchUpInside)
        button.frame = CGRect(x: 0, y: 0, width: 44, height: 44)

        let cartBarButton = BBBadgeBarButtonItem
        (customUIButton: button)
        cartBarButton.badgeOriginX = 0
        cartBarButton.badgeOriginY = 0
        navigationItem.rightBarButtonItem = cartBarButton
    }

    func cartButtonTapped(sender: UIButton) {
        print("showCheckoutScene()")
    }

    func refreshCartCount() {
```

```
        guard let cartBarButton = navigationItem.
        rightBarButtonItem as? BBBadgeBarButtonItem else {
            return
        }

        cartBarButton.badgeValue = "\(cartStore.count())"
    }
}
```

The setup method is called in `viewDidLoad`:

```
override func viewDidLoad() {
    super.viewDidLoad()
    title = "ASAP"
    setupCart()
```

Every time a product is added or removed from the cart, the refresh count must be called:

```
override func collectionView(collectionView: UICollectionView,
didSelectItemAtIndexPath indexPath: NSIndexPath) {
//...
    refreshCartCount()
    collectionView.reloadData()
}
```

If you run the app, you'll notice that it works smoothly:

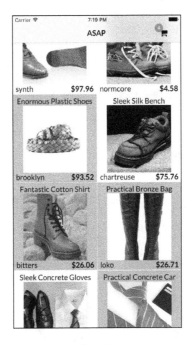

You can find the code for this version at `https://github.com/gscalzo/Swift2ByExample/tree/7_ASAP_4_AddToCart`.

Removing items from cart and checkout

To take a look at the details of the cart, we implement a new view controller that contains the products in the cart; let's call it `CheckoutViewController`:

In the Storyboard, don't forget to set `CheckoutViewController` as the custom class and the initial view controller.

We can now add the usual `factory` function to the class:

```
class CheckoutViewController: UIViewController {
    var cartStore: CartStore!

    static func instantiate() -> UIViewController {
        return UIStoryboard(name: "Checkout",
        bundle: nil).instantiateInitialViewController()!
    }
}
```

We will also add a `CartStore` property, which will be used to present the products.

To connect `EcommerceViewController` instead of using a plain segue, we use a trick that's been made possible by the protocol extension introduced by Swift 2.

Let's define an extension to `UIViewController` that adds a performing segue using `enum`:

```
import Foundation
import UIKit
```

```
protocol SegueHandlerType {
    typealias SegueIdentifier: RawRepresentable
}

extension SegueHandlerType where Self: UIViewController,
SegueIdentifier.RawValue == String {

    func performSegueWithIdentifier(segueIdentifier:
    SegueIdentifier, sender: AnyObject?){
        performSegueWithIdentifier(segueIdentifier.rawValue,
        sender: sender)
    }

    func segueIdentifierForSegue(segue: UIStoryboardSegue) ->
    SegueIdentifier {
        guard let identifier = segue.identifier,
            segueIdentifier = SegueIdentifier
            (rawValue: identifier)
            else {fatalError("Invalid segue identifier
            \(segue.identifier)")}
        return segueIdentifier
    }
}
```

In the e-commerce Storyboard, we add a segue from the view controller to the newly created **Storyboard** using ShowCheckoutScene as the identifier:

Then, in EcommerceViewController, we add an extension to handle the segue:

```
extension EcommerceViewController: SegueHandlerType {
    enum SegueIdentifier: String {
        case ShowCheckoutScene = "ShowCheckoutScene"
    }

    func showCheckoutScene() {
        performSegueWithIdentifier(.ShowCheckoutScene,
        sender: self)
```

```
        }
    }

    extension EcommerceViewController {
        override func prepareForSegue(segue: UIStoryboardSegue, sender:
    AnyObject?) {

            switch segueIdentifierForSegue(segue) {
            case .ShowCheckoutScene:
                guard let checkoutViewController = segue.
                destinationViewController as? CheckoutViewController
                else {
                    return
                }
                checkoutViewController.cartStore = cartStore
            }
        }
    }
```

Although this looks like a lot of code for a small value, this pattern will be really useful when several segues start from the view controller. This is because the compiler can check whether everything is correct, which cannot be possible using strings as identifiers.

Finally, implement the **Bar** button action:

```
    func cartButtonTapped(sender: UIButton) {
        showCheckoutScene()
    }
```

Let's move to **Checkout Storyboard** to lay out the components.

To do this, what we need is a button at the bottom and a table view to show the cart.

As you can imagine, we use a vertical **Stack View** where the height of the label is equal to 60; we add the leading and training constraints of the label to be equal to the container, the **Table View** width to be equal to the label, and the borders of UIStackView to be equal to those of the parent:

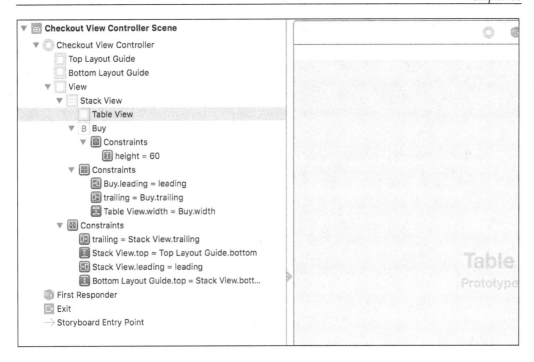

Since we already have `CartStore` in the view controller, let's lay out **Table View Cells** to present the contained products.

Let's add a `UITableViewCell` prototype, setting it as the `Basic` type and `Cell` as the identifier:

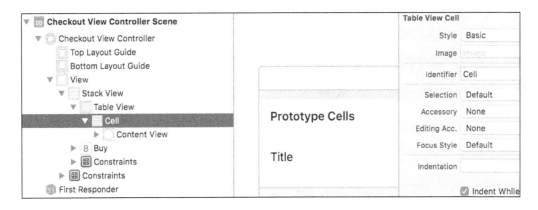

Next, select the **Table View** component, and set **Row Height** as 80.

Finally, set **View Controller** as the datasource whose function in the code will be as follows:

```
extension CheckoutViewController: UITableViewDataSource {
    func tableView(tableView: UITableView, numberOfRowsInSection
    section: Int) -> Int {
        return cartStore.count()
    }

    func tableView(tableView: UITableView, cellForRowAtIndexPath
    indexPath: NSIndexPath) -> UITableViewCell {
        let cell = tableView.dequeueReusableCellWithIdentifier
        ("Cell", forIndexPath: indexPath)
        let product = cartStore.allProducts()[indexPath.row]
        cell.selectionStyle = .None
        cell.textLabel?.font = UIFont.latoLightFontOfSize(15)
        cell.textLabel?.text = product.name
        cell.imageView?.sd_setImageWithURL(product.imageURL)

        return cell
    }
}
```

If you run the app after selecting a few products and going to the checkout, you'll see that the products are there, but there are a couple of problems: first, there is a gap on above the table, and second, empty rows are rendered:

To solve the first issue, select **View Controller** and uncheck **Extend Edges Under Top Bars**:

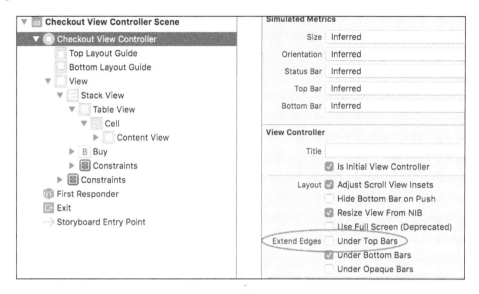

To solve the second issue, we need to set **Table View** as **Outlet** in CheckoutViewController and write the following code:

```
class CheckoutViewController: UIViewController {
    var cartStore: CartStore!

    @IBOutlet var tableView: UITableView!{
        didSet {
            tableView.separatorInset = UIEdgeInsetsZero
        }
    }
}
```

Let's also set the button as **Outlet**, so that we can set the font as well:

```
@IBOutlet var buyButton: UIButton!  {
    didSet {
        buyButton.titleLabel?.font = UIFont.latoFontOfSize(24)
    }
}
```

As per our requirement, the total amount is the title of **View Controller**.

Now, we'll add the function in `CartStore` in order to know the functional power of Swift:

```
class CartStore {
    var total: Double {
        get {
            return products.values.reduce(0) { partial, product in
                return partial + product.price
            }
        }
    }
}
```

Instead of a temporary variable as an accumulator, we use the `reduce()` function of a list, which iterates it and accumulates the result of the block; the accumulator will then be passed as a parameter in the next call.

In **View Controller**, we write a `refreshTotal()` function, which sets the total of the articles as the title:

```
private extension CheckoutViewController {
    func refreshTotal(){
        title = "Total: $\(cartStore.total)"
    }
}
```

This function is called in `viewDidLoad()`:

```
override func viewDidLoad() {
    super.viewDidLoad()

    refreshTotal()
}
```

One of the reasons to have the **Open Cart** view is the possibility of changing the products that are contained; in our simplified version, we want to allow the user to delete a product, and we want to use the slide-to-left gesture.

For the *TodoList* app, we used an external library because we wanted only the slide-to-left gesture (this library adds a slide-to-right gesture as well); we can use `editActions` of `TableViewDelegate` also:

```
extension CheckoutViewController: UITableViewDelegate {
    func tableView(tableView: UITableView,
    editActionsForRowAtIndexPath indexPath:
    NSIndexPath) -> [UITableViewRowAction]? {
        let delete = UITableViewRowAction(style: .Default,
        title: "delete") {
```

```
        [weak self] action, index in
        guard let product = self?.cartStore.
        allProducts()[index.row] else {
            return
        }
        self?.cartStore?.removeProduct(product)
        self?.refreshTotal()
        tableView.reloadData()
    }
    return [delete]
    }
}
```

This call basically creates an action that, when triggered, will remove the product and refresh the total.

We also need to set **View Controller** as UITableViewDelegate in **Table View**.

Because we change the store, we need to refresh the product collection in EcommerceViewController:

```
override func viewWillAppear(animated: Bool) {
    super.viewWillAppear(animated)
    refreshCartCount()
    collectionView?.reloadData()
}
```

The last missing feature is the buy action, which just calls the store and presents an informative popup:

```
@IBAction func buyTapped() {
    cartStore.buy()

    let alert = UIAlertController(title: "Done",
    message: "Thank you for buying at ASAP!", preferredStyle:
    UIAlertControllerStyle.Alert)
    alert.addAction(UIAlertAction(title: "OK", style:
    UIAlertActionStyle.Default, handler: { _ in
        self.navigationController?.
        popToRootViewControllerAnimated(false)
    }))

    presentViewController(alert, animated: true,
    completion: nil)
}
```

This code completes the app with the help of a local storage.

The following screenshot shows the Storyboards used in the app:

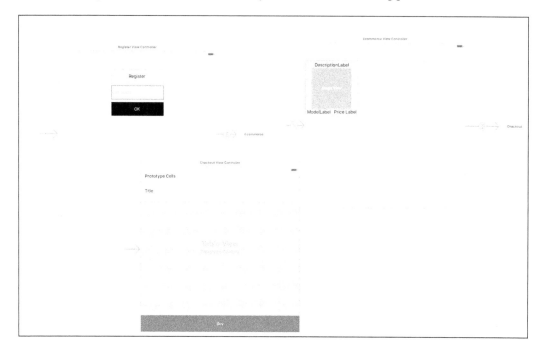

As you can see, using Storyboard references for the Storyboard is really clean, and it is really easy to see how the view controllers are connected together.

Et voilà, the *ASAP* app is now complete!

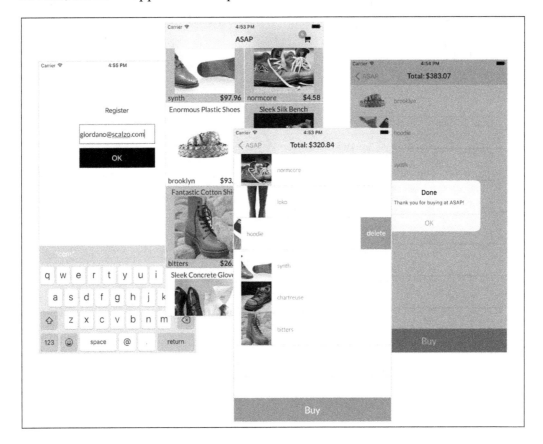

 You can find the code for this version at `https://github.com/gscalzo/Swift2ByExample/tree/7_ASAP_5_Checkout`.

Summary

Another long chapter I know, but full of information on implementing the skeleton of a real client server app: given these patterns, adding more functionalities, it is just a matter of adding new **View Controllers**, new stores, and new gateways, without the need to bloat the existing **View Controllers**.

In the next chapter we'll see how to use Swift to implement a Linux Server to give a real backend to *ASAP*.

11
ASAPServer, a Server in Swift

During the 2015 WWDC keynote, exactly one year after Swift was announced, Apple made another astonishing announcement: Swift will be open source!

Apple will release a first Linux version, which is completely decoupled from the Cocoa Foundation, and move the development and evolution of the language to the hands of the community.

As mentioned, the first Linux release will be done by Apple, but in the future, we can see Swift running everywhere: Windows, Android, and so on—everywhere the community of developers wants to create a version.

In early December 2015, Apple finally kept its promise and released the source of Swift on GitHub: `https://github.com/apple/swift`.

Apple also released a long-awaited packed manager, a sort of official CocoaPods, called **Swift Packet Manage**, which will help release modular software without using Xcode.

The Linux version is still in its infancy and is not ready for production; nonetheless, it's good enough to start experimenting with it preparing for Swift 3.0, which should be the first production-ready release for the server.

The interface of the ASAP Server

In the previous chapter, we implemented the app using a local storage, and now we want to implement a server in Swift to handle the products and the cart.

The actions that we want to handle are as follows:

- Getting the list of the products
- Adding a product to the cart

- Removing a product from the cart
- Creating and ordering from the cart

Using the REST architectural paradigm, we design our server to handle the following actions:

- **HTTP GET** of the `/products` URL, which returns the JSON of the product in the exact format we used in the previous chapter
- **HTTP POST** of the `/customer/<useremail>/cart/<productID>` URL, which creates a new relationship between the cart of the user and the product
- **HTTP DELETE** of the `/customer/<useremail>/cart/<productID>` URL, which removes the relationship between the cart of the user and the product
- **HTTP POST** of the `/customer/<useremail>/orders` URL, which creates a new order based on the customer's cart and resets the cart itself

One skeleton server for two OSes

Before implementing the server, we need to prepare a build environment for both OS X and Linux; also, let's prepare a `HelloWorld` server, which handles a `GET` and `POST` request in a predefined URL.

An OS X skeleton server

The Swift open source version for OS X can be downloaded from `https://swift.org/download/#latest-development-snapshots`; however, because a new version is released every week, it could be too complicated to be aligned with the version.

Preparing the OS X environment

Fortunately, taking inspiration from projects in different languages, such as PyEnv for Python, Kyle Fuller released a useful version manager for Swift called **Swift Version Manager**, which can install and manage different versions of Swift on the same machine, optionally tying a particular version of the language for each project.

The GitHub page of the project, `https://github.com/kylef/swiftenv`, shows different ways to install it, although I suggest that you do it via Homebrew using this command:

```
$ brew install kylef/formulae/swiftenv
```

If you don't have Homebrew installed (and you should), you can install it using the instruction on the brew home page `http://brew.sh`, which is basically just this command:

```
$ ruby -e "$(curl -fsSL https://raw.githubusercontent.com/Homebrew/
install/master/install)"
```

The first thing to do is install the Swift version we'll use in our server:

```
$ swiftenv install swift-2.2-SNAPSHOT-2016-01-06-a
```

This command downloads the version of Swift referenced as a parameter — `swift-2.2-SNAPSHOT-2016-01-06-a` in this case, a version ready to be linked to a project or to be made global.

After this, we create a folder for our *ASAPServer* project, where we set the Swift version using this command:

```
$ swiftenv local swift-2.2-SNAPSHOT-2016-01-06-a
```

Running the `swiftenv` local command, we should verify that the version is exactly what we need.

The HelloWorld skeleton server

Now we are ready to implement our *ASAP* server.

The first thing we do is prepare `makefile` to help us save a few keystrokes during the compilation and run of the server:

```
build:
    swift build
run: build
    .build/debug/ASAP
```

If you are not familiar with the `makefile` syntax, this file basically defines two commands, `run` and `build`, which can be called using the make `run` or `make build` command.

Moreover, the `run` command depends on the `build` command, so before running the server, the compiler builds the app if required.

As mentioned earlier, Swift comes with a **Swift Package Manager**, which needs the list of the external sub packages to build the app.

For our implementation, we are going to use a Sinatra-like server application written by Shun Takebayashi called **Swiftra**, and for the JSON handling, we will use a package part of the Zewo suite called **JSON**.

Let's add the two packages in the `Package.swift` file:

```
import PackageDescription

let package = Package(
    name: "ASAP",
    dependencies: [
        .Package(url: "https://github.com/zewo/JSON.git",
        Version(0, 1, 0)),
        .Package(url: "https://github.com/gscalzo/swiftra.git",
        Version(0, 0, 8))
    ]
)
```

The format is auto explicative; there are just two things to note: the first is that every package has a version that is the tag of the version we want to use, and the second is that the project has a name, *ASAP* in our case: a name that must be the same as the name of the directory under `Sources`, where we place the sources of our code.

Now let's create a `Sources` directory and then create a directory called `ASAP`, under which we place a `main.swift` file.

If you are familiar with Sinatra, you may notice that the format of `swiftra` is pretty similar:

```
import swiftra
import JSON
import Foundation

#if os(Linux)
    import Glibc
#endif


get("/hello/:name/:surname") { req in
    let response = "Hello \(req.parameters["name"])
    \(req.parameters["surname"])"
    print(response)
    return response
}
```

```
post("/hello/:name/:surname") { req in
    guard let name = req.parameters["name"],
    let surname = req.parameters["surname"] else {
        return Response(.BadRequest)
    }

    let responseJSON: JSON = [
        "greeting": "Hello",
        "name": .StringValue(name),
        "surname": .StringValue(surname),
    ]
    print("Created object: \(responseJSON.debugDescription)")
    return responseJSON.description
}

print("Starting...")
serve(8888)
```

After the requiring import files, we define two handlers: one for GET and the other for POST requests.

The parts of the URL preceded by a semicolon are the parameters that will be extracted by swiftra and put in a dictionary in the Request object, where they are accessible to be handled.

If we run the commands as shown in the following screenshot using make run in a terminal window, firstly, the packages are downloaded, then, the sources are compiled, and then the server is run.

Open a new terminal that we can connect to the server using curl commands:

```
→  Swif2ByExample   curl http://localhost:8888/hello/james/bond
Hello Optional("james") Optional("bond")%
→  Swif2ByExample
→  Swif2ByExample
→  Swif2ByExample
→  Swif2ByExample   curl -X POST http://localhost:8888/hello/james/bond
{"greeting":"Hello","surname":"bond","name":"james"}%
→  Swif2ByExample
→  Swif2ByExample
```

And this is the output in the terminal window where the server runs:

```
Linking Executable:  .build/debug/ASAP
.build/debug/ASAP
Starting...
Hello Optional("james") Optional("bond")


Created object: {
    "greeting": "Hello",
    "name": "james",
    "surname": "bond"
}
```

You can find the code for this version at `https://github.com/gscalzo/Swift2ByExample/tree/7_ASAP_6_ServerSkeleton`.

Preparing the Linux environment

The best way to verify that our code works in Linux would be to have a Linux machine; however, we can reach the same goal in a more convenient way using a Linux virtual machine running in our OS X environment.

We'll use VirtualBox as a virtualization system and Vagrant as the command-line interface for VirtualBox.

To install them, we can either go to their websites to download the packages or use Homebrew, like we did for SwiftEnv.

Firstly, we need to install `cask`, which is an extension of Homebrew:

```
$ brew install cask
```

Cask adds commands and packages to Homebrew, which permits us to install third-party binary programs.

Let's start with VirtualBox:

```
$ brew cask install virtualbox
```

Then, install Vagrant:

```
$ brew cask install vagrant
```

Now, we can define the configuration for Vagrant, which permits us to create preconfigured Linux images.

Let's create a directory and put the following Vagrant files inside it:

```
Vagrant.configure(2) do |config|
    config.vm.box = "https://cloud-images.ubuntu.com/vagrant/trusty/
current/trusty-server-cloudimg-amd64-vagrant-disk1.box"
    config.vm.network "forwarded_port", guest: 8888, host: 8888


    config.vm.provision "shell", inline: <<-SHELL
        export SWIFT_VERSION=2.2-SNAPSHOT-2016-01-06-a
        export SWIFT_PLATFORM=ubuntu14.04



        sudo apt-get --assume-yes install clang
        sudo apt-get install -y build-essential wget clang libedit-dev
python2.7 python2.7-dev libicu52 rsync libxml2 git


        curl -O https://swift.org/builds/ubuntu1404/swift-${SWIFT_VERSION}/
swift-${SWIFT_VERSION}-${SWIFT_PLATFORM}.tar.gz


        tar zxf swift-${SWIFT_VERSION}-${SWIFT_PLATFORM}.tar.gz


        sudo chown -R vagrant swift-${SWIFT_VERSION}-${SWIFT_PLATFORM}


        echo "export PATH=/home/vagrant/swift-${SWIFT_VERSION}-${SWIFT_
PLATFORM}/usr/bin:\"${PATH}\"" >> .profile
        echo "Swift has successfully installed on Linux"
    SHELL
end
```

This basically creates an Ubuntu image starting from a premade one and adds the required dependencies and the Swift binary on top.

Pay attention: if you want an updated version of the Swift binary, you need to change the SWIFT_VERSION variable; also, ensure that the version is the same as the one you installed in OS X, otherwise incompatibility issues can appear.

The last thing to note is the instruction:

```
config.vm.network "forwarded_port", guest: 8888, host: 8888
```

This command bridges the internal `8888` port to the external interface so that external apps can reach a server listening on this port.

Again, if you want to change the port of the server, don't forget to change this configuration.

 You can find the Vagrant file at `https://github.com/gscalzo/` `Swift2ByExample/blob/7_ASAP_7_LinuxSkeleton/` `LinuxSwiftVM/Vagrantfile`.

Now, take a look at this command:

```
vagrant up
```

With the preceding command, Vagrant creates the image and runs it as a daemon.

To log in to the Linux box, you must run the `vagrant ssh` command, and you are in.

Inside the terminal, we can copy or clone from the GitHub repository along with the code we just wrote and verify that connecting from another terminal in OS X with curl, the Linux server responds correctly.

If you are not familiar with the commands to clone a remote GitHub repository, the following commands should help you:

```
git clone https://github.com/gscalzo/Swift2ByExample.git
git fetch --all
git checkout 7_ASAP_6_ServerSkeleton
```

If you try to run the OS X server while Linux virtual machine is running, you'll notice that the `HelloWorld` server dies immediately; this is because the port is occupied by the Vagrant virtual machine. To free it, you need to suspend the virtual machine with this command:

```
$ vagrant suspend
```

To run it again, execute this command:

```
$ vagrant up
$ vagrant ssh
```

 You can find the code for this version at `https://github.com/` `gscalzo/Swift2ByExample/tree/7_ASAP_7_LinuxSkeleton`.

The ASAPServer

With the entire environment set, we can finally implement the *ASAP* Server.

The Products

In a real server, the products are probably saved in a database, but in our simple implementation, we will save the products in a file—the same file we used in the app.

So, let's start the implementation by saving the products.json file at the same level of makefile.

A DBRepository class will abstract the connection with the storage, making it easy to switch to a database, as we did in the app:

```
import Foundation

let dbRepository = DBRepository()

class DBRepository {
    func allProducts() -> String {
        print("Get /products")

        do {
            let productsAsNSString = try NSString(contentsOfFile:
"products.json",
                encoding: NSUTF8StringEncoding)
#if os(Linux)
            return productsAsNSString.bridge()
#else
            return productsAsNSString as String
#endif
        }
        catch {
            print("Error")
        }
        return "{ products: [] }"
    }
}
```

The only thing to note is that in Swift for Linux, at the time of writing this, the bridge between NSString and String is not automatic, so it must be made explicit by calling the bridge() function.

The main file is as simple as defining a call to the repository `allProducts()` function:

```swift
import swiftra
import JSON
import Foundation

#if os(Linux)
    import Glibc
#endif

get("/products") { req in
    return dbRepository.allProducts()
}

print("Starting...")
serve(8888)
```

The cart

The two functions to manipulate the cart are just two stubs in the repository:

```swift
class DBRepository {
    func allProducts() -> String {
        //...
    }

    func addToCartUser(userEmail: String, productID: String) {
        // add to cart of the user
        print("Add product \(productID) to cart of user \(userEmail)")
    }

    func removeFromCartUser(userEmail: String, productID: String) {
        // remove from cart of the user
        print("Remove product \(productID) to cart of user \
(userEmail)")
    }
}
```

In the `main` function, we need to extract the parameters from the request and then call the repository functions.

To avoid a typo in the name of the parameters, we use the usual pattern to create them as static constants in a `struct`:

```
struct ParamKeys {
    static let ProductID = "productID"
    static let UserEmail = "useremail"
}
```

In the routers, we set a `guard` statement to ensure that the parameters are valid:

```
post ("/customer/:useremail/cart/:productID") { req in
    guard let userEmail = req.parameters [ParamKeys.UserEmail],
        let productID = req.parameters [ParamKeys.ProductID] else {
            return Response (.BadRequest)
        }
    dbRepository.addToCartUser (userEmail, productID: productID)
    return "OK"
}

delete ("/customer/:useremail/cart/:productID") { req in
    guard let userEmail = req.parameters [ParamKeys.UserEmail],
        let productID = req.parameters [ParamKeys.ProductID] else {
            return Response (.BadRequest)
        }
    dbRepository.removeFromCartUser (userEmail, productID:
    productID)
    return "OK"
}
```

Note that if there is any error in the parameters, a `Bad Request` response is sent to the client.

The order

Finally, note that `createOrder` is a stub as well:

```
class DBRepository {
    func orderCreatedFromCartUser (userEmail: String) -> String {
        // create a new order from the cart
        print ("Create order from cart of user \(userEmail)")
        let orderID = "1"
        return orderID
    }
}
```

In a real implementation, `orderID` would be generated as `primaryKey` in the storage, but to show the decoupling between the API and the storage, a static hardcoded value is enough.

The main implementation notes more than a call to the repository:

```
post("/customer/:useremail/orders") { req in
    guard let userEmail = req.parameters[ParamKeys.UserEmail] else {
            return Response(.BadRequest)
        }
    return dbRepository.orderCreatedFromCartUser(userEmail)
}
```

The server can be tested using the `curl` command:

```
curl http://localhost:8888/products
```

```
curl -X POST http://localhost:8888/customer/james.bond@mi6.org/cart/123
```

```
curl -X DELETE http://localhost:8888/customer/james.bond@mi6.org /
cart/123
```

```
curl -X POST http://localhost:8888/customer/james.bond@mi6.org /orders
```

 You can find the code for this version at `https://github.com/gscalzo/Swift2ByExample/tree/7_ASAP_8_ASAPServer`.

Connecting the ASAP app

After implementing the *ASAP* server, let's add the capability of communicating with a server to our *ASAP* app.

The products

The first gateway to implement is the one that handles the product, implementing the `ProductGateway` protocol:

```
import Foundation

class ServerProductGateway: ProductGateway {
    func getProducts(completion: (String) -> Void) {

        let session = NSURLSession.sharedSession()
```

```
let task = session.dataTaskWithURL
(EndPoint.Products.url()) {
    (data, response, error) -> Void in

    if error != nil {
        print(error!.localizedDescription)
        return
    }

    guard let data = data,
    let products = NSString(data: data,
    encoding: NSUTF8StringEncoding) as? String else {
        return
    }

    dispatch_async(dispatch_get_main_queue()) {
        completion(products)
    }
}

task.resume()
}
}
```

To communicate with the server, we use NSURLSession, which is a powerful native way to make an HTTP request.

Note that the call is made in a thread that can be potentially different from the main thread; therefore, we need to call the completion() block in the main thread.

Also, you should notice that the URL is from an enum: this is a powerful way to build URLs in a static way, which is a pattern that was presented the first time in Chris Eidhof's blog post, http://chris.eidhof.nl/posts/typesafe-url-routes-in-swift.html, and implemented in the Moya library by Ash Furrow.

Basically, each URL is a case of an enum, and url() functions compose the actual NSURL from the baseURL and the parameters of the enum:

```
import Foundation

struct BaseURL {
    private static var baseURL: NSURL {
        return NSURL(string: "http://localhost:8888")!
    }
    static func appending(component: String) -> NSURL {
```

```
            return baseURL.URLByAppendingPathComponent(component)
        }
    }

    enum EndPoint {
        case Products

        func url() -> NSURL {
            switch self {
                case .Products:
                    return BaseURL.appending("/products")
            }
        }
    }
```

Although everything discussed till now might look overengineered for only one URL, it will become convenient when will add the others URLs.

Finally, we change the object to inject into the store in `EcommerceViewController`:

```
class EcommerceViewController: UICollectionViewController {
    let productStore = ProductStore(gateway: ServerProductGateway())
```

Running the app now will connect to the server instead of reading the products from the file.

The Cart

`ServerGateway` has a similar implementation, where we refactored the `NSURLSession` call to a common function with the `HTTP` method as a parameter:

```
import Foundation

class ServerCartGateway: CartGateway {
    private let userEmail: String?

    init(userEmail: String?) {
        self.userEmail = userEmail
    }

    func addProductID(productID: String){
        guard let userEmail = userEmail else {
            return
        }
```

```
        requestMethod("POST", URL: EndPoint.Cart
        (userEmail: userEmail,
            productID: productID).url())
    }

    func removeProductID(productID: String){
        guard let userEmail = userEmail else {
            return
        }

        requestMethod("DELETE", URL: EndPoint.Cart
        (userEmail: userEmail,
            productID: productID).url())
    }

    func buy() {
    }


    private func requestMethod(method: String, URL: NSURL){
        let session = NSURLSession.sharedSession()

        let request = NSMutableURLRequest(URL:URL)
        request.HTTPMethod = method

        let task = session.dataTaskWithRequest(request) {
            (data, response, error) -> Void in

            if error != nil {
                print(error!.localizedDescription)
                return
            }

        }

        task.resume()
    }
}
```

Also, we need to add a new entry to the EndPoint enum:

```
enum EndPoint {
    case Products
    case Cart(userEmail: String, productID: String)
```

```
func url() -> NSURL {
    switch self {
    case .Products:
        return BaseURL.appending("/products")
    case .Cart(userEmail: let userEmail,
    productID: let productID):
        return BaseURL.appending
        ("/customer/\(userEmail)/cart/\(productID)")
    }
}
}
```

Again, we change the injection in `EcommerceViewController`:

```
class EcommerceViewController: UICollectionViewController {
let productStore = ProductStore(gateway: ServerProductGateway())
let cartStore = CartStore(gateway:
    ServerCartGateway(userEmail:
    AppDelegate.appdelegate().userStore.userEmail()))
```

Running the app, we can see that it calls the server.

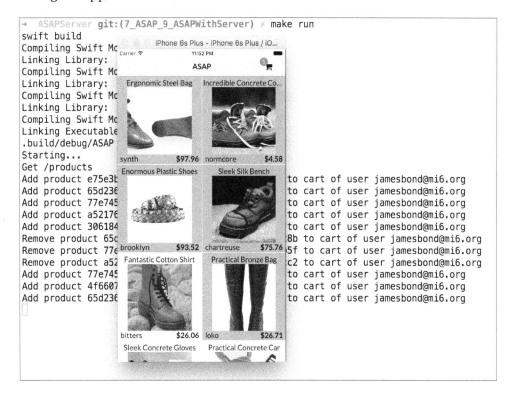

The order

The last command is order creation, which is just a new function in `CartGateway`:

```
func buy() {
    guard let userEmail = userEmail else {
        return
    }


     requestMethod("POST", URL: EndPoint.Orders
    (userEmail: userEmail).url())
}
```

A new endpoint is required:

```
enum EndPoint {
    case Products
    case Cart(userEmail: String, productID: String)
    case Orders(userEmail: String)

    func url() -> NSURL {
        switch self {
        case .Products:
            return BaseURL.appending("/products")
        case .Cart(userEmail: let userEmail,
            productID: let productID):
            return BaseURL.appending
            ("/customer/\(userEmail)/cart/\(productID)")
        case .Orders(userEmail: let userEmail):
            return BaseURL.appending
            ("/customer/\(userEmail)/orders")
        }
    }
}
```

With this, we conclude the building of our client-server e-commerce app.

 You can find the code for this version at `https://github.com/gscalzo/Swift2ByExample/tree/7_ASAP_9_ASAPWithServer`.

Summary

The Swift in the server is still in its infancy, and most features and performances are missing.

Nonetheless, we have understood that the possibilities are endless: can you imagine, for example, having the same code to serialize and deserialize the model between the client and the server? Or having web socket communication between apps with a server implemented in Swift? That would be really cool.

There are already a couple of projects that, with a different strategy, have the same goal: to be the best and most useful server framework for Swift. One is called Zewo, `https://github.com/Zewo`, which is basically a collection of small and effective modules to cover all the server needs from the HTTP to routers, web sockets, and so on, and the other is called Perfect, `https://www.perfect.org`, which has a more conventional and monolithic approach.

Both of them are still under heavy development, and the API compatibility is not a guarantee between the versions; nonetheless, they are already extremely powerful and flexible, and you can only imagine how they would be in the near future, when languages and tools will be mature enough.

With this chapter, we finish our practical introduction to Swift, which began with an introduction of the language and the most import features of Swift.

We then implemented different kind of apps, simple games, utility apps, 2D and 3D games, and finally, even a Linux server in Swift.

However, we just scratched the surface of our possibilities and all of these apps can be improved, extended, and remixed. And, of course, tons of different apps can be built using the programming bricks we learned together.

The code for the apps is available on GitHub at this link: `https://github.com/gscalzo/Swift2ByExample`.

I'll continue to update the code every time a new version of Swift breaks the compatibility, and you can reach me for any questions or feedback, either by opening a GitHub issue or sending me an e-mail — it shouldn't be difficult to find my e-mail address.

Now it's your turn to build the magic.

Index

A

Alamofire
about 137
reference link 61
app record
creating, on iTunes Connect 224-226
App Transport Security (ATS) 177
ASAP app, connecting
about 338
cart 340-342
order 343
products 338-340
ASAP cart
about 311
checkout 316
items, removing from 316-324
product, adding to 312-315
ASAP e-commerce store
about 298
e-commerce product list 299-301
product cell 303-306
products, parsing 307-311
products, storing 307-311
ASAPServer
about 335
cart 336, 337
interface 327, 328
order 337
products 335
Auto Layout 44
Automatic Reference Counter (ARC) 2

B

background image, weather app
downloading 159
searching, in Flickr 159-162
background, weather app
blurring 156, 157
Box2D
URL 181

C

Cartography
about 91, 137
reference link 135
closure 14
CocoaPods
about 98
URL 98
Cocoa Runtime 63
COLLADA
URL 252
concentration memory game
about 59
completing 86
dataSource, connecting 71-73
delegate, connecting 71-73
finishing 82
game logic, implementing 82, 83
game screen 66
menu screen 61
pair, obtaining 84, 85

skeleton, building 60
wrong turn, playing 85
Cube Runner app
about 237, 238
collision detection, implementing 269-271
cubes, adding 257-262
empty scene, building 239, 240
fighter, adding 252-254
fighter, moving 256, 257
Game Center integration 279-282
game over, implementing 272-274
game skeleton 243, 244
green torus, adding to scene 241
implementing 243
light, adding 242
light, moving 242
menu, implementing 245-249
music, adding 266, 267
obstacles, adding 263
real game, creating 269
scene, setting up 249-251
score, adding 264, 265
touches, adding 264, 275-277
world, texturing 254, 255

D

deck of cards implementation
about 73
assets, adding 78
CardCell structure 79-81
card entity 74, 75
card images, adding 78
deck, crafting 75
deck, finishing 77, 78
deck, shuffling 76
expected behavior, defining 73
touches, handling 81

E

e-commerce app
about 283
login and registration 284
open cart 286
products grid 285
register screen 286
skeleton app 286-298

enhancement, Flappy Bird app
adding 217
screen, shaking 221, 222
sound effects, adding 217-219
soundtrack, playing 219-221

F

fake user accounts
creating, to test Game Center 229, 230
fast enumeration 13
features, Game Center
achievements 223
leaderboards 223
multiplayer 223
Flappy Bird app
about 181
Bird node, adding 196-199
birds, colliding with pipes 212
code, explaining 190
collision-detection engine,
    setting up 206-210
completing 212
components, interacting 206
enhancement, adding 217
flight, implementing of bird 199, 200
flying bird 196
obstacles, adding 201
pipes node, implementing 201-205
player, authenticating 230-234
restarting popup, adding 214-216
score, adding 213, 214
scrolling, implementing 193-195
skeleton, building 182
stage for bird 189
three-dimensional world, simulating with
    parallax 191-193
Flat UI Colors
URL 64
FlickrKit 137
FXBlurView 137

G

Game Center
about 223
authentication 281
enabling 226-228

fake user accounts, creating to
test 229, 230
features 223
leaderboard, displaying 281
score, reporting 281
setting up 223, 224
game screen, concentration memory game
about 66
collection view, adding 68, 69
components, sizing 70
structure 66, 67
Grand Central Dispatch (GCD) 222
Guess the Number app
about 39, 40
code, adding 52-56
dots, connecting 47-52
graphic components, adding 43-46
skeleton app, building 41-43

H

HelloWorld skeleton server 329-332
High Order Function 34
HTTP DELETE 328
HTTP GET 328
HTTP POST 328

I

interpolation 13
items
removing, from ASAP cart 316-324
iTunes Connect
app record, creating on 224-226
reference link 225

J

JSON 330

L

Lato
URL 101
LatoFont 137
Linux environment
preparing 332-334

M

MACROs 29
menu screen, concentration memory game
about 61
basic menu screen, implementing 61-64
creating 64-66
MGSwipeTableCell
URL 109

O

Objective-C 2
Object library 45
Object-Oriented Programming (OOP) 34
OpenWeatherMap
URL 165
OS X environment
preparing 328, 329
OS X skeleton server
about 328
download link 328

P

Pamgaea
reference link 219
product
adding, to ASAP cart 312-315
properties 17

S

SceneKit 238
screen, TodoList app
building 103
datastore and View Controller,
connecting 105, 106
datastore, implementing 104
entities, adding 103
finishing touches 108
swappable cells 109-112
tableView, configuring 106, 107
skeleton app, TodoList app
building 90
empty app, implementing 90-97
third-party libraries, adding with
CocoaPods 98, 99

Todos View Controller,
    implementing 99-102
skeleton, Flappy Bird app
  building 182
  menu, implementing 184-188
  project, creating 182-184
skeleton, weather app
  assets, adding 137-139
  building 135
  project, creating 136, 137
SpriteKit 189
Swift
  about 1
  common behavior objects, defining 20, 21
  constants 5-7
  custom compound types, creating 16-19
  defining 2
  enumerations, on steroids 25, 26
  errors, catching 29-33
  existence, checking of optional value 24
  extended pattern matching 27-29
  flow, controlling 10-13
  functional programming patterns 33-36
  loose coupling, with protocols 22
  objects composing, protocol extensions
    used 22, 23
  URL 33
  using 1
  values transforming, functions used 14, 15
  variables 5-7
  variables, collecting in containers 8, 10
  Xcode, defining 3-5
Swift Package Manager 329
Swift Packet Manage 327
Swiftra 330
Swift Version Manager 328
SwiftyJSON 137

T

TodoList app
  about 87-89
  List View Controller 128-131
  reference link, for source code 131
  screen, building 103
  skeleton app, building 90

TodoDatastore, finishing 127
Todo task, adding 112
Todo view, adding 113-119
Todo View Controller, adding 120-126
type inference 7

U

UICollectionView
  reference link 59
UI, weather app
  completing 145
  CurrentWeatherView,
    implementing 145-148
  implementing 140
  in blocks 140-144
  next day's forecast, viewing in
    WeatherDaysForecastView 152-156
  WeatherHourlyForecastView,
    building 148-152

V

Vagrant file
  reference link 334
Value Type 17

W

weather app
  about 133, 134
  actual forecast, retrieving 165
  background, blurring 156, 157
  background image, downloading 159
  background image, searching
    in Flickr 159-162
  connecting, to server 173-177
  Core Location framework service,
    using 162-164
  CurrentWeatherView, rendering 168-171
  forecast, obtaining from
    OpenWeatherMap 165-168
  geolocalising 162
  skeleton, building 135
  UI, completing 145
  UI, implementing 140
  WeatherDaysForecastView, rendering 172

WeatherHourlyForecastView,
    rendering 171, 172
WeatherIconsKit 137
WWDC 2015
  URL 24

X

Xcode 7
  URL 3